THE CRIMEAN WAR
A Russian Chronicle

THE CRIMEAN WAR

A Russian Chronicle

ALBERT SEATON

B.T. BATSFORD LTD · LONDON

FIRST PUBLISHED 1977
ⓒ ALBERT SEATON 1977
ISBN 0 7134 0837 5

FILMSET IN 11 ON 13PT. MONOPHOTO EHRHARDT BY
SERVIS FILMSETTING LTD, MANCHESTER

PRINTED IN GREAT BRITAIN BY
J.W. ARROWSMITH LTD, BRISTOL
FOR THE PUBLISHERS
B.T. BATSFORD LTD, 4 FITZHARDINGE ST, LONDON W1H0AH

CONTENTS

LIST OF ILLUSTRATIONS

LIST OF MAPS

ACKNOWLEDGMENTS

Gratitude is expressed to the author and publisher and to Agence Hoffman of Paris for their kind permission to quote from *Tsar Nicholas I* by Constantin de Grunwald, published by Calmann-Lévy, Editeur, (in English by Douglas Saunders with MacGibbon and Kee). The photographs of Prince Paskevich and of the Russian column have been reproduced from Zaionchovsky. All other photographs have been taken from the St Petersburg three volume work *Sevastopol'tsy*. The jacket illustration is by kind permission of the National Army Museum, London.

NOTES ON SOURCES AND STYLE

Since the Soviet state archives are not available for public reference, this account of the Crimean War has, of necessity, been based largely on memoirs and articles that appeared in the Russian literary and military press between 1854 and 1870, contributed by those who had taken part in the campaigns. These Russian writers, all of them officers or soldiers, are of particular interest because they did not fear to criticize their superiors or the military system, and they expressed themselves with a candour rarely to be found in the military periodicals of any nation. For the tsarist journals of the day allowed their contributors remarkable freedom.

It is of course understandable that the accounts of the officers and men were often at variance with those of the senior commanders. But the generals themselves did not speak with a common voice. They were no less outspoken than their juniors and, uninhibited by standards of good taste or by laws of libel, their articles were sometimes personal and bitter attacks on their comrades, impugning not only their competence but their honesty, courage and honour. So it came about that when Lieutenant-General Kir'iakov, commanding the Russian left at the battle of the Alma, wrote a glowing and regrettably fictitious account of the part that he claimed to have played, Major-General Vunsh, the Chief of General Staff at the Alma, in replying, ridiculed Kir'iakov's version and accused him of running away during the height of the battle. For, according to Vunsh, Prince Menshikov, the Commander-in-Chief, found Kir'iakov alone and on foot, without staff or aides-de-camp, hiding in a hollow to the rear behind Telegraph Hill at a time when his leaderless troops were streaming from the battlefield. Nor was Kir'iakov the only general to desert his men.

Source material consisting merely of claims and rebuttals might prove difficult or even impossible to use, except that the editors of the literary and military journals published both charge and counter-charge with commendable impartiality and scant respect for rank or privilege, diligently seeking out further comment from other participants. When Lieutenant-

General Ryzhov described the glorious feats of valour of his own cavalry, the English or French reader might have had difficulty in recognizing the action as the field of Balaclava. But other Russian witnesses of the charge of the heavy and the light brigades have set Ryzhov's story aright. One lieutenant of Russian artillery standing with his battery at the end of the North Valley watching the approach of the light brigade almost to the muzzles of his guns, did not conceal his contempt for the superior numbers of Russian hussars and Cossacks who fled panic-stricken before 'a handful of red-coated desperadoes'. The present day reader, using probability as his criterion, will have little problem in evaluating these Russian accounts, however conflicting they may appear.

A number of Russian histories of the war have been used as reference works, and these have included the French edition *Défense de Sébastopol* of Totleben's work, Bogdanovich's *Vostochnaia Voina* and Zaionchovsky's *Vostochnaia Voina*. The main Soviet work consulted was Tarle's *Krymskaia Voina*, published in Stalin's lifetime. The only western source used has been de Grunwald's biography *Tsar Nicholas I*.

No attempt has been made to include the detail of the organization or of the actions of the allied forces, except insofar as they affect the continuity of the narrative and may be required by the general reader. There are, of course, occasional conflicts of evidence and claims; Russian stories of redoubts stormed and guns taken, where, according to allied histories, the defence was only a picquet and no artillery was in position. But, since this is a Russian chronicle, no cavilling footnotes have been appended. Such battle detail is, in any event, of minor importance. The book describes only the hostilities in the Crimea and not the general war in the Baltic, the Pacific, the Balkans and the Caucasus.

In transliterating Russian words and names the Library of Congress method has been followed except that the old-fashioned form of *y* has been used instead of *ii* at the ending of Russian surnames and the names of regiments. The German form of spelling has been retained for the names of German nationals; Russians of German descent have been described by the Russianized spelling they adopted. Some distinguished family names, e.g., *Dolgoruki, Lieven*, have been shown in the form familiar to the western world. Occasionally a family name has been introduced merely to identify the source of information, no comment or explanation being added as the name by itself is unlikely to be of interest to the general reader; further detail has, however, been included in the index. The use of Russian words in the English text has been avoided; in some instances, however, it has been necessary to do so for the benefit of the historian or specialist, in order that the translation of important quotations may be compared with the original expressions used.

At the time of the Crimean War there was a difference of 12 days between the Julian and the Gregorian calendars. All dates in the text are given according to the Gregorian (West and Central European) calendar.

The most important factors in the writing of history are sources, accuracy, impartiality and judgement; there can be no room for emotionalism or the striving for dramatic effect, for these are the province of the novelist. The accounts of those who fought in this war have, therefore, been reproduced exactly as they wrote them, for most of them wrote in all sincerity what they believed to be the truth: the truth is graphic and dramatic enough.

FOREWORD

This work could not have been completed without the assistance of a large number of people on both sides of the Atlantic. To all of them I express my gratitude.

I am greatly indebted to the Governing Body and the librarians of St Antony's College, Oxford, for the use of their resources. My grateful thanks go, too, to the staff of the Library of the University of Toronto and to the Librarian and staff of the Slavonic Section of the Bodleian Library, Oxford, to the Library of the School of Slavonic and East European Studies, London University, and to the Keeper of the Victoria and Albert Museum. In addition I most wholeheartedly thank the Chief Librarian and the Librarian in charge of the Library's Historical Section of the British Ministry of Defence Library (Central and Army) for generously making available to me Russian printed material and photographs.

Whereas I have relied almost entirely on my own research of Russian sources covering the war fought in the Crimea, I have made considerable use of secondary material describing the character of Nicholas I and of his court included in the Soviet study by Professor E.V. Tarle and in the French work by Constantin de Grunwald. This assistance I gratefully acknowledge.

Lastly I should like to thank my wife, who has typed and retyped the script many times and has shared with me so much of the detailed Russian research.

INTRODUCTION

Prince Alexander Mikhailovich Gorchakov, the celebrated Russian Chancellor and Foreign Minister under Alexander II, said that one of his principal contributions in the field of diplomacy was the coining and the use in Russian state documents of the expression 'The Sovereign and Russia'. Before he did so 'Russia' meant 'the tsar', for they were indivisible. So it was that Nicholas I *was* Russia and Russia was Nicholas, and the whole world, said Gorchakov, was aware of it.

The Crimean War might have been called Nicholas's War, for its causes lay rooted in Nicholas's expansionist aims and in the Franco–British attempts to curb them. In that war Russia lost over 100,000 men in battle, but the total casualty list through exposure and disease, typhus in winter and cholera in summer, was nearer half a million men. The Sevastopol siege was one of the bloodiest of the times. From this bitter and savage struggle comes an overwhelming picture of utter futility. At the end Russia did not gain a verst of territory. Yet the allies were no more successful in checking the Russian march of conquest, for, within two decades of the 1856 Treaty of Paris, Alexander II and Prince A.M. Gorchakov had contrived to annex vast territories far beyond Nicholas's most ambitious dreams. By then Russia knew how to use to its advantage Austria's preoccupation in Central Europe. For Russian sources have never made a secret of the importance of the role played in favour of the allies by the Austro–Hungarian Empire during the Crimean War; and there appears to be little doubt that the Austrian ultimatum sent to St Petersburg in December 1855 was the deciding factor which brought the Crimean War to a speedy close.

In the military field the story which unfolded was one of incompetence and cowardice on the part of the Russian High Command; in the Russian Army itself there was a total lack of determined leadership and professional ability. Yet many of the Russian generals were brave men and numbers of them were shot down leading their columns. The regimental officers and rank and file, ill-trained and ill-equipped, fought with their customary

doggedness. But, if the allies were incapable of exploiting their many vic-
tories in the field, the Russian Army of the Crimea was incapable of winning
one. Its only glory was in the closing stages of the defence of Sevastopol.

The heroes of this unhappy tale were the admirals, the officers and the
sailors of the Black Sea Fleet, who, fighting as infantry and artillerymen, by
their own efforts successfully held Sevastopol after the Russian Army of the
Crimea had abandoned it to the enemy. These men, armed only with musket
and cutlass and serving guns ill-suited to the land battle brought ashore
from their ships, defended unfinished earthworks against an enemy superior
in numbers and in armament. By their example they showed the defeated
Russian Army of the Crimea that the enemy was not invincible. Totleben
was the only army officer who was to prove a leader of ability and renown
in the defence of Sevastopol. But the Black Sea Fleet provided many such
leaders, men of outstanding moral and physical courage, of energy and genius,
officers capable of inspiring the rank and file by their presence and example.
The three greatest captains of them all, the admirals Kornilov, Nakhimov
and Istomin, stand in stone in a Sevastopol park not far from their graves
on the St Vladimir Hill, watching over the naval base in death as they did
in life.

CHAPTER I

* * * * *

TSAR NICHOLAS AND THE ARMY

Nicholas, the third son of Tsarevich Paul and the grandson of Catherine the Great, was born on 18 July 1796, and, according to his grandmother, was a remarkable child at birth; for he was enormous, and at eight days could eat gruel, 'has an astonishing bass voice, takes stock of everybody and moves his head just·like me'. Whereas his two elder brothers, Alexander and Constantine, had been removed from the care of their parents to be raised and educated at Catherine's court, Nicholas was to spend his early childhood with his father and mother.

Tsarevich Paul had no sympathy or affection for the mother who had usurped his throne; she, for her part, had little regard for his talents yet was apparently fearful in case he should oust her. Because of the peculiarity of the precedents and of the law relating to the imperial succession, the monarch assumed the right to nominate his or her successor; Paul suspected, not without reason, that Catherine intended to disinherit him in favour of his own son Alexander. This preyed on his mind so that, resentful of his exclusion from the councils of state, he withdrew from the St Petersburg imperial court of Tsarskoe Selo and the Winter Palace and moved with his wife and entourage to Gatchina, about fifty miles south-west of St Petersburg, remaining there in seclusion until the 42nd year of his life.

The tsarevich was a man of unstable temperament who could by turn be vindictive and cruel, generous and humane. Paul considered himself a liberal in that he sympathized with the Poles and made no secret of his opposition to the war being waged against them by his mother; and he regarded the French as the oppressors of Europe and disapproved of his mother's reluctance to enter the allied coalitions against the revolutionaries. The young court at Gatchina was thus conducted in opposition to Catherine's at Tsarskoe Selo; at Gatchina there was no brilliance, ostentation or luxury, no loose morals or debauchery; instead there was frugality, simplicity and order. Paul had great admiration for Germany, and in particular for Prussia, and, like his father and great-grandfather, he liked to play the soldier, running his household, his suite and the Gatchina court on Prussian military lines. A corps of about 3,000 troops had been stationed at Gatchina and the tsarevich was permitted to command and administer it at his pleasure; by his direction, the training system and the uniform of the troops were altered to conform to the Prussian pattern, so that by degrees the Gatchina corps became a distinct body set apart from the Russian Army. The tsarevich was fascinated by the minutiae of military rules and dress regulations, an absorption which he passed on to his third son Nicholas.

The military standards of this little Potsdam of the north were harsh, even allowing for the conditions of the time, for Paul was under the influence of his colonel of artillery, an able martinet named Arakcheev. This man was later to be responsible for Russian military development over a period of a quarter of a century, and the little corps at Gatchina was eventually to serve as a model for the Russian Army. In the atmosphere of such a household, where the day was regulated by the beat of the drum and by the call of the trumpet, amidst shouts of command and the challenge of sentinels, the young Nicholas lived out his earliest years. At the age of three he was fitted for his first military coat, that of an officer of the Horse Guards; a few years later this child, who, said a visitor, 'presumed to speak at table about political affairs in so decisive a tone', was given the uniform of a general.*

Nicholas's mother was German and his paternal grandmother was the daughter of a Prussian field-marshal; from his parents, and more particularly from his German governesses, Nicholas learned something of German morality and 'correctness' based on self-respect and dignity, and of the importance attached to work and duty. His first tutor was General Lambsdorff, a Baltic German from Kurland, under whose direction the prince learned to ride, to dance and to fence, to speak French and English and to practise on the piano, this last exercise being regarded by the youthful Nicholas as particularly useless since he preferred to play the drum.

In 1796 the Empress Catherine died without dictating her wishes as to the succession, and Paul was proclaimed tsar. The Gatchina battalions in their obsolete and cumbersome Prussian-type uniforms moved to St Petersburg and took over the guard duties on the royal palaces.

Paul had long feared that his claim to the throne would be set aside and that he would be imprisoned or murdered by Catherine's successor, fears which were not entirely baseless for Peter III and Ivan VI had been done to death with the complicity, if not at the instigation, of Paul's own mother. Yet, after Paul had become tsar, his terrors of a usurper were magnified; he

* De Grunwald, *Tsar Nicholas I*, pp. 21–4.

became increasingly eccentric and his method of government took the form of a stream of arbitrary edicts which alienated him from all classes of society. Although not opposed to serfdom, Paul attempted to restrict many of its abuses and this displeased the landowning nobility. He made no secret of his dislike of the regiments of the imperial guard and he gave preference to the officers of his own Gatchina corps; he imposed the Gatchina methods and style of uniform on the rest of the army. Many of Paul's actions were rational and some of them were just, but he lost the goodwill of many factions and failed to make good his threat, in the interest of his own safety, to exile the guard regiments to the distant outposts of the empire. In 1801 Paul was murdered in a palace *coup* instigated by Pahlen, the Governor-General of St Petersburg, together with a small group of army officers and the Semenovsky Guard Regiment. He was deposed, it was suspected, with the foreknowledge of his son and successor Alexander.

The new tsar Alexander was outwardly friendly and modest, going to great lengths to avoid giving offence, and had succeeded, when Catherine was alive, in remaining on good terms both with the empress and with his father. Exuding charm and grace he was a secretive dissimulator and accomplished actor, forming his opinions slowly and trusting no one. More cautious and rational than his father, he resembled him in his many inconsistencies and extremes; he could be autocratic or liberal, strong or weak, obstinate or malleable. Like his father, his mind was continually troubled by secret fears. In military matters Alexander, in his turn, came under the influence of Arakcheev, who, indifferent to the opinions of others and revelling in his own unpopularity, was blamed by the army for Alexander's deficiencies.

Russia's military fame during the first half of the nineteenth century rested on the victory won over Napoleon in 1812; Alexander was regarded as the saviour of Europe, while Russia was held to be the strongest military land power in the world. Nicholas, to his chagrin, took no part in the Napoleonic campaigns since Alexander would not permit him to do so.

In 1815 Nicholas married Charlotte, daughter of the King of Prussia, and thereafter he usually spoke German in his family circle. His obsession for certain aspects of army life continued to grow and it was at about this time that his mother, the dowager Tsarina Marie, wrote to him about her fears lest 'military trifles should interest him more than they ought', hoping that military service would not cause him to adopt a brutal, harsh and imperious manner, for 'this is unpleasant in anyone but unbearable in one of your birth'. But Nicholas was developing two characters, one of charm, known to his family and to the ruling circles in Europe, and the other kept for Russia, hard, severe and gloomy. If, as he said, he was happy amongst his soldiers, 'where all was order and logic', his countenance rarely revealed it. General Mikhailovsky-Danilevsky said of him, that this well-educated man exasperated the officers by assuming the bearing and staccato speech of a sergeant-major; certainly no one knew better than he the regulations, the finer points of drill and the handling of arms. Countess Nessel'rode commented: 'People say that Nicholas is wrong in his behaviour, making himself detested, and they report that he flies into rages, and is severe, vindictive and mean'.* These words might equally have been used to describe his father.

In 1818 Nicholas had been appointed Inspector-General of Engineers and then Colonel of the Ismailovsky Guard Regiment. By 1825 he had been promoted a lieutenant-general.

Alexander was childless, and his brother Constantine, the Viceroy of Poland, who had already married a Polish commoner, told the tsar that he was unwilling to succeed him. By what subsequently became known as the secret manifesto of 1823, Nicholas was named as Alexander's successor, although Nicholas himself was not informed of the decision or invited to his brother's councils of state. When Alexander died in 1825 the Russian Empire was without a tsar for several weeks while the throne was offered between St Petersburg and Warsaw, both Constantine and Nicholas refusing to accept it. The indecision, and the fact that Nicholas was believed to be more autocratic and reactionary than his brother Constantine, brought the Decembrist plotters out into the open with a mutiny of troops in St Petersburg. On 26 December, immediately after he had been proclaimed as sovereign, Nicholas appeared on horseback in the Senate Square escorted by a few generals and aides-de-camp. There, facing the mutineers in the presence of death, he calmly gave orders 'and showed composure and courage that impressed the spectators with profound admiration; from that moment he grew in greatness'.

Nicholas was frequently to give proof of his bravery, firmness and presence of mind; yet, at the same time, he was highly-strung and nervous and incapable of restraining his first impulses, for he was certainly in error when he personally examined several of the accused mutineers. This monarch, who later in life congratulated himself that the death penalty had been abolished in Russia, was capable of ordering a thousand lashes, a punishment which often ended in death, so earning Tolstoy's epithet of 'the flogger'. Yet, as Grunwald has pointed out, even Presniakov, the Soviet

* De Grunwald, *Tsar Nicholas I*, p. 33.

historian, believed that Nicholas 'used every endeavour to avoid all shedding of blood'. Only five of the Decembrists were executed, and those survivors who wrote their memoirs could complain only about military eccentricities, 'that Nicholas was harsh and unfair, strict and vindictive, that he struck soldiers and told the officers of a Finnish regiment that they were pigs'. A more objective description by the Polish Prince Lubomirsky, who was once close to Nicholas, depicted him as 'a bizarre mixture of defects and qualities, of meanness and greatness, brutal and chivalrous, courageous to foolhardiness yet faint-hearted as a poltroon, just yet tyrannical, generous and cruel, fond of ostentation and liking simplicity'.*

The December uprising profoundly shocked Nicholas, for many of the officers involved were known to him personally Nicholas understood that the salvation of the tsarist state and his own safety must depend on the loyalty of the army, and the mutiny reinforced in Nicholas's mind the need to impose on the troops a stricter form of discipline; this, so he apparently believed, could be achieved only by long hours spent each day on the drill ground. Initiative on the part of commanders or troops was to be suppressed in favour of unquestioning obedience. Benckendorff, the Chief of Police, began to recruit informers from within the army to spy on the officers.

* * *

After his succession Nicholas continued to think of himself as primarily a soldier, for he believed that the military life was the most noble calling in the world. He was usually in uniform and much of his day was spent in the *manège* or on the parade ground that echoed to his sonorous voice; his taste was for spartan austerity, and he habitually slept on a camp bed or a mattress filled with straw.

Since Nicholas had, until the time of his accession, been almost fully employed on military duties, he found it difficult, or was unwilling, to alter his method of work and his daily routine after he became tsar. He commanded and administered the Russian Empire as though it were a regiment so that Pushkin characterized him as 'the execrable sovereign, but distinguished colonel'. With Catherine, the rank and title of *general-adiutant* had been given to her favourites; under Alexander, it was bestowed on senior field commanders; Nicholas used generals aide-de-camp for any business he had on hand, military or civil. The members of his military suite thus became his envoys, sometimes his plenipotentiaries, throughout the empire and Europe, twenty-two new generals aide-de-camp being created in the

* De Grunwald, *Tsar Nicholas I*, pp. 32–4.

first year of his reign. The household guard was greatly increased and Nicholas's entourage was almost exclusively military. His civilian ministers were granted only one audience a week and, by 1840, 10 of the 13 ministerial portfolios were held by generals aide-de-camp, the only civilian ministers being those for foreign affairs, education and justice.

Not content with imposing a military rule over the ministries, Nicholas required his subjects to conform to certain quasi-military regulations; he ordered a uniform for nobles, functionaries, professors and students; no civilians were permitted to wear moustaches. Nicholas regarded dress coats, grey hats and 'Jew or French-like' beards as symbols of indiscipline, and this mania grew to such an extent that the tsar would order the guardroom arrest of citizens for what he considered to be irregularities in their appearance or dress, and would have offenders, who in his opinion would profit by the experience, enrolled for a period of military service as private soldiers.

Nicholas rose early, long before dawn, and, after a short walk in the garden of the Winter Palace, set to work in his candle-lit study, dealing with affairs of state until after midday when he received his military leaders. He later let himself out, by a private staircase, to wander alone through the streets of St Petersburg in a threadbare tunic and grey cape with a cap or pointed Prussian helmet; his figure was well known to the citizens who bared their heads respectfully as he passed. Unannounced, he visited and inspected public institutions, schools, hospitals and barracks, nothing escaping his notice. Such behaviour, and in particular his arbitrary punishments of thirty days' arrest, soon ceased to astonish and shock public opinion in the capital.

There was much about the tsar's eccentricity to suggest that he had taken for his models Frederick the Great and Frederick-William of Prussia. Nicholas worked harder than most of his subjects and liked to identify himself with the people; he would help a peasant lift a heavy sack on to his shoulders or walk with the lonely hearse of some forgotten pauper, until accompanied by an ever-growing crowd, he would arrive at the burial place heading a cortège numbering several thousands.

According to Count Zichy's report to Metternich in 1827, military matters occupied three-quarters of Nicholas's day, and he seemed 'to have more talent and better judgement than the generals around him'. Twelve years later, the German General von Gagern reported that 'at first the tsar says he will leave everything to the generals, but hardly an hour goes by and he takes command himself – he cannot help it!'. The French Ambassador said that Nicholas went out of his way to win the army's loyalty, and every year on 26 December, the Decembrist anniversary, he and the tsarina drove in an unescorted carriage to meet the officers and men of the Preobrazhensky and thank them for their loyalty at a time when other guard regiments had mutinied.* Nicholas made some efforts, too, to punish the peculation of officers and functionaries and improve the conditions for the soldier by reducing the enlistment term to fifteen years – but only for those soldiers of excellent conduct who had reached the rank of sergeant, a record that was difficult to achieve.

Nicholas made a number of changes in senior military appointments. Arakcheev was removed because he was unpopular with the army and because Nicholas was averse to sharing his power with anyone. Prince Menshikov, a prominent member of the old Russian party who had been out of favour with Alexander, was recalled to the service; his first mission was a diplomatic one to Teheran to conduct negotiations with the shah. Baron Diebitsch, born in Prussia and educated in a Prussian cadet school, became the chief of the tsar's military staff, and Paskevich, a veteran of Austerlitz and Borodino, was given the key command in the Caucasus. Although Nicholas had rid himself of Arakcheev, in reality the army did not alter much for Nicholas's attention was taken up with ceremonial and with trivialities nearly a century out of date; drill and the field of formal manoeuvre were Nicholas's domain, and he rarely touched upon the real sinews of war, that is to say the development of weapons, tactics and military organization.

Paskevich defeated the Persians in 1826 and 1827 and then attacked the Turks in Caucasia, taking Kars and Erzerum. During the 1828 Turkish War in the Balkans, Nicholas went campaigning, the only time in his life he was to do so, and, true to his nature, he took the direction of operations out of the hands of Wittgenstein, the Commander of 2 Army. Nicholas tried, most unsuccessfully, to run the war and the Russian Empire from his tent, eventually being forced to return to the capital leaving Diebitsch to the field command. In 1829 he recalled Diebitsch to St Petersburg to resume his duties as the head of the military staff before being appointed, two years later, as the Russian Commander-in-Chief responsible for quelling the Polish uprising. Diebitsch died of cholera during the course of the campaign and was replaced by Paskevich, who, on overcoming the Poles, had waged three victorious wars in succession. As a reward the grateful tsar created him Prince of Warsaw, Viceroy of Poland and Commander-in-Chief of the Active Army. Paskevich was to hold this post until the end of the Crimean War. Although Nicholas relied largely on the advice and judgement

* De Grunwald, *Tsar Nicholas I*, pp. 61–82, 135–6.

of this old warrior, Paskevich was unlikely to keep abreast of military thought since his jealous and suspicious nature demanded unthinking obedience from his subordinates. Nor was the field-marshal prepared to oppose his sovereign's caprice. For a quarter of a century he and Nicholas set the pattern for the Russian Army.

The supreme control of the Russian Army was vested in the tsar, and to assist him Nicholas used the services of a Main Staff of His Imperial Majesty consisting of the Minister for War, who acted as the tsar's immediate deputy, the General Master of Ordnance, the Inspector-General of Engineers, and generals of His Imperial Majesty's Suite and a number of other functionaries. The staff had, however, no peacetime administrative function and was merely an advisory and consultative body. Paskevich was usually absent from the capital and was not represented on the main staff.

The Ministers for War during Nicholas's reign, Count Tatishchev, Count Chernyshev (from 1827–53) and Prince Dolgoruki, were responsible only to the sovereign and not to Paskevich or members of the main staff. The Minister of War handled personnel, supply, financial and legal matters connected with the Russian Army, so that he was in fact the tsar's military administrator and deputy, without having, however, power of command over the Commander-in-Chief of the Active Army or over the other members of the main staff, all of whom had direct access to the tsar. Although Paskevich was designated as Commander-in-Chief of the Active Army, he commanded only the troops in Western Europe since all the guard, grenadier and reserve cavalry corps and the military commands in the south-east and the interior came directly under St Petersburg.

The Russian general staff was still in its infancy and its development had suffered a check following the Decembrist rising; for in government and military circles there was a reaction of distrust against the intelligentsia and intellectuals. Although a general staff academy had been founded during Nicholas's reign, the general staff was held in little regard and few officers chose to serve in it; in 1851, for example, there were only 10 staff college graduates from the academy. The Prussian-born Diebitsch, however, knew how to make good use of his few staff officers and this was true also of Prince M.D. Gorchakov, the field commander in the Balkans in 1854. But most of the senior commanders, following Paskevich's lead, affected to despise the officers of the general staff and declined to employ them in their proper role. So the generals went into battle without a planning or command organization, relying entirely on their own judgement in their hour of need; the responsibilities of their immediate circle, usually aides-de-camp and mounted officer gallopers, were rarely clear.

The small staff organization in the capital known as His Majesty's Suite for Quartermaster Affairs was the only permanent general staff body in existence, but its responsibilities covered the movement and quartering of troops, reconnaissance, intelligence and finance. So it came about that the general staff had little training or experience in operations, reconnaissance or topography as applicable to the conditions of war, since the Russian Army's main training ground was the drill square; even its battle tactics were performed as parade evolutions.

About one in five of the regimental officers had entered the army from the *corps des pages* (for the regiments of the guard) and from the military cadet schools (for the line), nearly all of them belonging to the *dvorianstvo* or hereditary nobility, which differed from the aristocracy elsewhere in Europe since it formed no more than a titular or petty *noblesse*, having neither wealth nor land and not being part of the court. The majority of the officers, however, were other rank volunteers, many of these also, according to Lieutenant-General Bogdanovich, coming from the nobility of the fourth class (the sons of army officers or civil servants), who before being commissioned had to pass a qualifying examination and serve in the ranks as *junker*. The *junker* was neither officer nor conscript, and his duties approximated to those of a senior sergeant; on service he usually lived with the officers.

Another method of officer recruitment was by the direct entry of former non-commissioned officers 'without status or fortune', who had qualifying service of ten years in the guard or twelve in the line and who could pass a simple examination. Some of these non-commissioned officers were 'cantonists', the sons of military colonists, trained as soldiers from the age of six and known among their fellow officers as 'bourbons' because of their imperious and unmannerly behaviour. The commissioned cantonists were usually unthinking automata, prized by regimental commanders because of their readiness to perform all the irksome routine duties. According to Captain Chodasiewicz, infantry line regiments held a high proportion of these promoted non-commissioned officers.

Some celebrated nineteenth-century Russian writers and composers had been army officers, but they were not typical of their class, for most officers appear to have been without higher education or intellectual development. Little was demanded of them beyond obedience and the performance of routine duties according to the regulation; youthful enthusiasm was soon dulled by boredom and drink. Except in the guard and grenadier corps and in certain cavalry regiments, officers were without independent means; promotion was slow and pay was poor, hardly a third of that of Prussian officers, and it differed little according to rank, for a Russian colonel's salary was only twice that paid to a lieutenant. Prussian officers were obliged to live frugally; the Russian officer could hardly exist on his pay, and this was possibly a contributory cause of the corruption and dishonesty often found among army officers and officials in the Russian Empire. But the Russian officer shared the virtues as well as the characteristic defects of his men; he did not lack courage or hardiness, he was generous and had his own conception of honour; if he was unfitted for war it was because his training rarely extended beyond the parade ground and the office. Yet the command organization would probably have worked efficiently if its generals had been men of ability, which they were not: they were products of a military system which regarded any tendency towards independent thought as heresy, and which was a false imitation of the Prussian in that it failed to understand and copy the lesson of German efficiency, honesty, integrity and leadership by example.

Some of the tsars and part of the court nobility were German by birth, and numbers of German officers had been induced to enter the Russian service. These were greatly outnumbered, however, by Russian nationals of German origin, the descendants of earlier generations of immigrants who had come into Russia or the Baltic provinces; many of these settlers had remained as close-knit foreign communities, retaining even their language. Officers of Russian stock called them the *liebe Brüder* and resented their presence, for according to popular belief promotion was assured only for those with German names.

By the 1831 military service law, about 80,000 conscripts were taken into the army each year for a period of colour service of 25 years in the line and 22 in the guard. Recruits were selected at the age of 20 from those who paid poll tax, from town-dwellers and peasants, many of whom were serfs. The main burden of military service fell, however, on the poorer peasants of Russian nationality, and their selection was left mainly in the hands of the village elders of the communes in that these worthies appear to have been allowed considerable discretion as to exemptions. The names of those eligible for service, the non-exempt, were then put into an urn from which the required number of recruits was drawn by lot. When a man left his home village he usually did so for ever, since if he survived his period of service he had little inclination to return to a community in which he was a stranger; and so he either re-enlisted or became a drifter or a vagabond.

After a medical examination and the administering of the oath by a priest, recruits were allocated to arms. Tall and well-built men went to the guards; those who were literate went to the engineers or became clerks;

lighter men, particularly those who had been brought up with horses, were despatched to the cavalry or artillery; when the cavalry and supporting arms had taken their pick, the remainder, the great mass, went to the infantry. In the early days of their service the recruits were kept under close guard in case they should desert.

The training system was harsh and unimaginative, the commanders of all arms being obsessed by the requirements of the parade ground – posture, carriage, arms drill and the precision goose-step, and the slapping of the ground with the sole of the boot peculiar to the Russian service. Even after the Crimean War Alexander II was still recounting with pride how his former Semenovsky drill instructor would place a glass full of water on the top of his shako and drill, turn and march, his legs raised in turn parallel to the ground as he goose-stepped 'without spilling a drop'. Officers, even generals, were abused and ridiculed on parade in front of their troops; other ranks received 'the toothpick', the smashing blow on the jaw, or were flogged, or made to run the gauntlet.

Although at the time it was widely believed in Europe that Russia had very large armed forces, the military historian Bogdanovich, who once served in Nicholas's army, maintained that the tsar, if he had been challenged, could hardly have put more troops into the field than either Austria or France. For, said Bogdanovich, the establishment of the regular army was only 494,000 men, and this figure included the 135,000 already with the reserve; of this reserve, 46,000 men were required to bring the regular units up to their war establishment leaving only 89,000 to replace casualties or to raise new formations.* This reserve was a doubtful asset since most of the 135,000 reservists were past their 45th year and too old for campaigning, yet the regular army could not go to war without it; in 1849 Paskevich had insisted that his corps must be reinforced even by these over-age veterans before he could move his troops to assist the Austrians in suppressing the Hungarian uprising.

Professor Zaionchovsky's study, published in 1908, made use of official Russian sources that had not been available to Bogdanovich, for neither Nicholas I nor Alexander II permitted the disclosure of the true Russian strengths. Zaionchovsky put the roll of the Russian Army considerably higher than that estimated by Bogdanovich, maintaining that the 'one million army' was a fiction only insofar as in reality the figure was an under-estimate; the active strength of the Russian Army, he said, stood at 834,000 men on 1 January 1853, while the regular reserve numbered a further

---

* Bogdanovich, *Vostochnaia Voina*, Vol. 1, Ch. 4 (*Prilozhenie*).

159,000 officers and men bringing the total to nearly a million. To this figure Zaionchovsky, unlike Bogdanovich, has added the so-called irregular troops, irregular only in name since they comprised the non-Russian regular regiments of the standing army, mostly of cavalry, and the powerful reserve forces of the Cossack hosts; for the Cossacks had their own system of short service conscription, all able-bodied men of the host undergoing three years' full-time military training before going to the reserve. Although the peace-time strength of these irregular troops stood at only 90,000 this could be increased by the calling up of Cossack reserves to nearly a quarter of a million men.* Lastly there were the 146,000 men of the corps of internal defence, a properly organized military body although poorly trained and equipped, that brought the total active and reserve strength to 1,400,000 men.

By the mere threat of the use of such a force Nicholas virtually controlled the destinies of the peoples of Central and Eastern Europe for more than a quarter of a century. Yet, as was to be proved, the Russian armed forces were in no way ready for modern war, and, when put to the test, were incapable of giving substance to Nicholas's grandiose political designs. And, whatever the numerical strength of the Russian Army, Nicholas had insufficient troops when he entered upon the Crimean War for he had to find his reinforcements between July 1852 and December 1854 by six com-pulsory levies, requiring the Russian provinces to furnish numbers based on a percentage of their population: these gave him recruits but not soldiers.

The Russian long service recruiting system could not build up a trained reserve in peace sufficient in numbers to reinforce and expand the army in war. On the other hand, Nicholas's military organization was eminently suitable for maintaining internal security and suppressing disorders and it met the peculiarly Russian requirement, caused by the great distances and the lack of railways to bridge them, that armed forces should be in existence and ready for action both on the frontiers and at communication centres in the interior. An army based on short service conscription could certainly have provided the reserves required for European war, but it would have proved difficult to mobilize and deploy these reserves at short notice. Moreover, the introduction of general conscription would have given rise to further political and social problems, in that the raising of a citizen army could have led firstly to a loosening of the disciplinary code and then to subversion and civil war – for this was one of the courses which had been advocated by some of the Decembrists. And, since by law a man

* Zaionchovsky, *Vostochnaia Voina*, Vol. 1 *Prilozheniia*, pp. 484–6.

ceased to be a serf as soon as he entered the army, general conscription would presumably have meant the end of serfdom.

The peacetime regular army consisted of the guard reserve cavalry corps (St Petersburg) and one guard infantry and one grenadier corps (Novgorod), all three corps coming under the immediate control of Nicholas. Paskevich commanded the four infantry corps, the so-called Active Army stationed in Central Europe for the defence of the western frontiers, but the control of 5 (Odessa) and 6 (Moscow) Independent Infantry Corps was retained by the tsar through the Minister of War; 1 (Novomirgorod) and 2 (Kharkov) Line Reserve Cavalry Corps came under the Inspector of Reserve Cavalry. The Caucasus, Orenburg and Siberian Corps were responsible direct to the sovereign.

The organization of the Russian field formations was common to that of the other European powers, the infantry corps consisting of three divisions each of four regiments of three battalions, to which were added one corps rifle and one corps sapper battalion, making a total of 38 battalions in all. Infantry corps, except that of the guard, had in addition a light cavalry division of 32 squadrons. The guard reserve cavalry corps consisted of one cuirassier and two light cavalry divisions, while the line reserve cavalry corps each had two or three cuirassier, uhlan or dragoon divisions.

The infantry division, whether guard, grenadier or line, had two brigades each of two infantry regiments, the regiments consisting of three, or sometimes four, battalions. The brigades, regiments, and even the companies within the battalions, might be designated grenadier, carabineer, eger, fusilier, or infantry (musketeer), but these titles had only a traditional significance since the organization, armament and function of all of them were identical. Infantry battalions usually consisted of four companies each of 250 men when at full establishment, but an infantry regiment rarely numbered more than 2,500 men. A cavalry division had two brigades each of two regiments; heavy (cuirassier) and guard cavalry regiments had six squadrons, light (hussar) and lancer (uhlan) regiments had eight, and mounted infantry (dragoons) had 10 squadrons; a squadron numbered 170 men.

The artillery brigades in an infantry corps were grouped under an artillery division commanded by a major-general; although he could exercise direct control over the deployment of the batteries, this was properly the task of the commanders of the artillery brigades organic to the infantry divisions. The artillery brigade usually had two 12-gun field batteries, each of six 12-pounder guns and six 18-pounder howitzers, and two 12-gun light batteries, each of eight 6-pounder guns and four 9-pounder howitzers. Horse and Cossack batteries had only eight guns or howitzers, usually

6-pounder guns and 9-pounder howitzers. Guns and howitzers were smooth-bore, brass muzzle-loaders, fired with a slow match and mounted on wooden gun carriages; all could fire cast-iron roundshot and case-shot, musket balls packed into a light canister which broke up on firing. Field pieces, except the 6-pounder guns, could also fire a fused high-explosive shell which relied for its anti-personnel effect on the breaking up of the shell casing, and a form of high-explosive shrapnel shell filled with musket balls. The maximum range of this field artillery varied from 900–1100 yards, but the flying fragments of a bursting shell could cause casualties over a radius of 500 yards. The rate of fire, even of the light 6-pounder gun, was not more than two rounds a minute. Each gun required a draught team of four horses (six for each of the field and horse battery guns), and three for each of the two-wheeled ammunition caissons. Horsed artillerymen carried a pistol and a light cavalry sword, but all foot artillery were unarmed except for a short half-sabre hardly longer than a bayonet.

Most Russian infantry were equipped with smooth-bore muzzle-loading muskets recently converted from flint-locks by the replacement of the flint mechanism by a percussion striker and firing capsule. This modified weapon fired a .700-inch spherical bullet, and, as its flat trajectory was only 150 paces and it had no ranging sight, it was rarely effective above 200 paces; its weight together with the bayonet was nearly 12 pounds. Reloading was difficult and slow and could only be done from a standing position, the maximum rate of fire being one round a minute; after firing several rounds the barrels became so scaled up that it was difficult to insert the bullet into the muzzle, while a damaged or lost ramrod made further firing impossible. By 1 January 1853, nearly all the regular infantry corps had received the converted muskets. All other infantry formations and nearly all the line cavalry went to war armed with flint-locks.

The few rifle battalions, one to each corps, were completely equipped with rifled weapons, and each line infantry and cavalry regiment held a few score rifles for long range fire. All Russian rifles were muzzle-loaders, the cavalry marksmen being equipped with 1818 pattern .675-inch eight-groove carbines which had an effective range of only 400 paces. The infantry and rifle battalion rifle was the 1843 percussion fired Littikhsky, although some Gartung rebored dragoon muskets were also in use. Both the Littikhsky and the Gartung were of .700 inch calibre, the rifling consisting of two broad spiralling grooves into which were seated the two projecting lugs of the bullet. The maximum range of the Littikhsky was 1,120 paces.

*   *   *

The field training of the Russian foot had progressed little since the Napoleonic Wars, being based on a set of drill movements. Since the musket had little range and such a poor rate of fire, infantry were forced to rely on the shock action of the bayonet; so it came about that the main tactical manoeuvre was directed towards closing with the enemy, the advance to contact and attack being based on Carnot's dense columns of the French Revolutionary Armies of the previous century. The column, formed up line behind line almost in the fashion of a square or of an ancient Macedonian phalanx, would advance on the enemy with a regular and measured step, the musket, with bayonet fixed, being carried in a vertical position close to the soldier's right side, the right arm, held stiffly to the side, grasping the weapon by the small of the butt, the left arm resting across the chest and holding the upper part of the musket by the stock. Only the front rank of the column marched with the point of the bayonet lowered towards the enemy in the 'on guard' position. In battle, as in ceremonial, the advance was carried out with drums beating and colours flying, this awe-inspiring sight being described by one enthusiastic contemporary Russian commentator as 'the spectacle of the gods'. Alabin, however, in passing a retrospective judgement on this battle manoeuvre, said contemptuously of it that 'the criterion of efficiency depended entirely on the style of marching and on the correct stretching forward of the toe'.

In the Napoleonic Wars the attack in close column had proved successful against defenders equipped with the short range and slow loading musket, for the effect of the steady advance, coupled with the fire of flanking artillery and skirmishers who covered the column, was often sufficient to demoralize the enemy before the battle was joined. In addition to its shock power and momentum the column had the advantage that it was easy to control, for no man could falter or run away; on the other hand it suffered from obvious disadvantages in that the serried ranks offered an easy target and that only the first two ranks were in a position to engage the enemy either with the bayonet or by musket fire. There were a number of different types of column, some of them very complicated; the company column was widely used in the advance to contact in order to cover the front and flank of the main shock force – which was usually in the battalion column – the company columns having the advantage of dispersal in that they were separated from each other by distances of 100 paces or more, but were still close enough to be mutually supporting by fire. The close battalion column remained the favourite, however, because of the ease with which it could be controlled; in this tactical formation the battalion of 800 men would attack in a phalanx which had a frontage of only 25 paces and a depth of 32 paces.*

The Russian Army persisted in its reliance on column, rather than on line or open order fighting, partly because of the poor quality of its small-arms and partly because it was, as yet, unacquainted with the capabilities of modern rifled weapons. The regulations, admittedly, had once made it obligatory to train 48 of the best marksmen in each company as skirmishers for open order fighting, and the line formation, in two or three ranks, had been practised as a drill movement when it was necessary to illustrate the theory of maximum concentrated fire; but the line formation was never used in the field because the Russian tended to rely on the defence by counter-attack.

In the period between 1815 and 1850 Russian Army training had been directed towards fighting the Turk, and Paskevich emphasized in his 1853 series of tactical regulations that formations must move and fight *en masse* in order to counter the mobility of the Turkish cavalry and infantry who attacked in scattered groups from all sides.† Paskevich ordered that Russian troops must avoid operations in open order, even in broken or close country, because they fought best in tight formations. Instead of throwing out a line of skirmishers, protection had to be found by using company or half-company columns out to the front or flanks; even cavalry were not allowed to open up into extended order, but had to operate by half squadrons. Paskevich included detailed rules for the movement and deployment of all formations and units, arbitrarily regulating the exact distances to be maintained between them and prescribing the methods to be used to repel each type of Turkish attack. Paskevich allowed only the Don Cossacks to operate singly or in small groups, because he believed them to be the finest troops in Europe for outpost work of this type.

The development of small-arms had been neglected for decades in the Russian Army and there had been strong opposition to the introduction of breech-loading weapons on the grounds that they would encourage the infantryman to shoot off his ammunition and make him disinclined to close with the enemy. The bayonet was the master and, according to Bogdanovich, recourse to fire-arms was scorned by the infantry of the line. Such firing as was done was by volleys, troops 'discharging more blank than ball, so that it was not unusual to find infantrymen of many years' service who had rarely fired their muskets; each was allowed only ten rounds a year, but this was often used for other purposes'. Tactical training took place on the parade

---

* Zaionchovsky, *Vostochnaia Voina*, Vol. 1, p. 529; Vol. 1 (*Prilozheniia*), No. 186.
† *Rukovodstvo dlia boia protiv Turok*, 1 August 1853.

ground or on open and flat fields and no use was made of obstacles or ground. Battle formations and inter-arm co-operation were conducted according to an unalterable system and laws, there being five set battle orders for infantry supported by artillery, and four for cavalry supported by artillery. Deviations were not permitted.

The Russian cavalry force was the largest in the world, totalling 60 regiments made up of 454 squadrons. The cuirassier heavy cavalry was meant primarily for shock action and was armed with a heavy straight sword; the front rank usually carried a lance but, other than the non-commissioned officers, all of whom had pistols, the cuirassiers had no fire-arms. The dragoons, who could fight both mounted and on foot, were armed with a musket and bayonet and a light cavalry sword. The light cavalry, that is to say the hussars and the uhlans, had a sabre and cavalry carbine, all uhlans having in addition the lance. Cavalry fought in column or in two ranks. By European standards the Russian cavalry horse was indifferent in quality, being small and light of bone.

Russian cavalry suffered from the same sickness which had taken hold of the infantry, for too much of its training was directed towards displays, reviews and ceremonial occasions; covered *manège* volutions were considered to be more important than field-day riding across country. The horses became sleek and soft through underwork and the daily hours of grooming, and the cavalryman's idea of mounted movement was a leisurely walking pace with the singers out ahead; even trotting was forbidden. Too much was artificial and had no bearing on war. On campaign the horses suffered early casualties due to their lack of fitness and being overloaded, for they carried rider, kettles, rations, blankets and fodder; more Russian horses died during the short subtropical summer than in the long and bitter winters. Lord Lucan, the commander of the British cavalry in the Crimea, had been present with the Russian Army during the Turkish War of 1829, and he described the regular Russian cavalry as 'being as bad as could be, but the Cossacks could be damnably troublesome to an enemy, especially in a retreat'.

The Cossacks occupied a unique position in the Russian forces for they were recruited under special terms of service from the Russian and Ukrainian settler hosts that once guarded the frontiers of Old Russia. Military service had long been compulsory for all Cossacks so that it had become part of their way of life; to be rejected by the authorities on medical or other ground was regarded as a slight both on the man and on his family, for the Cossack's father provided, at his own expense, the horse, saddlery, uniform, sabre, lance and other equipment, only the carbine being supplied by the government. In return for a grant of common land and exemption from taxes, the Cossack was held to be at the service of the tsar for as long as he could sit a horse, but by the amending law of 1835 the recruit served full-time for only three years, after which he went to the reserve, remaining available for colour service until his fiftieth birthday. The Cossack was not the wild savage sometimes described by West European writers, for he was usually more intelligent and better educated than the Russian cavalry or infantry of the line; on the other hand, he was less amenable to the harsh and rigid discipline of the Russian troops, and, if he was a recalled reservist rather than a recruit on his initial period of colour service, he soon lapsed into his frontiersman's ways with a looser and more informal relationship with his officers and junior leaders. On service he wore what he pleased, and his mount was an unkempt, diminutive and scrubby little pony often recently broken from the wild steppe herds and sharing with its rider an extraordinary stamina.

These characteristics, bred into the soldier by his birth and surroundings, separated the Cossack troops from the Russian mass. The Russian infantry-man was unthinking and obstinate in defence; the Cossack, on the other hand, was observant, cautious and independent, with a highly developed instinct for self-preservation, for he saw no virtue in dying where he stood when by removing himself a verst to the rear he could continue the fight. Although the Cossack mounted regiments were organized in much the same fashion as the line cavalry, they had little value for shock action since they usually lacked the necessary discipline and training. But, as Paskevich and Lucan were agreed, there were no better troops than Cossacks for raiding, for seeking out gaps in defence lines, or for pursuit.

CHAPTER 2

* * * * *

DIPLOMACY AND THREATS

When, in 1552, Ivan the Terrible overcame the Tatar Khanate of Kazan, five hundred miles to the east of Moscow, the last barrier was removed to Russian expansion into Asia; thereafter colonizing families made their way beyond the Urals, spreading almost spontaneously eastwards across the wastes of Asia to the Bering Sea and beyond. Since this movement met no serious resistance it remained without centralized government direction from Moscow, the real work of settlement being left to the colonists themselves, the merchant adventurers and the Cossack hosts.

To the north-west, the west and the south of European Russia the situation had been different, for tsarist expansionism, entirely deliberate in its nature, had been opposed by Swede, Lithuanian, Pole, Austrian and Turk. Undeterred by this resistance, the successors of Peter the Great had stubbornly and systematically sought to advance their frontiers along the Baltic and the Black Sea coasts in order to gain access to the oceans of the world, while to the west of Muscovy they tried to project their borders into the heart of Central Europe. Nicholas improved on the methods of his predecessors when he based his claims on the romantic and self-assumed roles of protector of the Slavs and of defender of the Greek Orthodox church.

When the great visionary Alexander I died, the Austrian minister Metternich said that 'the romance is ended and the story now begins', for Metternich saw Nicholas as a soldier and man of action. Yet in reality Nicholas was more gifted as a diplomat than as a soldier for he was energetic and tenacious and had quick wit and fluent speech in many tongues: he was cunning and devious and he shamelessly flattered the heads of state and their diplomats in the pursuit of his own ends; and he spoke 'with great clarity, briefly and simply, his arguments being closely reasoned and shrewdly worked out'. The tsar was sometimes majestic, sometimes condescending, apparently frank – even ingenuous – usually charming to foreigners, and with his eye ever on Russia's interests.

Nicholas's courage and determination might have brought lasting benefits to Russia if he had not been a man of impulse 'in whom passion often swept away reason'. Then the soldier ousted the diplomat and Nicholas assumed the guise of the menacing warlord, promising to put 300,000 Russian troops at the disposal of the Austrian Emperor, the King of Prussia or the King of the Netherlands; and although he probably had no intention of sending a man, the threats were not forgotten elsewhere in Europe. He was, thought Grunwald, a bad psychologist who wanted to impose his own ideas on the whole world; war would probably have broken out earlier were it not for the judgement and efforts of Nessel'rode, his German-born Chancellor.*

Catherine the Great had secured part of the south coast of the Baltic Sea by the annexation of Kurland from what had formerly been Poland, and Alexander had further improved the Russian hold by incorporating Finland into the Russian Empire. In 1831 when the Kingdom of Poland lost its constitution, the western frontiers of the Russian Empire bordered on East and South Prussia, Silesia and Austrian Galicia. To the south, further Russian encroachment was blocked by the Ottoman Empire which still stretched from Bosnia, Serbia, Wallachia and Moldavia to Arabia and Tunisia: since the sultan controlled the straits to the Mediterranean, the Black Sea was virtually a Turkish lake.

Nicholas believed that the Ottoman Empire was dying fast and must shortly disintegrate, and it was he who coined the description 'the sick man of Europe'. But although Nicholas sympathized with the aspirations of his Greek co-religionists in their struggle for independence against Moslem oppression, he could not bring himself to support revolutionaries against the Sultan of Turkey whom he regarded as the Greeks' lawful sovereign. Nicholas preferred what he believed to be the more open and honest course, conquest or partition by intimidation. He told the Austrian Ambassador in 1829 that the Turkish Empire was 'about to fall', and he asked the question: 'Would it not be better to forestall the people who would fill the vacuum?'. The tsar was in favour of sharing the fruits of conquest with any power that would assist him, but after his unhappy experience in the early Turkish wars he was disinclined to undertake the task alone. It was for this reason that he listened to Nessel'rode's advice and gave up the idea of annexing the Danubian Principalities of Moldavia and Wallachia (those territories which, after the Congress of Berlin in 1878, were to form modern Rumania).

* De Grunwald, *Tsar Nicholas I*, pp. 179–84.

In 1833 the sultan appealed to Nicholas for help when his capital was threatened by the rising of Mohamet-Ali, the Pasha of Egypt. Nicholas saw the uprising as sedition, 'a germ of evil and disorder . . . if Constantinople is lost then we shall have as neighbours a nest of stateless persons', and he ordered Admiral Lazarev's squadron to land an expeditionary force on the shores of the Bosphorus. In July of that year the thankful sultan agreed the Unkiar-Skelessy treaty of friendship and alliance between Russia and Turkey, proclaiming 'the exclusive predominance of Russia in the affairs of the Ottoman Empire' while a secret clause closed the Black Sea to foreign warships. Overnight the sea had been transformed from a Turkish to a Russian lake. The treaty was ill received elsewhere, for in France the government and public were hostile to Russia and sympathetic with the rebellious Poles, to many of whom they had given sanctuary; in London, statesmen were sensitive about Russian inroads into Persia and suspicious of Nicholas's naval pretensions. The worsening of relations with these two maritime powers made Nicholas seek a better understanding with Austria and Prussia. But he made his own position clear with regard to the Ottoman Empire when he told the Austrian Ambassador 'I do not meddle with Spain and Portugal, but as to Turkey that is my own affair'.

The Russian Navy had been much neglected since the death of Peter the Great and one of Nicholas's earliest actions had been to institute far-reaching naval reforms, appointing one of his favourites, Major-General Prince Alexander Sergeevich Menshikov, to implement the naval re-organization and re-equipment programme. Menshikov had been born in 1787 from a line of princes of Russia and the Roman Empire, a descendant of Peter the Great's crony Field-Marshal Prince Alexander Danilovich Menshikov, he who, originally of humble origin, purchased a Swedish soldier's wife at the sack of Marienburg and subsequently, on Peter the Great's death, secured the throne for her as Empress Catherine I and became himself the virtual ruler of Russia. His descendant Prince Alexander Sergeevich had entered the college of foreign affairs as a diplomatic *junker* in 1805, and was later attached to the Russian Embassies in Berlin and London. In 1809 he entered the artillery of the guard as a second lieutenant, seeing service in Moldavia and becoming an aide-de-camp to Alexander I; three years later he transferred to the Preobrazhensky Guard and was appointed as the divisional staff officer of operations of a grenadier division at Borodino; at the battle of Leipzig in 1813 Menshikov was accredited to the staff of the Crown Prince of Sweden, and in 1814 was wounded during the march on Paris. In 1816, six years after being commissioned, he was already a major-general on the operations directorate of the tsar's military staff, the next year being appointed *general-adiutant* to Alexander, whom he accompanied on missions at home and abroad. In 1823 he was seconded to the Ministry of Foreign Affairs, but, as a result of Arakcheev's intrigue, he fell from grace the next year and was 'released from the service due to domestic circumstances'.* Nicholas, on his accession, had recalled Menshikov to his own military staff and restored him to favour.

Although Menshikov knew nothing of maritime affairs Nicholas transferred him from the army to the navy with the rank of rear-admiral, appointing him in 1829 Chief of Naval Staff and Naval Member of the Committee of Ministers, action so unusual that the English newspapers of the time carried caricatures showing Menshikov booted and spurred and riding the decks of a warship on a horse. Menshikov continued to serve with the navy for more than a quarter of a century; although Austrian diplomats reported him to be a naval administrator of ability, the correctness of these opinions must remain in doubt.

In 1839 Nicholas, the astute opportunist, altered his stance in the affairs of the Middle-East where the situation had undergone a radical change. Mohamet-Ali had routed the sultan's forces and extended his power over Asia Minor and Arabia as far as the Persian Gulf; this put the British and French in disarray, for Paris wanted to support Mohamet-Ali, but London, fearing that India might be threatened, declared for the sultan and signed an agreement with Russia, Austria and Prussia, pledging help. In 1841, by a further protocol signed in London with the adherence of France and Turkey, Russia renounced the privileges given by the Treaty of Unkiar-Skelessy; henceforth the closing of the Bosphorus and the Dardanelles to foreign warships was recognized as fundamental to international law. Nicholas thus sought to drive a wedge between Britain and France, even at the cost of losing the Russian protectorate over Turkey and military access into the Mediterranean. The tsar showed himself to be a realist in that he understood that his own Black Sea Fleet would have been powerless against the British naval forces in the Mediterranean and that British help was indispensable whether Russia were to take military action against the sultan or against the Turkish and Egyptian insurgents. Ignoring the hostile London press, Nicholas continued to court Victoria and Palmerston, and he pressed for military alliances and commercial treaties between the two countries. In 1844 when the tsar visited Britain he protested to Prince Albert and British statesmen that he was 'an honest and sincere man and not the impostor he was generally considered to be', adding that 'he did

---

* *Morskoi Sbornik*, 1869, T. 102, No. 5; *Russkii Invalid*, 1869, No. 2.

not want an inch of Turkish territory but would not allow others to seize it'. Nicholas's real intentions were scarcely concealed, for Palmerston wrote that 'one is denying the teaching of history if one believes that Russia is not thinking of extending to the south . . . for all governments, especially absolute governments, think of increasing their territory for political rather than economic reasons'. According to Palmerston, Russia, by which he presumably meant Nicholas, was 'just a great humbug'.

In February 1848 came the revolution in Paris and the setting up of a new republic in France, events which Nicholas viewed with anxiety. The following month the revolutionary disorders in Berlin prompted the tsar to issue a manifesto threatening 'the revolutionary presumption which dares, in its madness, to menace Russia'; this proclamation caused alarm elsewhere because it was feared that the manifesto might presage armed intervention by Russia in the affairs of its neighbours. Nor was this concern unjustified for, in July of the same year, Russian troops re-entered the Danubian Principalities since Nicholas was afraid that they would lapse into anarchy. By the Treaty of Balta-Liman which Russia imposed on the Porte, Moldavia and Wallachia were deprived of their elected assemblies.

Towards the end of 1848 the Hungarians rose against Austria in defence of the 1848 constitution; Nicholas was at first reluctant to interfere. Early in 1849, however, a few Russian troops were sent into Transylvania to quell the fighting between Hungarians and Rumanians, and the Austrian Emperor Francis-Joseph appealed to Nicholas for armed assistance against the Hungarians, emphasizing that the success of the revolution must endanger both of their thrones. Numbers of Poles, former subjects of the tsar, were prominent among the Magyar insurgents and there had been outbreaks of violence involving Poles and Ruthenians in Lithuania and Galicia. In May Nicholas ordered Paskevich into Hungary, explaining to the world in his imperial manifesto that the intention was 'to annihilate the audacious anarchists who threaten the peace of our frontiers'. London was unwilling to permit the Austrian Empire to be broken up and was particularly disturbed that many of the revolutionaries were indeed motivated by anarchism; for this reason the British Government was at first sympathetic to Russia's action and Nicholas lost its goodwill only when he demanded from Turkey the extradition of those insurgent Poles who had taken refuge there.

Russia's relationship with Prussia became strained during this period, for Nicholas suspected that the Prussian territories of Posen, or what was then known as South Prussia, were a breeding ground for Polish subversion inside Russia; and the tsar mistrusted any proposal for German unification.

Nicholas sent bellicose demands to his brother-in-law Frederick-William in 1848, at the time of the Prusso-Danish War, and again in 1850. That same year the tsar favoured Austria when he arbitrated at Olmütz in a dispute between Vienna and Berlin, an action described by Bunsen, a Prussian, as an imposed solution 'worse than the partition of the world between Alexander and Napoleon'. Some Prussians began to think of their own state as an appendage, a province of Russia, 'governed by hereditary regents of the house of Hohenzollern'. Even Albert, the Prince Consort, wrote that 'the Emperor Nicholas is master of Europe'. The situation was best summed up by Stockmar when he said that Nicholas had improved on the methods of Napoleon, for he had undertaken no campaigns and, unlike that emperor, had not even had to raise a succession of new military forces; Nicholas had attained more important results without striking a blow, merely by diplomacy and threats. Such power, according to Stockmar, seemed unexampled.†

*   *   *

The immediate cause of the Eastern War against Turkey centred around the quarrel between the Greek and the Latin churches over the custody of the holy places in Jerusalem and Bethlehem. In 1841 the French had proposed that Jerusalem should be made a free city and, ten years later, the King of Prussia suggested that the five major European powers should be jointly responsible for protecting the Christian inhabitants of the Ottoman Empire. In Nicholas's view, however, he alone was answerable for those subjects of the sultan who were members of the Greek Orthodox church; indeed, he appeared to think that the Koutchouk-Kainardji Treaty made between the Porte and Catherine the Great, on which he based his claim, could be extended to include *all* Christians living in the Turkish Empire. The tsar was obsessed by the belief that the Polish *émigrés* living in Constantinople had a hand in every intrigue against him. At first the sultan gave in to Nicholas's demands, but a few weeks later he revoked his orders, and, on the urging of the French Ambassador at the Porte, withdrew the concessions he had made to the Orthodox church only to grant them to the Catholics. It was apparent to Nicholas and to the outside world that the sultan intended to be independent of St Petersburg.

Nicholas had aged prematurely, and with the years came a marked eccentricity. The Prussian military attaché, reporting on him at this time, thought him, 'passionate, conceited, unfair, indiscreet and intractable'. In 1852 the French Minister saw him as 'difficult to understand, with incon-

† De Grunwald, *Tsar Nicholas I*, pp. 198–200.

gruous qualities and defects, the simplest and best of men who inspires fear in all around him, friendly, romantic, harsh and unforgiving'. Nicholas had, thought de Castelbajac, something about his character resembling 'Peter the Great, Paul I and a knight of the middle ages, but in ageing it is Paul I who is the strongest in him'. Intoxicated by his diplomatic successes between 1848 and 1852, Nicholas saw himself as the overlord of Europe. From 1852 onwards he became obsessed with Slavophilism, persuading himself that the millions of Christians in the Turkish Empire regarded him as their saviour. Since such an attitude was foreign to his government and court and was unlikely to have been encouraged by the German-born tsarina, Grunwald has surmised that Barbette Nelidov, the tsar's mistress, may have encouraged Nicholas in these fantasies.

In January 1853 the tsar, addressing the British Ambassador Sir Hamilton Seymour 'as a friend and a gentleman', was sufficiently imprudent to tell him that it was Russia's duty and right to watch over the interests of the many millions of Christians within the Turkish Empire; if anyone should contest this right then he, as tsar, would not shrink from a temporary occupation of Constantinople. The Danube Principalities, he continued, were 'already independent under Russia's protection'; Serbia and Bulgaria should similarly become independent states; England, thought Nicholas, should perhaps be offered Egypt and Crete.

A few months later the tsar wrote to the Austrian Emperor telling him that the populations of Moldavia, Wallachia, Bulgaria, Greece and Serbia were about to rise and throw off Turkish domination, and he hinted that the European powers should accelerate the process by recognizing the independence of each of the newly emerging states; Constantinople, suggested Nicholas, should be declared a free city and the defences along the straits razed to the ground. By November, however, Nicholas's opinions and resolutions had hardened, for he said that he intended to forestall the machinations of the British Government and invite the Christian nations to join with Russia in a holy crusade towards achieving a sacred aim, the liberation of all Christians, irrespective of their particular faith, who were subject to Moslem domination in Europe.

Early in 1853 Nicholas had sent Prince Menshikov on a mission extraordinary to Constantinople to present his case and, it was widely believed, to intimidate the sultan. Menshikov who, according to the diplomat Meyendorff, had great talent for repartee but a negligible mind and a dubious character, had neither the frankness nor the honesty to command respect, and Grunwald has quoted the view of Mandt, Nicholas's physician, that Menshikov did not take his mission seriously, 'it simply furnished him with a fresh excuse for witticisms and jokes'. Although it is true that Men-shikov caused great offence to the sultan and his court by his brutal arrogance, he was carrying out Nicholas's instructions: 'if Turkey did not yield, then the ambassador extraordinary must threaten the destruction of Constantinople and the occupation of the Dardanelles'. Nor were these empty threats, for the tsar was actually planning a sudden *coup* by the Black Sea Fleet and the landing of several divisions at the Bosphorus; the operation was abandoned only in April because Paskevich succeeded in persuading his master that general war might follow.*

Nicholas did not want war, although it was part of his political strategy to bring Europe to the brink of hostilities in his efforts to intimidate those who opposed him; he would undoubtedly have taken even greater risks if only France and Turkey had been involved, but he was worried by the close interest taken by the British in the Middle East, for the islanders were already openly assessing the armed strengths there and did not conceal their low opinion of the value of the Black Sea Fleet. Russian warships, they thought, were slow and 'since many of the hulls were constructed from pine' must have a short life whether in or out of battle; nor were they impressed by ships' crews who lacked ocean going experience and who, until they joined the Russian Navy, had never seen the sea. Nicholas was well aware of this, for, two years before, when Palmerston had insisted that a Portuguese Jew, a native of Gibraltar, was entitled to the same protection as an Englishman, Nicholas had written to Paskevich that the incident had served as a lesson to him 'for one can expect anything of this government of pirates'.

Before Menshikov departed for Constantinople the tsar had disclosed his latest ideas on the partitioning of the Turkish Empire: the Principalities should go to Russia, and Serbia and Bulgaria would be independent; the Adriatic was to be ceded to Austria; Egypt, and perhaps Cyprus and Rhodes, should be given to England; Crete was to go to France. Constantinople was to be made a free city with a Russian force on the Bosphorus and an Austrian garrison at the Dardanelles. But Menshikov's mission was a failure for Lord Stratford, the British Ambassador to Turkey, thwarted his every move, so that the tsar's ambassador extraordinary had to leave Constantinople empty-handed. When the tsar received Menshikov's report, he is said to have burst out: 'I feel the five fingers of the sultan on my face'.†
By then Nicholas knew that it was his last chance to withdraw, for he wrote

---

* Zaionchovsky, *Vostochnaia Voina*, Vol. 1, *Prilozheniia*, p. 599.
† De Grunwald, *Tsar Nicholas I*, pp. 260–3.

to Paskevich saying that 'it is easy to begin war but God alone knows how to end it'.

Nicholas had sought only to check the growth of French influence at the Porte and restore Russia's dominant position there so that he might preside at the partition of the Ottoman Empire – an event which he believed to be inescapable; if the Turkish Empire were not partitioned it would, he thought, disintegrate and fall into the hands of 'stateless persons, anarchists and Poles'. The tsar believed that a display of force would be enough to make the sultan yield, and this was his intention when, on 28 and 29 May, he and Paskevich drew up new plans for three phases of operations; the first was to be the occupation of the Principalities as a means of compelling the Turks to accept Russian demands. If this measure failed to secure the desired results, the tsar proposed to blockade the Bosphorus 'and threaten to declare the independence of the Principalities and Serbia'. The third stage would be to make good this threat and 'to make a start on the destruction of the Ottoman Empire'. But, added Nicholas, 'I am not yet of a mind to proceed to such extreme actions'.* Eleven days later these plans were sent to Prince M.D. Gorchakov, the Commander of the Russian troops bordering on the Principalities.

Nicholas knew that the reaction in France would be hostile, but he counted on the neutrality of Britain and relied on the support of Prussia and the friendship of Austria. Nicholas had offended the Emperor Napoleon III by the cavalier tone of his personal communications; but he had also come to be disliked by the Emperor Francis-Joseph for his patronising and protective airs – what Grunwald calls 'his Cossack courtesy' and poor taste – for Nicholas had even begun in his diplomatic utterances to couple Austria with Russia's intentions, 'what suits one, suits the other'; Nicholas had incurred the hostility of the King of Sardinia by striking his name off the list of honorary colonels of the Russian Army because the tsar disapproved of the king's progressive form of government; he had refused to accredit a diplomatic agent to the King of the Belgians because the king had Polish officers in his service; Sweden still resented the 1809 annexation of Finland, a territory that had never been Russian, and Nicholas had done little to improve relations in that quarter. In Central Europe, and in particular among the peoples of Prussia and Austria where Nicholas thought he was assured of friends, there was also 'a growing unpopularity of Russia, a hate and fear which governments were incapable of combating'. Nicholas himself was regarded as an ambitious tyrant, 'covering his plans of conquest

---

* Zaionchovsky, *Vostochnaia Voina*, Vol. 1 (*Prilozheniia*) pp. 603–4.

and invasion with a mantle of religion'.

It is believed that Nicholas's embassies abroad did not serve him well in that their political assessments were inadequate or wrong. But, even if the tsar had been misinformed, he was to an even greater extent self-deluded concerning the attitudes and intentions of the European nations. Nessel'rode, his counsellor, no longer had much influence, and Nicholas only aggravated the situation by his bombastic and violent outbursts in which an insulting epithet was added to every name. Undeterred by Austrian coolness, he suggested to Francis-Joseph the strategy to be used by Austrian troops 'in occupying Serbia and Herzogovina' in return for which service Nicholas would put Russian troops at Austria's disposal 'in case of subversion in Italy'.

On 2 July Nicholas ordered Russian forces across the Pruth and into the Principalities, and on the following day he had a manifesto read in all the Russian churches declaring that the tsar had no intention of starting a war.

> By the occupation of the Principalities we desire such security as will ensure us the restoration of our dues. It is not conquest that we seek but satisfaction for a just right so clearly infringed. We are ready, even now, to halt the movement of our armies . . . But if blindness and obstinacy decide to the contrary, then, calling God to our aid, and in full confidence in His power, we shall march forward for the sake of the Orthodox church.

The tsar's action united his adversaries. At first it appeared as if the European powers might agree on a formula agreeable to both parties, but the sultan required certain alterations to what subsequently became called the Vienna note; these alterations were unacceptable to the tsar. In early October, the Porte issued an ultimatum demanding the evacuation of the Principalities within fifteen days, and, as the Russians took no steps to comply, Turkey declared war on 23 October 1853. Eight days later Nicholas had Nessel'rode issue a circular to the foreign embassies in St Petersburg, in which he declared that 'as far as the tsar's dignity and interests would permit, Russia would abstain from the offensive and would content itself with maintaining its position in the Principalities'.

Five days after the declaration of war Turkish troops under Omar Pasha crossed the Danube and entrenched themselves near Kalafat. On 4 November the Russian 4 Infantry Corps under General of Infantry Dannenberg counter-attacked the Turkish forces near Oltenitsa, to the south of Bucharest, and lost heavily in casualties, being forced to break off the action and retire. Nor was *General-Adiutant* Count Anrep more successful when, at the turn of the year, he attacked the main Turkish lines at Kalafat, for he was defeated with great loss after a four day battle. Another force, under Baumgarten, had been surrounded and was only extricated with difficulty.*

At the beginning of February 1854 Nicholas had instructed the 72 year old Field-Marshal Paskevich to return to St Petersburg to confer on the prosecution of the war. Paskevich was opposed to mounting an immediate offensive towards Constantinople because he was fearful of Austrian and Prussian intervention, for the Russian troops in Wallachia had made little headway against the Turks and would have been in a perilous situation should Austrian troops have attacked out of the Banat. The main threat, Paskevich told Nicholas, was from the powerful ground forces of Austria and Prussia and not from French or British sea landings at Odessa or in the Crimea, for these could be contained 'merely by allocating 35,000 men to each place'. The field-marshal believed it necessary to lay siege to Silistria and take Turtukai, since this might entice the British and French to land in Dobrudja in order to assist their Turkish allies; the Russian forces would then be in a position to crush all three forces in a single theatre; but Paskevich stressed to the tsar once more that it was most important to have sufficient Russian troops kept in reserve to the north of the Principalities in case of war with Austria and Prussia. Subsequent events showed that Paskevich was against making *any* move to the south, and it is probable that he suggested an attack on Silistria only because Nicholas demanded it. Nicholas had reservations about Paskevich's appreciation, but he intended in any event to lay siege to Silistria, particularly since this would protect the Russian flank against an allied landing at Varna. The tsar wrote to Prince M.D. Gorchakov on 13 February that Paskevich was unnecessarily pessimistic, for Austria was sending 'very friendly assurances to Russia'.†

On 30 November 1853 Vice-Admiral Nakhimov's six sail of the line had arrived before Sinope, the Anatolian naval port on the southern shore of the Black Sea, and in a sharp battle had destroyed the entire Turkish force at anchor there, including seven frigates and a number of transports; the loss of life on the Turkish side was put at 4,000 killed. Although Nakhimov's raid was a legitimate act of war, it was regarded in London and Paris as deliberately provocative and entirely contrary to Nessel'rode's circular of 31 October, and it was resented all the more as British and French fleets were standing by in the straits near Constantinople in case they should be needed to support the sultan. On 4 January the allied warships entered the Black Sea, bent on clearing the waters of Russian vessels. Nicholas thereupon recalled his ambassadors from London and Paris; the western powers

---

* Bogdanovich, *Vostochnaia Voina*, Vol. 1, pp. 131–8 and 167–83.
† Zaionchovsky, *Vostochnaia Voina*, Vol. 2 (*Prilozheniia*), p. 313.

followed his example. Since Nicholas declined to reply to an Anglo–French ultimatum that he should withdraw his troops from the Principalities, on 27 March Britain and France declared war on Russia. During that month Austria had reinforced her armies on the Wallachian frontier, calling a further 95,000 men to the colours, and on 20 April Austria and Prussia signed a defensive alliance stating that an attack on the one would be regarded as an attack on the other.

Paskevich's fears of Austrian intervention were justified and his advice to the tsar to evacuate the Principalities, if it had been taken, would have done much to extricate Russia from a difficult diplomatic situation. The field-marshal had no confidence in Nicholas's plans and no liking for the role which the tsar had given him, for he remained disinclined to pursue the war against the Turks with the vigour required by Nicholas, for fear that an attack by the Austrians should find him with his reserves committed. Paskevich, the elderly, tired and timid bureaucrat, remained in command, but at the same time delayed Shil'der and Gorchakov in their offensive preparations; his fault, according to Prince Vasil'chikov, who was part of his staff, was in his lack of moral courage in not tendering his resignation to the tsar.

Whatever Paskevich might have told his sovereign, it would appear that he wanted to disengage from operations against the Turk and to avoid being involved in hostilities against the British and French. On 23 April he wrote to Menshikov, newly appointed as Commander-in-Chief West Crimea, a consoling letter making light of the allied threat: Paskevich's real intention, however, was to make clear to Menshikov that the Crimea could expect no help from the Active Army or from the Army of the Danube, except by such reinforcement as might be ordered by the tsar.

I have been most closely involved with field operations [in the Balkans] during the last year, but you, most honoured Prince Alexander Sergeevich, can be assured of my sympathy at the predicament in which you find yourself . . . The English, of course, will try to come to grips with our Black Sea Fleet. But you will take care of that! An allied landing is hardly likely to cause you any trouble after you have received the brigade from 17 Infantry Division [about 6,000 men], which I have sent to you in accordance with the tsar's orders. Unfortunately we now find marshalled against us not only the maritime powers but also Austria supported, so it appears, by Prussia. England will spare no money to bring Austria in on her side, for without the Germans they can do nothing against us. From the newspapers I see that £6,000,000 sterling has been allotted for this purpose. You, my dear Prince, will already know of the latest protocol concluded by the four powers with the object of forcing us out of the Principalities. If we are going to find all Europe ranged against us then we will not fight [the main continental enemies] on the Danube.

Nicholas, too, was grasping at straws. At first he could not believe that the Austrians would side against him; later he was sure that Prussia would break with Austria at the decisive moment. But then, on 27 April, he wrote to Paskevich a letter which appeared to confirm the field-marshal's forebodings: 'There are indications', Nicholas said, 'that the Austrians might attack on 20 May'. But the tsar was already showing signs of strain and instability, for two days later he became temporarily reconciled that Austria might be added to the list of Russia's foes and he sent off another note to Paskevich saying:

If the Austrians treacherously attack us, you have only to engage them with 4 Corps and the dragoons; that will be quite enough for them! Not one word more, I have nothing more to add!

Shortly afterwards Paskevich became a casualty to anxiety, for suddenly, during the siege of Silistria, he said that he had been hit by a shell fragment, although he was in fact unwounded; he gave up his command to Prince M.D. Gorchakov, and rode off in his carriage back across the Danube.* On Nicholas's orders the siege was raised.

In St Petersburg there was a general consensus of opinion that the Russian reverses were due to poor diplomacy, in that Russia found itself isolated in Europe; the high command, too, was censured for the blundering failures in the Balkans and for the folly of raising the siege of Silistria 'at the moment of success'. The Russian Army, however, was still considered to be invincible, since the great victory of 1812 was foremost in everyone's mind; Nicholas had been at pains to mention it in his manifesto and in his letter to Napoleon III; the public were continually being reminded of it and it was the theme of the discourse of what Tarle calls 'enlightened society', for writers and poets harped on it. 'How could the nephew, this little Napoleon, succeed when his distinguished forebear had failed?'. During the eighteen months between Constantinople and the battle of the Alma this spirit of optimism continued everywhere and the Russians persuaded themselves that if they did not want war it was from feelings of humanity and not from any doubt about the outcome.

There was also an influential section of opinion that regarded a war as

* Bogdanovich, *Vostochnaia Voina*, Vol. 2, pp. 90–2.

being essential to Russia's expansion. Prince Mikhail Pavlovich Golotsin, being in St Petersburg and close to the tsar, was in a position to see and hear most of what occurred; he noted that the tsar was uneasy in his mind, but he himself, like the rest of the court, had no doubts. On 17 August 1853 he wrote to Menshikov:

> People of the German party in touch with the Austrian and Prussian Embassies are busy trying to steer the tsar away from the war, and make much play on the humanity aspect. It is a misfortune that nobody seems to want or believe in war, and this at a time when Russia needs a war!

Countess A.D. Bludov, 'the perpetual guest at the Winter Palace', believed not only that Russia should go to war, but that it would be a great pity if Austria did not summon the necessary courage to declare war on Russia, for she saw much benefit in engaging France, England, Turkey and Austria at the same time. And this buoyancy was common throughout official circles during the first half of 1854, notwithstanding the rumours of Paskevich's pessimistic frame of mind, the failure of Count Orlov's mission to Vienna and the reported doubts of the tsar. The gloomy Nicholas, in company with a select few, knew more than the court and Russian officials suspected.

According to Professor Tarle, Paskevich deliberately misinterpreted Nicholas's order to raise the siege of Silistria and, on his own authority, withdrew all Russian troops from the Principalities.* Such a view is, however, unsupported. It appears more likely that the withdrawal took place solely as a result of German pressure. On 3 June, Austria, with the support of Prussia, delivered an ultimatum to Russia, requiring a withdrawal. Vienna would listen to no terms or conditions and St Petersburg had to obey. Nicholas could not believe his own senses. When he appeared on a parade at the Winter Palace his face was almost unrecognizable with emotion, and, when he came back to his apartments, he turned Francis-Joseph's portrait to the wall and wrote across the back, in his own hand, '*Du Undankbarer!*'.

During June and July as the Russian forces withdrew from the Principalities, French and British troops landed at Varna. Austrian troops, with the agreement of the Turks, occupied Moldavia and Wallachia. The Danube campaign was at an end. From this time onwards the hands of the allies were freed, for there was now no question of supporting Turkish forces in the Balkans or of defending Turkey. The moment was opportune for a direct attack on Russian soil.

* Tarle, *Krymskaia Voina*, Vol. 2, p. 11.

* * *

The war against the Turks in the Caucasus had continued with varying fortunes. The commander there, Prince Vorontsov, had asked the tsar for reinforcements and the unwilling Nicholas had sent one division by sea from the Crimea. There were numerous engagements, mostly of a local nature, both against the Turks and against the indigenous mountain peoples, and although the Russian Army enjoyed considerably more success than it had in the Balkans, the casualties were not light. During the autumn and the winter of 1853, however, the Russian forts on the northern coast of the Black Sea, to the east of the Crimea, became increasingly isolated because of the difficulty of supplying them overland across the Caucasus range; in the previous September Paskevich had advised the tsar to evacuate them, but Nicholas strove to hold on to every inch of soil. The entry of foreign warships into the Black Sea gave encouragement to the Turks and to the rebellious tribes, and put the forts in such danger that Nicholas was finally compelled to order Menshikov to dismantle them and ship the garrisons and guns back to the Crimea. Meanwhile minor actions between Russian and Turk continued throughout the summer in Georgia, Kars and Erivan.

The Russian military command in the Caucasus, like that in the Balkans, feared that its theatre might be attacked by the Anglo-French expeditionary force; it was also uncertain of the attitude of Persia, its immediate neighbour. But Nicholas would not tolerate any suggestion of withdrawal or of evacuating further forts, and he told the commanders there 'to hang on and do the best they could'.

There were of course dangers nearer at home, for during the spring and summer of 1854 a British fleet was in the Baltic bombarding small ports and burning Russian vessels, and patrolling within sight of Kronstadt and the capital. A French force besieged and destroyed the fort of Bomarsund in the Aland Islands. The Russian Navy did not put to sea. One of the main purposes of the allied raiding was to encourage the entry of Sweden into the war; in this they failed. But, according to Russian accounts, the naval raiding actions were successful in that they tied down powerful Russian land forces in Finland and along the southern coast of the Baltic Sea; for St Petersburg was fearful in case Sweden should enter the war or the allies land an expeditionary force there. The threat to Russian soil was to come, however, in the Crimea, 1,200 miles to the south.

CHAPTER 3

*　*　*　*　*

FATAL OPTIMISM

When Menshikov returned from his unsuccessful mission in Constantinople he had been rewarded by Nicholas with the appointments of Commander-in-Chief West Crimea and Commander of the Black Sea Fleet; he was to hold these in addition to his many other posts. Tarle believed that Menshikov regarded all appointments as no more than his due, for he was a very rich and cultivated man, had a vast library and could read in many languages, and during his long life he had wanted for nothing except the crown. Enjoying the tsar's favour and confidence, Menshikov's careerist aims were such that he never declined an honour or refused a post, whether it was deserved or whether it was in his power to fulfil its duties. Although he was Commander-in-Chief of the Black Sea Fleet and of the Crimean Army, Minister for the Navy and Governor-General of Finland, he was neither sailor nor soldier, neither governor nor diplomat. Menshikov, thought Tarle, was gifted and malicious, foreign diplomats 'lending a very attentive ear to this sharp and tricky prince'. In 1853 one such diplomat, General de Castelbajac, wrote of Menshikov:

> He has a nice wit and has, with his simple and polished manners, the air of one of our great lords of Louis XV's court. He loves women, gambling, horses, good and bad company. But if he has faults, he has also qualities, contrary to his compatriots who generally have only faults. He has integrity and independence of character and spares no one in his witty and caustic repartee.

Unhesitatingly and with no self-doubts Menshikov continued his own life style and course, being careful only in his relationship with the tsar. But he was harsh in his criticism of Nicholas's other favourites and ministers for their worthlessness, their servility, their fraudulent dishonesty, their conceit and their stupidity. Menshikov made a joke of Chernyshev's military pretensions and condemned Vronchenko, the Minister of Finance, for having no knowledge of finance in general or Russian finance in particular, unmindful that he himself was similarly placed in respect of naval, army and Finnish affairs; he mocked his colleagues, his staff and his subordinates, the allies and the Russian troops in Turkey and the Caucasus. Everybody and everything were the butt for the jokes and sneers of this intellectually destructive Sybarite.

It was known in Russia that the allies might try to seize Sevastopol since this course had long been advocated in the western press. In April came the allied bombardment of Odessa from the sea, and on 18 May Menshikov reported to St Petersburg the presence of reconnoitring enemy vessels off the Crimean coast; such sightings became a common occurrence during the following two months.* With the raising of the siege of Silistria in June it became increasingly clear that the next allied attack must fall on Sevastopol. Yet, according to the memoirs of Miliutin, the latter-day War Minister, 'there was a great calm both in St Petersburg and in Sevastopol notwithstanding the wealth of news we got from abroad about the enemy's preparations'. However, continued Miliutin, not everybody was satisfied with the Commander-in-Chief West Crimea 'for following the arrival of visitors and letters from the south there arose in Peterhof serious criticisms of Prince Menshikov, accusing him of apathy and irresponsibility, of distrust of his subordinates and lack of attention to the troops'. Military opinion in the capital 'was puzzled because Menshikov could not bother to form a headquarters and staff, so that his command appeared to be entirely disorganized'; and Menshikov insisted, in the fashion of the diplomatic corps, on calling those around him a 'chancellery' and not a *shtab*. At about this time a lampoon was said to have been circulated among the officers of the Ministry for the Navy which took the form of a mock naval directive to Menshikov. It read as follows:

Your Highness should have no difficulty in destroying the [Russian] Baltic Fleet by your own direction. Should it turn out somewhat differently with the Black Sea Fleet then the responsibility will lie with [the former Commander-in-Chief] Lazarev, with Nakhimov, the present Commander of the Black Sea Fleet, and with Kornilov, the Chief of Staff.

Whether or not Menshikov really believed that an allied landing was imminent during the late summer and early autumn is uncertain. There is no doubt that in his correspondence with Nicholas, Paskevich and Prince M.D. Gorchakov, Menshikov bemoaned the weakness of his forces and clamoured for reinforcements before the allies should invade the Crimea.

* Menshikov, *Morskoi Sbornik*, 1854, No. 4.

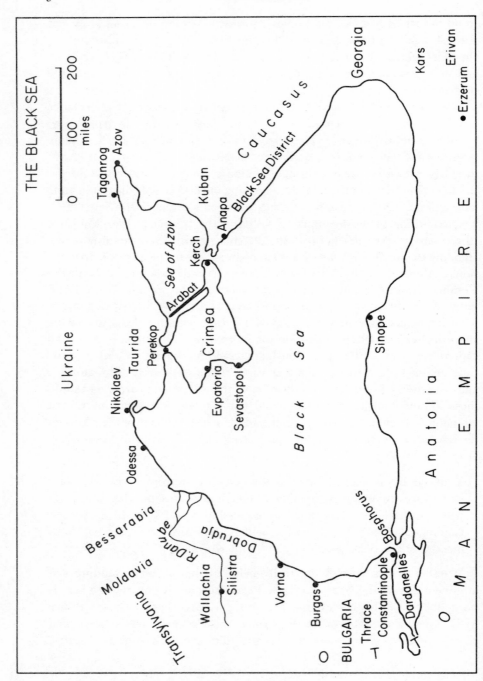

THE BLACK SEA

0 100 200
miles

On 30 June, for example, he wrote a pessimistic and complaining note to Gorchakov in Bessarabia, saying that the enemy might land '60,000 men not including the Turks'; against such a force he could only muster 22,700 infantry, 1,100 cavalry and 36 guns. Again, on 11 July, Menshikov told Nicholas that 'among the dangers threatening the Crimea' he counted on 'an attempt against Sevastopol and the Black Sea Fleet', and he sent his son Vladimir Alexandrovich as a personal envoy to Gorchakov to plead for help. Yet there is much other evidence to suggest that these official letters gave little indication of his real opinion.

Two of the outstanding military leaders of the Crimean War were the vice-admirals Nakhimov and Kornilov, considered by Tarle 'to be pupils of Lazarev and men of the new school, out of the run of the usual type of Nicholas's generals and admirals'. Nakhimov, the senior of the two, was the *de facto* Commander of the Black Sea Fleet, a plain-spoken and able sailor who was liked and respected by his men. Kornilov, the Chief-of-Staff of the Black Sea Fleet, was more reserved by nature but had both a wider and a more specialized education than Nakhimov, being an excellent organizer and administrator. Although Tarle considered that neither of these admirals had any faith in Menshikov, his character or ability, Tarle is probably describing a situation which was to exist *after* the battle of the Alma, for Kornilov's diary indicates that before 20 September the writer believed that Menshikov had both experience and ability in army matters.

Kornilov was among those who had been pressing since 1852 for the introduction of steam screw vessels into the Russian Navy and for the strenghtening of Sevastopol, since at the time the base stood almost defence-less. Because it was proving difficult to get financial approval from the capital for new fortifications, Kornilov drew up a subscription list of officers and civilians in Sevastopol willing to meet the cost from their own pockets. But when he put the proposal to the Commander-in-Chief, Menshikov rejected it with great indignation, saying that he 'did not wish to see a list of cowards'. Since, in Kornilov's view, Menshikov had no real understanding of the danger threatening Sevastopol, the Chief of Naval Staff persisted and eventually persuaded his superior to permit the merchant contractor Volokhov to build a coastal fort at his own expense to protect the Sevastopol roads. This fort, named the Volokhov after its generous subscriber, was completed only two days before the allies landed and was one of the principal forts which held off the allied fleet during the first bombardment.

As the summer progressed a careless and fatal optimism took hold of Menshikov and this happy frame of mind spread to his suite, for Komovsky, 'laughing merrily, made fun of the news received from the Danube that the

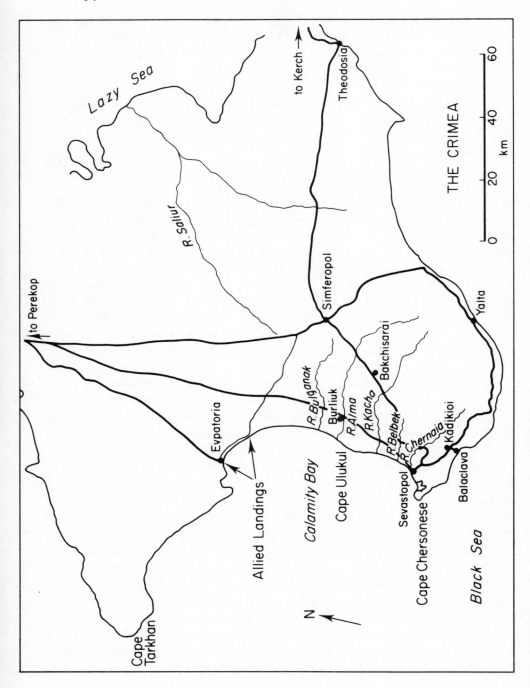

allies were embarking from Varna and setting sail for the Crimea'. When Prince M.D. Gorchakov, with selfless concern, sent his own engineer adviser Lieutenant-Colonel Totleben post-haste to Menshikov to assist with the construction of the Sevastopol defences, Totleben was ill-received. For when, on 22 August, Totleben handed to Menshikov Gorchakov's letter of introduction, he was told curtly that 'Prince Gorchakov, in his absent-mindedness, has apparently forgotten that I have my own sapper battalion; I suggest that you take a rest and then return where you came from'. Although Totleben was eventually allowed to stay in Sevastopol, he remained virtually unemployed until after the battle of the Alma.

After the war, in 1869 when Menshikov was still alive, Totleben wrote to General Gersevanov a private letter not meant for publication, in which he said that 'the prince really did not expect an invasion of the Crimea and this was proved irrefutably by witnesses and documents and by his own actions before the landing; to maintain the contrary is to deny the truth'. When an estate owner on the Bulganak, a personal friend of Menshikov's, asked the Commander-in-Chief whether he should evacuate his family from the Crimea the admiral replied that 'the enemy could not make a landing with less than 40,000 men, and he has not got that number'. And, only two days before the allied invasion, Menshikov wrote to *General-Adiutant* Annenkov 'my assumption that the enemy will never dare to land has been proved entirely correct'. 'In any event', concluded Menshikov, 'with the lateness of the season a landing is no longer possible'.

Although Menshikov was to be censured by many Russian historians for these incautiously expressed opinions, at the time many of his views were supported by other leaders. Bogdanovich has told of the commonly shared belief among military men that it was impossible to land a force of more than 30,000 men from the sea or supply them across the exposed beaches during the violent Black Sea autumn storms. It is true that the solicitous Prince M.D. Gorchakov was uneasy concerning the safety of Sevastopol and frequently warned Menshikov about possible allied intentions, but even he supposed, as did many others in St Petersburg, that the worst danger to be feared from the allies was a short term raid on the Crimea; on 22 September, after the battle of the Alma – for the news of the defeat had not of course reached Bessarabia – Gorchakov wrote to Menshikov in this vein, hoping that Menshikov 'would exact revenge before the allies re-embarked'.

* * *

The peacetime garrison of the Crimea had originally consisted of 13 Infantry Division, but after this formation was shipped to the Transcaucasus in

September 1853 for service against the Turks leaving behind only its reserve
infantry brigade, a brigade of 14 Infantry Division was brought into the
Crimea from Odessa to replace it. Both of these divisions belonged to
5 Corps. The steadily deteriorating situation, caused by the Russian failure
in the Balkans and by the entry of France and Britain into the war, forced
Nicholas to reinforce the Crimea further, and 16 and 17 Infantry Divisions,
based in peace on Yaroslavl and Moscow and forming part of 6 Corps,
were ordered to move into the peninsula together with two regiments of
Don Cossacks.

There was no railway south of Moscow and all troops and supplies had
to go to the theatre of war on foot or by horse. The Tarutinsky Regiment,
which was part of 17 Infantry Division, had left its peacetime quarters at
Nizhnii-Novgorod on 2 December 1853 on the long route to the south.
All ranks knew that the regiment was going to war against the Turks, and
on the first day's march, in spite of the cold and the snow, the wives and
families accompanied the columns for many miles before taking their leave
and turning back. The regiment went on, covering from ten to twelve miles
a day, marching five days in every seven. In Old Russia they were welcomed
and vodka and cakes were brought out for the troops while the landowners
put their houses at the disposal of the officers. By the spring the regiment
was in the Ukraine where the inhabitants were more reserved and the land-
scape took on a different appearance; villages became further and further
apart and few people were met on the roads. The regiment was then rerouted
from Bessarabia to the Crimea across the steppe, the many Tatar barrows
(*kurgany*) surmounted by stone monuments being objects of wonder to
the Russian troops. It was the end of April before the regiment finally
reached its destination.

By 10 September 1854 there were 34 battalions in the Sevastopol area
and another eight on the march south of Perekop, in all about 38,000 troops
and 18,000 seamen under Menshikov, the Commander-in-Chief of the
West Crimea. There were a further 12,000 men in the Kerch-Theodosia
area, but these came under General of Cavalry Khomutov's East Crimea,
which formed a separate military district together with the Kuban and the
North-West Caucasus.

Bogdanovich believed that the first intelligence of the imminence of the
allied landings was brought to Menshikov on the night of 11 September
when the Commander-in-Chief was present at a ball given by the officers
of the Borodinsky Regiment in honour of the name day of its chief. But since
the allied fleets were still far out to sea, about thirty leagues from Cape
Tarkhan, the report could have described only the movement of four enemy

vessels carrying the allied commission selecting the point of disembarkation on the west coast. In any event, Menshikov took no action on this information.

At ten o'clock on the morning of 13 September watchers from Sevastopol could see the smoke of a fleet above the distant horizon, and between noon and six o'clock in the evening the coastal semaphore telegraph station at Ulukul, near the mouth of the Alma, sent a succession of sightings reporting in all a hundred enemy vessels moving in a north-easterly direction towards Evpatoria, about 45 miles north of Sevastopol. In Bogdanovich's opinion, a rapid review of the military situation was called for, 'this being the task of the general staff, but instead of submitting the problems of the conduct of operations for the consideration and advice of officers of experience, delegating to them executive responsibilites, Menshikov carried out all the planning and command functions himself, using [his chief-of-staff] Colonel Vunsh as his confidant and aide'. The only action taken by Menshikov appears to have been to send his aide-de-camp Stetsenko, a naval lieutenant, to Evpatoria, with orders to keep the enemy fleet under observation and return Cossack gallopers with the news. Stetsenko rode to Evpatoria, which he did not reach until dusk, and he sent back only two reports, one to Menshikov, that 'the enemy was lying just off Evpatoria and appeared to be on the point of disembarking a land force', and the other to Kornilov, that 'the enemy fleet stood so crowded and in such disorder that it might be possible to use fire-ships against it'. These messages were received in Sevastopol during the course of the night. Meanwhile Menshikov began to concentrate troops on the west coast to the north of Sevastopol between the Alma and Kacha rivers, a further 24 battalions arriving there on 13 and 14 September to reinforce the eight already on the ground.

A lieutenant of guard artillery, Shcherbachev, arrived in Sevastopol on 13 September after a two month journey from St Petersburg, bringing with him the 600 Congreve rockets which had been specially requested by Menshikov. The city was full of excitement and the wildest rumours, for Shcherbachev was told that an enemy landing party had rowed ashore further to the north and, taking possession of a coastal telegraph station, had sent a message to the naval base, 'We shall soon be with you', receiving in return the reply, 'You will be made welcome – we have been expecting you for a long time!'. When Shcherbachev reported to the Commander-in-Chief that day he found him easy in his manner and pleased at the prospect of a land battle. This confidence was shared by Menshikov's staff; Zholobov, a captain of cuirassiers and aide-de-camp who was to be killed a few days later on the Alma, was so certain of victory that he was ruminating, perhaps with himself in mind, on the selection of the lucky staff officer who would be sent to St Petersburg to carry the despatches and good news to the sovereign. Shcherbachev was won over by these 'noble and persuasive' views and was surprised to find that they were not shared by the gloomy Totleben.*

That same evening Shcherbachev went to the theatre to see a play, Gogol's *Inspector-General*, Admiral Staniukovich, the governor of the naval dockyard, being present in a box with his family. At the end of the third act a messenger arrived from Menshikov with the information that the enemy was about to disembark at Evpatoria. Staniukovich left immediately. The news, said Shcherbachev, 'ran round the house like electricity'. The show was abandoned and the theatre emptied rapidly. And, as Shcherbachev walked home, the Ekaterininsky road presented an unusual spectacle, for lights were on in all the houses and there were groups of officers at each cross-road discussing the situation. Seamen and soldiers stood to that night to prepare for battle, so that few in the garrison got any sleep at all.

In the Tarutinsky Regiment the news of the earlier fighting against the Turks in Caucasia had strengthened the belief of the rank and file in the invincibility of Russian arms. According to one non-commissioned officer, the men were already beginning to fear that their regiment would never see any action, when, on the night of 13 September, ball ammunition was issued to all ranks and arms and equipment were inspected. The next day the troops were told that they were going to fight the French, and, 'by ten o'clock everyone was strutting about the camp in marching order, ready at a moment's notice to put on their packs'.

The enemy fleet could be seen quite clearly on the horizon moving towards Evpatoria while his steamers were poking about close to the shore. Just after midday came the order 'Take up packs!'. We formed companies in front of our tents and then joined up by battalions. The drummers, as though for the sake of propriety and of course to give them something to do, then beat the alarm . . . Some of our officers, although themselves ignorant of the use of the bayonet, gave us advice of this sort: 'Be careful not to hold the thrust position too long – jab quickly and withdraw. There is no doubt that we will beat the enemy hollow'.

The non-commissioned officer continued:

Although none of us had ever seen battle, there was a surfeit of such

* Shcherbachev, *Artilleriiskii Zhurnal*, 1858, No. 1.

advice; all of us, officers and men, were confident in our own strength, and openly voiced it; only the battalion commander, Lieutenant-Colonel Gorev, said nothing, but sat there on his horse, glowering and silent.

The patriotic fervour was such that Russian civilians began to arrive in the camp asking to be enlisted on the spot. Volkov, the regimental commander, selected a few of the better looking, and one strapping fellow was alloted to No. 1 Company 'where everyone regarded him as a very brave sort'. However the bloody battle of the Alma soon changed his mind and 'in order to escape further service he falsely claimed that he was a casualty'. These volunteers, thought our non-commissioned officer, served no useful purpose, 'but at the time their appearance certainly cheered the men in the ranks'.*

Menshikov was subsequently criticized in the Russian military press for not moving part of his forces to the port of Evpatoria to oppose the landings. Totleben took the view, however, that allied sea-power gave the enemy a decisive strategic advantage since he could move his troops along the coast much faster than the Russian troops could march. By this logic Totleben reasoned that the Evpatoria landing, and indeed the main disembarkation which began on 14 September across the open beaches in the area of the old Genoese fort about 12 miles to the south of Evpatoria, could have been a feint designed to draw Russian troops to the north. Evpatoria was sufficiently distant for the allies to have re-embarked in order to seize the unguarded base of Sevastopol before Menshikov's forces could have appeared on the scene. The beaches in their disembarkation areas were controlled by the fire of the ships' guns, and this made it doubtful whether the Russian troops could in fact even have delayed the landing of the allied troops.† Totleben believed that such an unfavourable encounter before the campaign had started might have affected the morale of the Russian Army in the Crimea, for it was essential to keep the land forces intact and in good heart until they could be reinforced from European Russia. The Russian Black Sea Fleet sheltering in Sevastopol, fourteen men-of-war and seven frigates, all of them sail, could not have engaged the allied fleets with much hope of success.

Information about the strength of the enemy had been difficult to get at first, for the only Russian troops in Evpatoria had been 200 convalescents under a Major Branitsky of the Tarutinsky Regiment who vacated the town together with most of the Russian population as soon as the enemy fleet

---

* *Voennyi Sbornik*, 1863, No. 6.
† Totleben, *Défense de Sébastopol*, Vol. 1, p. 154.

appeared. But as the allies took no steps to seal off Evpatoria, Russians and Tatars were free to come and go as they pleased and Don Cossack vedettes soon appeared on the skyline outside the town. Then, on 15 September, a detachment of 57 Don Cossack Regiment took prisoner eleven French soldiers who were foraging for provisions in the Tatar settlements, and these, when interrogated, estimated the strength of the allied force at between 50,000 and 100,000 men. From these reports and from the count of ships Menshikov came to the conclusion that his own force was likely to be much outnumbered, and he sent a second request to General Khomutov asking for 60 Cossack Regiment, the Moskovsky Regiment and a field artillery battery to be sent to Sevastopol from the area of Kerch.

Menshikov, according to Totleben, knew that the allied goal was Sevastopol, and he considered that the only course open to him was to bar the enemy route on such features to the north of the city as were suitable for defence. He decided to use all available field troops for this purpose, leaving only part of the reserve infantry brigade of 13 Infantry Division and naval detachments inside the base. All the reservists needed to man the Sevastopol batteries had already been called up, and Kornilov had ordered the naval force to immediate readiness. Menshikov's report and appreciation, sent to the sovereign on 15 September, said that the enemy fleet lay off Evpatoria and that a considerable force, together with cavalry, had landed between Evpatoria and the Kontoygan estate. Menshikov added: 'Not having the means to attack the enemy on the open beaches that are covered by the guns of the fleet, I am concentrating my force on an advantageous position from which to give battle'. Three days later the Commander-in-Chief sent a further report, saying that the enemy had completed his disembarkation but had not yet moved, and that the Russian troops were being assembled on the Alma near the village of Burliuk on the main Evpatoria-Sevastopol highway.

In St Petersburg and Moscow all hung upon the news. Aksakov, a writer tolerably well informed about the allied forces, but, like everyone else, having no idea at all how few Russian troops there were in the Crimea or of the weakness of the Sevastopol defences, wrote on 28 September:

All our feelings and attention are now turned to the Crimean shores where the cholera has not prevented the allies from carrying out this terrible landing about which you have read in the newspapers. The fate of the campaign and of the Crimea is in the balance. Without doubt the enemy's troops are better organized than ours, his weapons and shells are superior and he has the support of a huge fleet with guns which can cover the beaches at a range of two versts [2,300 yards]. But we are on our home ground and we have fresh troops; the first storm will separate the enemy from his fleet and he may be cut off. It is not known how many troops we have in the Crimea; if we have a large force, say 100,000, then the enemy may be annihilated. Sevastopol is fortified from the land. The people are delighted with Menshikov's orders of the day and I myself expect much from him; such a talented and fine officer could not fail to rise to the occasion and either make his fame immemorial or die a hero's death. He has just sent an encouraging and cheerful letter to Moscow.

As Tarle has said, Alexander Sergeevich could always discourse brightly, send cheerful letters and write orders of the day which stirred the *bourgeoisie*, and this did not change even after the landings or the defeats that followed.

The news of the landings, which did not reach St Petersburg until 23 September, alarmed and depressed Nicholas and he sent off an order to Krasnov, the *ataman* of the Don Cossacks, telling him to move all available troops to aid 'the remnants (*ostatki*) of Prince Menshikov's corps, in case the enemy – which God forbid – should take Sevastopol'. And Dolgoruki, the new Minister for War, feared to despatch a government messenger to Perekop in case the allies should have already blocked the route.

The build-up of Menshikov's force was rapid, for on 14 September there were already 20,000 men at the Alma. Six days later his numbers had increased to 35,000, two hussar regiments arriving on 15 September, Popov's 60 Don Cossack Regiment coming from Perekop on 18 September and Tatsyn's 57 Don Cossack Regiment and the Moskovsky Regiment arriving from Kerch on the night of 19/20 September, the morning of the battle, after a forced march of 160 miles in five days.

By 20 September Menshikov's troops on the Alma comprised 6 Corps, commanded by General of Infantry Prince P.D. Gorchakov (the elder brother of General of Artillery Prince M.D. Gorchakov in Bessarabia and the cousin of the diplomat Prince A.M. Gorchakov), consisting of Lieutenant-General Kvitsinsky's 16 Infantry Division and Lieutenant-General Kir'iakov's 17 Infantry Division. In addition to these two divisions of 6 Corps, Menshikov commanded a detached brigade of 14 Infantry Division, a hussar brigade, two Don Cossack regiments, four separate infantry battalions of reservists two from the Belostoksky and two from the Brestsky all from the reserve brigade of 13 Infantry Division, a rifle battalion, a naval battalion and some sapper companies. Menshikov's force totalled 42 battalions of infantry, 16 squadrons of light cavalry, 11 squadrons (*sotni*) of mounted Cossacks and 10 batteries numbering 84 guns.

*   *   *

Russian commanders and historians were subsequently agreed that the line of the Alma River offered Menshikov the most favourable defensive position to the north of Sevastopol.

On the south bank of the Alma where the river ran into the sea was a high headland crowned by the ruins of a wooden Tatar fort, with only a narrow and difficult pathway leading from the fort down to the beach; this promontory gave an excellent view not only along the coast to the north and south but also to the east over the lower stretches of the river. The coast to the south of the headland was bounded by cliffs inaccessible from the sea except in the area of the Ulukul Valley where the bed of a dried-up stream ran down to the beach about a mile south of the Alma estuary.

The water of the Alma was not a great obstacle for the dry summer weather had lowered the level so that it could be forded in a number of places; but the strength of the position lay in the fact that the line of the river was covered on the southern side by a steep-edged plateau, precipitous near the sea-shore and running inland for 2,000 yards almost cliff-like at a height of nearly 150 feet, the overhanging edge of the plateau being so close to the river that a soldier on the cliff edge could hit an enemy on the north bank by short-range musket fire. Thereafter, as one moved further eastwards, the plateau fell back to the south-east, away from the river, so that the basin of the Alma became wider and the approach to the plateau much less steep. On the plateau itself were further hills, some rising to about 350 feet. The area to the north of the Alma formed an open tableland sloping away from the coastal cliffs downwards towards the east, becoming a low-lying and open steppe visible for many miles from the commanding plateau on the south bank.

The sheer northern edge of this plateau running from the Tatar fort along the south bank of the Alma was intersected between the Alma estuary and the village of Alma-Tamak, nearly 2,000 yards upsteam, by three narrow and steep ravines cutting into the vertical sides of the plateau, these deep gullies being known colloquially as *balki* by the Russian troops. The first of these ravines, although it was deep and long with a very difficult bottom, was not as steep as the two neighbouring gullies upstream. Further to the east, near a fourth ravine opposite Alma-Tamak, the edge of the plateau lost its cliff-like character and changed direction at an outlying spur known to the British as Telegraph Hill, so-called since it had near its summit the half-completed Alma telegraph station; the plateau then ran diagonally south-eastwards along the main Evpatoria-Sevastopol road in a series of jutting but more gradually sloping hillocks. The main road, which stretched roughly from north to south, crossed the Alma by a wooden bridge near the village of Burliuk and then climbed up on to the plateau, rising along the bed of a long valley named 'the Causeway' by the British, with open rolling terrace-like slopes. To the east of the road was a range of hills of irregular shape called the Kurgan, stretching down on all sides at first fairly steeply and then in a gentle incline. Forward of this range was an exposed and high knoll, beyond which ran the track from the inn (*traktir*) near Tarkhanlar, south towards the Kacha River. Numerous Tatar bridle and cart tracks ran over the plateau and hills both to the east and the west of the Evpatoria-Sevastopol road, southwards down into the Ulukul Valley and beyond. There were at least three fords across the Alma, all of them used by Tatar carts, one at Tarkhanlar above the bridge and two lower downstream, that at Alma-Tamak opening on the track which climbed the steep sides of the southern plateau by way of the fourth ravine.

The two principal villages on the north bank of the river, Alma-Tamak and Tarkhanlar, had Tatar mosques, although they were only a half-mile collection of straggling one-storied buildings separated by stone walls and overgrown gardens; Burliuk was roughly similar in size. These villages were connected by an almost continuous belt of vineyards on the north bank, about 300–400 yards in depth and coming down to the water's edge; inside the vineyards were a few farm buildings and trees and more stone boundary walls. Except in two isolated places, in the loops of the river immediately to the west or Burliuk, there were no vineyards on the south bank of the Alma; this bank was open and without any form of cover.

Menshikov intended to defend the high plateau to the south of the Alma and the range of hills to the east of the Evpatoria road, for this commanding ground dominated the right bank of the river and gave excellent observation over the miles of open steppe to the north. Moreover, the coastal cliffs on the left flank south of the Alma estuary were so high that, so the Russians believed, they screened the plateau from the aimed fire of ships' guns and from observation from the sea, except at mast-top height, so that the troops on the plateau could only be engaged by high-angle naval gun-fire, and then only at venture. Between the Tatar fort and Alma-Tamak the river cliffs offered a similar advantage to the defender and presented a formidable obstacle to an attacker from across the Alma; east of Alma-Tamak, where the cliffs gave way to steep slopes, reserves in depth could be held behind the crest or on the reverse incline of the plateau hidden from enemy observation. The main disadvantage in basing a defence on the plateau was that the position could be turned on the right flank if the enemy should seize the

Kurgan, and it was therefore necessary for Menshikov to occupy this feature or cover it by extending his right along the banks of the Alma towards Tarkhanlar. This was about five miles from the sea, making the frontage very wide for the small and poorly armed Russian force.

Menshikov did not use a council of war and does not appear to have taken his senior commanders into his confidence; nor did he make use of a staff in preparing his plans. Because his appreciation was unrecorded, the defects in his plan are at first sight more apparent than its logic; for Menshikov decided against defending the cliffs on the south bank of the Alma on his extreme left flank, a decision which was to lose the battle for the Russians. Except for a single infantry battalion which he posted near the village of Akles in the Ulukul Valley covering the *seaward* approach a mile south of the Tatar fort, Menshikov rested the left of his line on the fourth ravine opposite Alma-Tamak, about 2,000 yards from the sea. The river cliffs remained undefended.

Menshikov divided his force into two main parts, the right wing and centre under Prince P.D. Gorchakov consisting of 16 Infantry Division, commanded by Lieutenant-General Kvitsinsky (the Suzdal'sky, Vladimir-sky, Kazansky and Uglitsky Regiments); Kvitsinsky's division, except for two artillery batteries covering the Burliuk bridge, stood on the right hand side of the main Sevastopol-Evpatoria highway. The left wing was the respon-sibility of Lieutenant-General Kir'iakov, the Commander of 17 Infantry Division, who could muster both of his brigades but only three of his four regiments (the Borodinsky, Moskovsky and Tarutinsky); but he had, in addition, the four reserve battalions of the Brestsky and Belostoksky. Kir'iakov was removed from Gorchakov's command and came directly under Menshikov. The boundary between Gorchakov's and Kir'iakov's troops was subsequently in dispute, but, according to the original deploy-ment, it would appear to have been the main road leading down to the Burliuk bridge. The Commander-in-Chief's two subordinates seem to have been permitted little initiative, since they were required merely to conform to the plan issued by Menshikov, individual regiments being sited and deployed before the battle as instructed by Vunsh and Zalesky, his two principal staff officers.

For over a century Russian military writers have speculated on the reasons that caused Menshikov to deploy his troops in the way he did and to leave unguarded his left flank, the river cliffs west of Alma-Tamak. Bog-danovich considered that 'if Menshikov had thought it necessary to give battle on the Alma, engaging much superior forces, then he should have investigated the value of the position in all its detail and strengthened its natural features, instead of leaving the reconnaissance of the position to a subordinate staff officer, Lieutenant-Colonel Zalesky, merely accepting his report that the heights on the left flank were unassailable'. 'For', continued the writer, 'to leave heights uncovered is much like leaving a castle un-defended, relying on its walls to keep the enemy out'. Menshikov may have taken exaggerated counsel of his fears of the casualties likely to be inflicted by sea bombardment; in reality such losses, thought Bogdanovich, would probably have been acceptable, 'as the valiant Shchegolev battery had already proved at Odessa'.*

Captain Enisherlov of the Uglitsky Regiment, who served throughout the battle as a staff officer to Kvitsinsky, the Commander of 16 Infantry Division, thought that no troops were positioned on the 2,000 yards of river cliff east of the mouth of the Alma because 'of the prevalent opinion that the heights were unscalable and that it was impossible to turn this flank by land'. Menshikov had ordered that an infantry company should be stationed at the old Tatar fort, but on the morning of the battle, on 20 September, this post was abandoned at the approach of enemy warships. Enisherlov could see little sense even in posting a company at the fort, for he reasoned that if its mission had been merely to observe, this was a task which could have been better performed by a few Cossacks; if, on the other hand, the intention had been to defend the Tatar fort headland from a land assault, at least a battalion of musketeers and a score of riflemen should have been deployed there, well protected by earthworks and covered approaches.†

Menshikov did not deign to answer his critics. Vunsh, his chief of staff, came to his aid, however, in the Russian military press, explaining that Menshikov's intention was to remain on the defensive and keep his force intact until reinforcements should arrive; at the same time he intended to cover Sevastopol and inflict losses on the enemy. But Vunsh could provide no answer to those who criticized the Commander-in-Chief's tactics in not resting the left flank of the Russian defence against the sea, except that he, too, postulated that 'this would have been difficult because the enemy was likely to cover the coastal area with his guns'. Although Russian sources make no mention of it, de Bazancourt has said that on topping the cliff the French skirmishers surprised 'fifty or so Cossacks' whom they drove off with rifle fire. If Cossacks were in fact posted to give early warning of the enemy approach they apparently failed to do so.

---

* Bogdanovich, *Vostochnaia Voina*, Vol. 3, p. 32.
† Enisherlov, *Voennyi Sbornik*, 1859, No. 1.

Kir'iakov, who was in command on the left flank, subsequently said that all the advantage of ground lay with the Russians and that the defensive line could have been made impregnable if field works had been prepared during the six days before the battle. Well-sited epaulements and trenches would, thought Kir'iakov, have done much to nullify the superiority in range of the enemy's rifles, as the experience in defending Sevastopol was later to show. By 8 a.m. on 14 September most of the Russian troops had been concentrated on the Alma; but, according to Kir'iakov, 'they lay in no military order whatever, just as they had been disposed by Lieutenant-Colonel Vunsh; there was no preparation or digging, and only on 18 September did we receive any form of plan. On that day stakes were driven into the ground to mark out the positions the units were to take up on the morning of the battle'.*

While the troops sat in idleness, Menshikov, according to Vunsh, 'spent several days in considering the deployment'. He was aware of the danger that the enemy might attempt to turn the left flank 'by a landing in the valley of the Ulukul', and for this reason he stationed a battalion at Akles to observe the seaward flank and meet the enemy with volley fire as they emerged out of the dried-up bed of the river. Vunsh said that Menshikov had not entirely discounted the possibility that the allies might attack frontally across the river with their right hard against the coast. Should this happen, part of Gorchakov's reserve would be switched from the rearward position on the main Sevastopol road over to the far left flank. It was intended, continued Vunsh, that these troops should take up their position on the extreme left 'at the very moment when the enemy columns would begin to appear on the plateau, so masking the fire of their own ships' guns'.† Vunsh did not explain how these Russian reinforcements were to be brought from a position over two miles away, in time to reach the cliff edge at this precise and critical moment.

The Russian Commander-in-Chief appears to have been convinced that the cliff-like barrier on the Russian left would force the enemy to make his main offensive in the centre along the easier approach of the Sevastopol road and the Kurgan: Menshikov decided to fight his defensive battle there and win it by inflicting heavy casualties on the allies as they crossed the river. The corps commander Prince P.D. Gorchakov subsequently explained:

It was the intention of His Highness [Menshikov] to hold the ground in

---

* Kir'iakov, *Russkii Invalid*, 1856, No. 136.
† Vunsh, *Voennyi Sbornik*, 1858, No. 3.

front of the river only as long as it suited him, and then to fight the main battle preferably when the enemy was crossing the river. With this in mind he sited 18 light guns near the main road at about 300 sazhens [700 yards] from the bridge, so that both the bridge and the road were enfiladed, and 12 field guns further to the right in the epaulement [known to the allies as the Great Redoubt] to engage the area of the bridge and ford with roundshot and case-shot. Near this battery stood the composite naval battalion, the Kazansky, the Vladimirsky and the Suzdal'sky Regiments, and all except the Suzdal'sky stood in battalion column ready to counter-attack. The purpose was to exploit the inevitable disorder of the enemy when he crossed the river and, striking him a swift blow, drive him back. All this was laid down quite clearly by Prince Menshikov and was repeatedly brought to the attention of unit commanders by me.*

Enisherlov confirmed this when he said that 'Gorchakov's plan was based on keeping up a rapid artillery defensive fire with case and shot and, when the enemy gained the left bank, delivering a counter-attack with the bayonet; if this were to be done successfully two or three times it might eventually so weaken the enemy that the Russians would be able to go over to the counter-offensive'.

Menshikov had complete confidence in defence by counter-attack and in the tactics of the column assault, and they formed the basis of his plan. His tactical talent may not have been of a high order but he was not alone in this for nearly all Russian military men, Enisherlov said 'even those of genius', fully accepted the Suvorov maxim that 'the bullet is a fool, but the bayonet a fine fellow'. The development of the rifle in Russia had been much neglected and, until the day of the Alma, the Russian Army held firmly to its old faith in the bayonet used in attack column. No commander could imagine that rifle fire was going to decide the coming battle or understand that in future neither infantry nor artillery could defend ground without the protection of entrenchments. This was the reason why the vineyards, stone walls and villages on the north bank of the river were not levelled to the ground. The destruction of the area had indeed been discussed by commanders, but no action was taken because no one had realized the skilful use that enemy riflemen would make of this cover. In consequence peacetime regulations prevailed, and, so the story has it, the Russian troops were forbidden even to collect firewood from the vineyards on the right bank.

No serious consideration was given to the possibility that the enemy

* P.D. Gorchakov, *Russkii Ivalid*, 1856, No. 101.

might envelop the whole Russian line by bypassing it to the east; to do this the allies would have to make a long and circuitous march over waterless steppe separated from the fire and victualling support of the fleet, where, with unfit horses, they were vulnerable to the superior numbers of the Russian cavalry. If, however, such an envelopment had been attempted, Menshikov intended to withdraw southwards without giving battle.

* * *

The Russian Commander-in-Chief's final tactical battle plan accepted that the river cliff from the mouth of the Alma to Alma-Tamak should be undefended. The sector from the fourth ravine opposite Alma-Tamak eastwards almost as far as Telegraph Hill, a distance of over 2,000 yards, was defended by the four reserve battalions of the Brestsky and the Belostoksky, all in company column drawn up on the lower slopes about 400 yards from the river; behind these reserve battalions about 200 yards to their rear in the second defence line stood the Tarutinsky in battalion column of attack. To the right and upstream of the Belostoksky, the Borodinsky was deployed in battalion column in the first line on the lower slopes of Telegraph Hill, while to its front, little more than 200 yards from the water and 600 yards from the Burliuk bridge, were positioned two light batteries of 16 Artillery Brigade. These batteries, though sited in Kir'iakov's 17 Infantry Division sector, were part of Kvitsinsky's 16 Infantry Division and were to become known to the British as 'the Causeway batteries'. Both stood in the open uncovered by epaulements. The Moskovsky with a light battery formed Kir'iakov's left flank reserve, and this was kept well to the rear of Telegraph Hill.

Telegraph Hill, held by the Borodinsky, was to prove the key to the defensive system in the centre, yet there appears to have been some confusion as to whether Kir'iakov or Kvitsinsky was responsible for it. Since the Borodinsky belonged to 17 Division, it might be supposed that Kir'iakov's right boundary extended to the main road; his neighbours certainly said so and blamed him for the failure of that regiment. On the other hand the Causeway batteries, which lay about half a mile to the west of the road and formed the pivot of the fire defence of Telegraph Hill, belonged to Kvitsinsky. Nor was Vunsh's subsequent definition any more precise when he said that Gorchakov (and therefore Kvitsinsky) was responsible for the *centre*, which Vunsh said was the road and bridge, and the *right*, the area of the ford upstream; Kir'iakov was to cover the *left*, described by Vunsh as 'the ford downstream and the Alma heights'. Kir'iakov later denied that the Borodinsky had anything to do with him.

Except for the two Causeway batteries, Kvitsinsky's 16 Infantry Division was deployed to the right of the main Evpatoria-Sevastopol road. On the north-west slope of the Kurgan, within case-shot range of 600 yards from the bridge, was an epaulement, a breast-high earthwork to cover the twelve guns of the field battery of 16 Artillery Brigade. This became known to the British as 'the Great Redoubt'. Flanking both sides of the epaulement and about 200 yards to its rear stood the four battalions of the Kazansky in the first defence line, drawn up in battalion column of attack. To the right and rear of the redoubt near the crest of the Kurgan was a second epaulement sheltering a light battery of 14 Artillery Brigade, this earthwork being known to the enemy as 'the Lesser Redoubt'. Yet further along the crest to the right of the Lesser Redoubt another light battery of the same brigade was deployed in the open; immediately to the rear of this battery and sheltering in the dead ground behind the crest the Suzdal'sky Regiment was drawn up, partly in company column and partly in battalion attack column.

On the southern slope and behind the crest of the Kurgan, in Kvitsinsky's second line, stood the Vladimirsky and Uglitsky in battalion column of attack; in a hollow behind the Vladimirsky waited two Don Cossack batteries. The right open flank beyond the Suzdal'sky was covered by Tatsyn's and Popov's Don Cossack regiments. Contrary to what Anichkov has said, there were no line troops on the right flank between the ridge of the Kurgan and the Alma.

In the general reserve on the left hand side of the main road, stood a brigade of 14 Division, consisting of the Volynsky and the Minsky (less the battalion detached to the Ulukul on the left flank) with a light battery of 17 Artillery Brigade. On the right of the main road was concentrated the hussar brigade (also part of the general reserve) consisting of two regiments, the Kievsky and the Ingermanlandsky (Duke of Saxe-Weimar) together with a light horse battery. This general reserve, which stood astride the main road, was theoretically under Gorchakov's command; in fact when the battle was joined Menshikov used both this general reserve and Kir'iakov's left flank reserve (the Moskovsky) as a force at his own disposal. The Cossack regiments were deployed forward on outpost duty as far north as the Bulganak; when they came under enemy pressure they were to retire to the open right flank.

A sapper headquarters was set up at the bridge together with two sapper companies. Forward of the river an outpost line, formed by the riflemen of 6 Rifle Battalion and 6 Composite Naval Battalion, took up its position in the gardens of Alma-Tamak and Burliuk.

In his initial deployment Menshikov had retained the divisional infantry groupings although he did not necessarily keep the regiments within their own brigades; this meant that the brigade commanders were unemployed during the battle. Menshikov was even less fortunate in allotting artillery, for this soon took on such an irregular pattern that infantry regiments fought supported by guns other than their own affiliated batteries or without any artillery support at all. But Menshikov's chief fault lay in failing to define the responsibilities of command and staff; Kir'iakov held the left and Kvitsinsky the right, but their troops, and presumably their responsibilities, overlapped at Telegraph Hill; Prince P.D. Gorchakov, the corps commander, who should normally have commanded three divisions, was in charge of the defence of the centre and of the right, but the only troops under him were those of the right – Kvitsinsky's 16 Infantry Division, so that this unfortunate division was to suffer from the immediate control of two commanders. Menshikov's own staff lacked any organization or defined duties and the Commander-in-Chief used the general staff officers and naval and army aides-de-camp indiscriminately as messengers. Control, co-ordination and liaison were poor for, as Enisherlov said, 'there was no comprehension in the Russian Army of the golden rule that formation commanders should apprise each other as frequently as possible of major developments during the battle. The reverse was indeed the case, for it was regarded as an insufferable burden to keep one's neighbours informed, particularly when one might suppose that if nearby commanders had only used their eyes they should have seen the events from their own positions'. The exchange of liaison officers was unknown in the Russian Army at that time.

Notwithstanding these strictures, an examination of Menshikov's deployment serves to confirm the logic of his plan, based though it was on a tactical fallacy. The short range of the Russian smooth-bore musket made it necessary to rely on artillery to inflict casualties on the attacking infantry as it came across the river and climbed the slopes; the Russian guns were therefore sited in front of the foremost line where they had good observation and fields of fire; Menshikov was not to know that British rifles outranged Russian guns. Before the battle started nearly two-thirds of the Russian artillery had been deployed forward in this way covering the area of the bridge, the Causeway road and the north-west slopes of the Kurgan. From the siting of the artillery it can be deduced that Menshikov did not expect an attack between the sea and Alma-Tamak and that he considered a major attack unlikely between Alma-Tamak and Telegraph Hill, for the reserve battalions of the Brestsky and the Belostoksky, armed only with flintlocks, had no artillery covering that front.

* * *

The Congreve rockets brought to Sevastopol by Lieutenant Shcherbachev could not be used in the field for, due to an oversight, the launching frames had been left behind. Nor, because of their limited range, were they of any use to the coast batteries. Not wishing to remain unemployed, Shcherbachev asked Menshikov to let him join the field force and, on 16 September, he was instructed to report to Major-General Kishinsky, Menshikov's director of artillery.

From the beginning Shcherbachev's position was, as he expressed it, 'very unpleasant'. The cut of his guard artillery jacket displeased the officers of the army artillery, a dislike which they did not conceal; because of their attitude Shcherbachev declined to join a battery, and Kishinsky kept him at his own headquarters as an adjutant. Shcherbachev's duties made it essential, however, that he should be mounted, but, as saddle-horses could not be got, he was forced to take an animal broken to shaft and trace offered to him as a pack-horse. For this 'absolute jade' Shcherbachev had to pay 100 silver rubles.

When the poorly mounted Shcherbachev arrived on the Alma he rode up and down the positions to familiarize himself with the ground. But this officer of the guard was without professional or intellectual pretensions, for he knew nothing about the enemy, his characteristics or strength and could, in any case, make little of the Russian defensive deployment; nor does he appear to have asked Kishinsky to enlighten him. He could only conclude that it was Menshikov's intention 'to hold on to the ground which he had occupied'.

The morale of the troops, according to Shcherbachev, was excellent, 'for they were ready to die for tsar and country and were indignant on account of the enemy invasion'. The party of convalescents coming from Evpatoria had brought disturbing news of the murder of Russian sick by Tatars and Jews, and though this had angered the men it had made them more resolute. Captain Chodasiewicz, a Pole with the Tarutinsky, said much the same; many of his fellow officers, the so-called *burbony*, in their morale-boosting talks with the men had stressed the inferior quality of the British troops when removed from warships or facing any enemy other than savages. One cheerful materialist in the ranks summed up the situation rather differently when he said that all were in high spirits, for the weather was fine and the food good 'and there was even a cup of vodka to be had'.

On 16 September Kornilov was still in Sevastopol supervising the hurried construction of fortifications. On that day he entered in his diary:

According to information from the [Alma] camp, the enemy has brought

fresh troops ashore and prepares to attack us; but the position selected
by the prince is particularly strong and we are therefore quite content.
The defences of Sevastopol proceed at a good pace.

The next day he wrote a cheerful and confident letter to his wife at Nikolaev,
hoping for a Russian victory. On 18 September the admiral rode out at
dawn to the Alma camp. He again recorded in his diary:

> I found everyone there unconcerned and in the best of spirits, the prince
> being quite satisfied – indeed even merry. His tent was pitched on a
> prominence [Telegraph Hill] from which it was possible to see 30 versts
> [20 miles], for there was a huge telescope near it trained on the enemy's
> camp and fleet. The allies certainly have many troops, with fresh ones
> continually arriving.

Nor were Menshikov's generals less displeased with their chief, for
Gorchakov and Kvitsinsky appear to have been satisfied with Menshikov's
plan, both before and after the battle. Nor at the time, according to Vunsh,
did Kir'iakov raise any objections; indeed, having received his orders, he
exuded a breezy confidence, and 'was the first to echo that with one battalion
[at Akles] he would soon settle the hash of any enemy ascending the heights
from the sea'. Chodasiewicz, too, commented on Kir'iakov's boastfulness
before the action. Two years after the battle, however, Kir'iakov said that
he was the only general who had any misgivings about Menshikov's orders,
for he did not agree with the deployment of the left wing and in particular
with the positions to be taken up by the Brestsky, Belostoksky and Borodinsky Regiments; and he 'made his views clear in the presence of a number
of people, among whom were Major Durnov, adjutant to Prince P.D.
Gorchakov, and Lieutenant-Colonel Zalesky, staff officer to Prince Menshikov'. Kir'iakov told them that 'if he was to fight in such a place, then
they, as officers of the general staff, had a duty to take all steps which might
be necessary to get the troops from the lower slopes back on to the plateau';
and Kir'iakov was of the view, so he said, 'that Zalesky did not disagree'.
Kir'iakov's letter to the *Russkii Invalid* continued:

> As for the detail of the deployment, I can give only that of the left flank
> which I commanded, that is to say, those troops to the left of the main
> road:
>   The Borodinsky in two lines
>   The Brestsky and Belostoksky in one line, and behind them the
>   Tarutinsky.
> These twelve [*sic*] battalions had no artillery – there were no epaulements

and all were in attack column – the first line being only 150 paces from the second and the riflemen only fifty paces out in front. . . . Because the troops were packed so tightly with the steep hill at their backs, the casualties were high. This was reason for the precipitate withdrawal which caused our men to seek the sanctuary of the heights.

The description of the lack of depth of the position may have been exaggerated; and although it is true that the Brestsky and Belostoksky had no artillery, there were two batteries of 16 Infantry Division (the Causeway batteries) in front of the Borodinsky. The letter is of importance, however, in that in it Kir'iakov accepts what he denied elsewhere, that the Borodinsky Regiment was under his command. In any event, as Vunsh pointed out in his reply in the *Voennyi Sbornik*, Kir'iakov should have voiced his disagreement to the Commander-in-Chief and not to subordinate staff officers.

* * *

On the morning of 19 September the allies began their march southwards from the left bank of the Bulganak towards the Alma, their warships moving off shore and accompanying the movement of the troops. The Cossacks fell back, and some hours later the enemy arrived at a point described by Kir'iakov as 'within twice the range of cannon shot, from where they could view all our positions'; Menshikov instructed Kir'iakov to drive the enemy back on the left 'and so discover his intentions'.

At midday Kir'iakov went forward from the Alma position taking with him the hussar brigade, nine Cossack *sotni* and a brigade of his own division; after covering a mile he reformed his troops into fighting order, the Borodinsky moving on the right in battalion column while the Tarutinsky advanced on the left in the same order, a light battery travelling in the centre, while the hussars covered the right wing and Cossacks the left wing. The dismounted part of the force then stopped some way from the Bulganak under the cover of a hill while the cavalry continued over the ridge. There they came face to face with four British squadrons. Both sides halted and threw out skirmishers and there was a desultory exchange of carbine fire. But since the enemy showed signs of bringing up infantry and guns to support his mounted troops, the Russian cavalry began to withdraw over the ridge on to their own infantry columns. Skal'kovsky, an officer with the Tarutinsky Regiment, said that 'this little cavalry affair' lasted about an hour and a half, but it was marred by an error of identification and poor control.* For the Kievsky Hussars had already put two squadrons out as

* Skal'kovsky, *C Peterburgskie Vedomosti*, 1855, No. 124.

part of the covering force prior to Kir'iakov's sally, and these were dressed in white linen tunics. The remaining Kievsky squadrons were wearing the dolman. The tunic-attired squadrons came in last, following on the others, and Kir'iakov, under the impression that the horsemen were French cuirassiers, ordered the battery commander Kondrat'ev to open fire. Several of the Kievsky men were killed or wounded by the Russian artillery. The sequel was that the enraged General Khaletsky, commanding the hussars, had to be restrained from cutting down Kondrat'ev with his sabre.

Shcherbachev, the lieutenant of guard artillery, was not privileged to be present throughout Kir'iakov's fighting reconnaissance, for this unlucky officer, whose accounts show to have been likeable and honest even if not very able, rarely seemed to know what was afoot. He had fallen asleep after his midday meal on the Alma position and was woken only by the sound of firing, and when he ran to his general's tent he found that Kishinsky had left with Kir'iakov some time before. Mounting his scarcely rideable horse he galloped off after the brigade; but, said Shcherbachev, 'the affair was over and when I met the formation it was already coming back; General Kishinsky listened to my excuses in silence'.

Kir'iakov's only success that day was the capture of de Lagondie (Lagonda), a French lieutenant-colonel of the general staff, who was apparently so short-sighted that he mistook the Kievsky for allied troops. He was taken prisoner by a hussar non-commissioned officer named Zarubin, who received 150 silver rubles as a reward.

On 19 September Prince Bariatinsky, newly appointed as a flag-lieutenant to Kornilov, was sent to Menshikov on the Alma bearing letters and messages from his chief, with instructions to return with the answers the same day. He, too, had a look at the advancing enemy through the big telescope in front of Menshikov's tent. Since Bariatinsky wanted above all else to be present during the coming battle, he begged Menshikov that he should be allowed to remain on the Alma and that another officer be sent back in his place to Kornilov. Menshikov readily agreed and appointed Bariatinsky to his own personal staff as an aide-de-camp. So it came about that this naval officer who had no army experience was used twenty-four hours later, at the height of the battle, to convey crucial and complicated word of mouth tactical orders to battalions under fire.

Bariatinsky described the arrival of the captured French officer in front of Menshikov's tent, very dishevelled and without a cap but still mounted on his horse. The Commander-in-Chief stood up, as did his staff. But when Menshikov asked the officer his name the only reply he got was one of indignation:

M. le Commandant-en-Chef! Je dois me plaindre de vos soldats, qui m'ont arraché les pans de mon uniforme!

'Of course', said Bariatinsky, 'no one took any notice'. Lagondie was so distressed at being captured that Menshikov's staff suggested that they might ease his plight by sending a messenger to the allies under a flag of truce asking for the Frenchman's personal effects. But, on consideration, Lagondie decided against it, saying that the French camp might take an unkind view of such a request. Lagondie was sent back to Sevastopol under escort to be lodged at Prince Bariatinsky's house there, since this was 'the only residence available with a staff of servants and cooks'.

Bariatinsky was to be fortunate enough to enjoy once more the comfort of his own Sevastopol home on the night of the 20 September. On the 19 September, however, he shared a tent with the other members of Menshikov's staff: Menshikov's son Vladimir Alexandrovich, Colonel Vunsh, Captain-Lieutenant Verigin and the adjutant Skolkov, the captains of cavalry Greig and Zholobov, and the state councillors Kospovsky and Grot. For some it was to be their last night alive. By the light of the dying sun Bariatinsky could distinguish the red jackets of the English and the red trousers of the French troops who were bivouacing on the plain only three to four versts away. With the darkness, sounds became more distinct and Menshikov's staff could even hear the rumbling of the movement of enemy guns, shouts and the neighing of horses.

Shcherbachev put the enemy camp at a distance of between three and five miles and, he concluded weightily, 'it was obvious that there must be a battle the next day'.

In the evening we and the enemy lit countless fires, and going round the bivouacs of the various Russian regiments I watched the happy faces of the choirs as they sang, and I listened to the hum of the talking as the old soldiers relived their past battles in recounting them to the young. Enthusiasm and confidence were to be seen on every face. The battery officers were discussing at length what might happen the next day; only one, the Commander of 3 Battery of 14 Artillery Brigade, whose name I have forgotten, although normally of a cheerful disposition took no part and withdrew; the following day he was killed by a bullet in the chest, a most remarkable affair because the battery was not engaged and no other man was killed or wounded. Then finally, little by little, the fires and the talk died down and all went away to their tents.

A non-commissioned officer, describing the same scene, commented on the cheering and rejoicing late that evening at the arrival of some of the Moskovsky Regiment in their distinctive tall headdress 'rather like high shakos', after their long forced tramp from Kerch. He continued:

That evening a military band played marches near the Commander-in-Chief's grey tent and a choir sang old Russian songs. A number of our men were then detailed for picquets over the river forward of the village and the order was given to put out the fires – only a few being left alight. At the evening meal many of the soldiers ate little, and night came on in a weariness of waiting. We could hear the barking of hungry dogs roaming the deserted village down below. As we lay down to sleep, dressed in our field marching order, for the first time there arose a feeling of apprehension and uncertainty.*

Late that same night, in his candle-lit study in the Sevastopol garrison, a tired Kornilov wrote in his diary:

God does not abandon the righteous and we therefore await the outcome calmly and with patience. In 1812 Russia was in a worse position and yet maintained – nay – even increased, its greatness.

* *Voennyi Sbornik*, 1863, No. 6.

CHAPTER 4

*   *   *   *   *

THE ALMA

When, well before dawn, Shcherbachev reported for duty to the army headquarters he found Prince Menshikov and his staff already at work; Prince P.D. Gorchakov was there doing duty as Menshikov's deputy, and the army and corps staffs and aides were acting as a single team, for *Fligel'-Adiutant* Lieutenant-Colonel Isakov, chief of staff to Gorchakov, on learning that Shcherbachev had come for orders, instructed him to send off all artillery transport to the rear and have the gun teams harnessed up. When Shcherbachev had done so, he returned to the headquarters at about 8 a.m. in company with Kishinsky, his chief, to wait until the enemy should show signs of movement.

In the Tarutinsky Regiment the order to send back all transport was given at 6.30 a.m. and half an hour later the regiment was paraded in the presence of Kir'iakov and the regimental colonel, Major-General Volkov, to celebrate the day of the birth of the Virgin Mary. Bariatinsky said that all the troops were in their long grey greatcoats and the flat peakless forage cap, for he saw none with the spiked Prussian-type helmet; by Menshikov's order all the officers wore other rank pattern greatcoats. A *Te Deum* was sung and the priest blessed the regiment and sprinkled holy water. Shortly afterwards firing could be heard from the sea and it was reported that the French were on the move.

About 2,000 yards to the east, to the right of the main road, Enisherlov was on the Kurgan with Kvitsinsky, the Commander of 16 Infantry Division, with whom he remained during the battle. Enisherlov said that he had a good view of all that happened on the right and centre, where the British were, but could not see the fighting on the French sector to the left of the Borodinsky beyond Telegraph Hill. The advance by Bosquet's French column along the coast, which started at about 5.30 a.m., was unnoticed from the Kurgan, and, said Enisherlov, would have been visible only from the area of the old Tatar fort, which was of course unoccupied. An hour later there was still no movement from the British bivouac area.

Enemy naval vessels had been firing earlier in the morning but the bombardment from the nine steamships lying between the Ulukul headland and the mouth of the Alma became particularly heavy at about 11 a.m., their shells reaching the area of the Brestsky battalions 2,000 yards inshore. By then, however, the whole of the allied army was on the move, the left (east) flank of the French force, still in column of route, stretching almost as far as Telegraph Hill. The movement of the British on the Russian right was centred on the Burliuk bridge, and this meant that they had farther to go than their allies; the pace of the redcoats was in any event slower and so it came about that the French, waiting for the British to come alongside, had to stop several times, once even to make coffee. Meanwhile Menshikov did nothing to alter his deployment. Although Menshikov did not know it, Bosquet had already arrived at the mouth of the Alma, putting out skirmishers and forming up his troops in two columns, Autemarre's brigade being directed on the ford and the steep ravine, while Buat's brigade was to move across a narrow sandspit where the river ran into the sea and then scale the cliffs near the ruins of the Tatar fort; Buat was to be followed by the Turkish division in his rear. After mustering his force below the Tatar fort Bosquet, according to the Russian reconstruction of the battle, resumed his advance at some time shortly after 11 a.m. In a few minutes the hardy Zouaves were over the river and up the cliffs, so that the amazed Bosquet, watching them, was to remark to his staff: 'These gentlemen undoubtedly do not want to fight'. The artillery followed Autemarre's brigade up the ravine and on to the plateau, coming into action gun by gun.

There appears to be little doubt that Menshikov knew nothing of the arrival of the French at the estuary until the enemy riflemen had crossed the Alma and scaled the cliffs. Admittedly, Stetsenko, one of Menshikov's naval aides-de-camp, subsequently said that Menshikov 'became aware' of the French *movement* 'at the eighth hour'; exactly what Stetsenko meant is, however, unclear. What is certain is that Stetsenko was sent to the left flank at about 11 a.m. to warn Kir'iakov of the French approach and that, according to Chodasiewicz, he found the divisional commander presiding over a little champagne party to celebrate the coming battle. Kir'iakov, whom Tarle considered to have been 'utterly ignorant, totally devoid of any military ability and rarely in a completely sober state', returned to Menshikov the answer 'that he could see the French and did not fear them'. On receiving this unsatisfactory reply the Commander-in-Chief called for his horse. But Bariatinsky is sure that Menshikov did not set off for the left flank until the news had been brought to him that enemy troops 'were making their way up the heights', and he believed that Menshikov had this

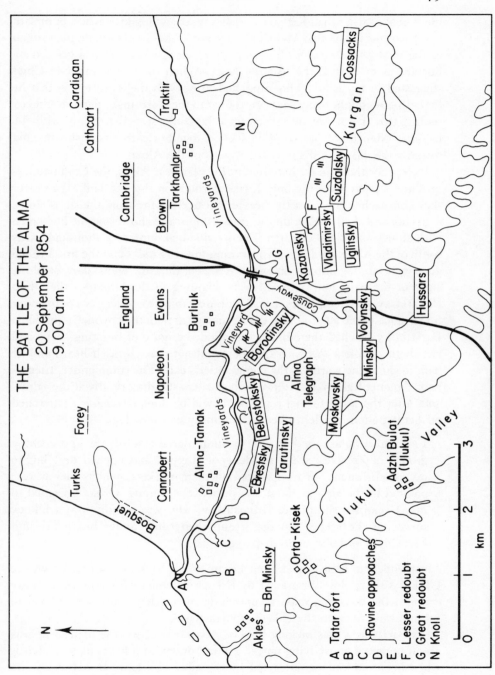

THE BATTLE OF THE ALMA
20 September 1854
9.00 a.m.

N

Cardigan
Cathcart

Traktir

Cambridge

Brown
Tarkhanlar

Vineyards

Cossacks

Kurgan

Suzdalsky
Vladimirsky
Uglitsky

F

Kazansky
G

England
Evans
Burliuk

Causeway
Hussars

Vineyard
Borodinsky

Volynsky
Minsky

Napoleon
Alma
Telegraph

Moskovsky

Forey

Vineyards

Belostoksky
Tarutinsky
E Brestsky

Adzhi Bulat
(Ulukul)

Valley

Turks

Canrobert
Alma-Tamak

Ulukul

Bosquel

D

C

◇Orta-Kisek

□ Bn Minsky

B

A

Akles

N

A Tatar fort
B ⎫
C ⎬ Ravine approaches
D ⎭
E Lesser redoubt
F Great redoubt
N Knoll

0   1   2   3
km

intelligence earlier than Kir'iakov. Skal'kovsky and Chodasiewicz, both with the Tarutinsky, said that Menshikov arrived at their regiment on the plateau to the west of Telegraph Hill at about 11 a.m., where he was greeted by hurrahs as he wished the troops victory. When the Commander-in-Chief suggested to Kir'iakov, who happened to be with the Tarutinsky, that he (Menshikov) might bring some guns over to the Tarutinsky flank, Kir'iakov replied that it was not necessary since he could stop the enemy with the bayonet. Menshikov passed on in silence, together with Kishinsky, making towards the coastal cliffs near the mouth of the Alma.

Except for the Minsky battalion in the rear near Akles, the Commander-in-Chief's party were the only Russian troops on the left flank; the nearer they approached the coast the heavier became the fire from the ships' guns, with shot and shell tearing up the grassy slopes and showering the horsemen with stones and clods of earth. Enemy riflemen, already a thousand yards south of the Alma, could be seen running towards Akles and the first French guns were coming into action near the edge of the cliff. Menshikov, catching sight of the battalion of the Minsky standing in the Ulukul Valley, told Bariatinsky, his temporary naval aide-de-camp, to order its commander 'to advance to the left and take the French guns with the bayonet'. But when Bariatinsky reached the Minsky battalion the noise of bursting shells and ricocheting bullets was such that he could not make himself heard and he had 'to shout the words in the commander's ear'. The commander, Lieutenant-Colonel Rakovich, listened to his orders standing rigidly at the salute, and, after the usual formal reply of 'It will be done (*sluzhaius*')', marched off his battalion in a left wheel. Bariatinsky continued:

> I sat and watched the battalion column march towards the approaching groups of Zouaves, when suddenly it stopped and opened fire; but to my astonishment our troops fired off their muskets, held as they were – pointed in the air – without any pretence at aiming. Or so it seemed to me. I rejoined the prince [Menshikov] who was standing on a hillock surveying the scene, but our group then came under heavy fire and Menshikov ordered us to disperse.

Meanwhile the Minsky battalion began to fall back in disorder down the Ulukul Valley, closely pursued by French riflemen who kept up a steady fire into the wavering mass of marching men. Menshikov sent Vunsh to try and rally them in the village of Orta-Kisek.

As Bariatinsky was picking his way eastwards across the plateau he was about to pass a figure lying on the ground under an other rank's greatcoat, when his attention was attracted by the edge of a familiar red jersey. As

Bariatinsky approached the body he caught sight of a shoulder-board bearing the monogram of the sovereign and he realized it was *Fligel'-Adiutant* Skolkov, lying in a pool of blood with his right arm blown off. Bariatinsky dismounted.

> Recognizing me, Skolkov asked to be got to a medical dressing station. Just then I caught sight of a [Russian] cart moving off in the distance, so I leaped on my horse and set off after it. Hearing a cry, I looked back and there was Skolkov running after me! But then he staggered and fell. Shells and bombs were falling everywhere. I caught up with the vehicle and, turning it round, brought it back for Skolkov.*

Meanwhile Vunsh was almost frantically engaged near Orta-Kisek, having been instructed by the Commander-in-Chief, so he said, to move in reinforcements 'in accordance with the pre-arranged plan'. At first only two battalions of the Moskovsky Regiment (Kir'iakov's reserve) were ordered over to the left flank, but the other two battalions had to follow, together with three battalions of the Minsky and several batteries from the general reserve. By the time they had arrived, between noon and one o'clock, all of Bosquet's division was on the plateau together with its artillery; in the meantime Canrobert had driven the Russian riflemen out of the vine-yards north of the Alma, and his troops, leaping down the steep banks into the water, were beginning to ford the stream near Alma-Tamak.

Bogdanovich believed that all redeployment to meet the threat on the left flank was done at Menshikov's personal order, and Vunsh said that the Commander-in-Chief moved about the battlefield at the gallop, watching the rear as well as the flank, and moving hussars and artillery into the Ulukul Valley in case the French should outflank the Minsky. According to Kir'iakov, Menshikov did not appear unduly perturbed when he first rode on towards the Tatar fort, accompanied only by Kishinsky and his aides; but it was the Commander-in-Chief himself who shortly afterwards sent back urgent messages for the Moskovsky, the Minsky and the artillery. The Commander of 17 Infantry Division thus confirmed that the fighting on this wing was directed personally by Menshikov and not by himself, for Kir'iakov, who was supposed to be in command of the left flank, had remained with the Tarutinsky, not yet under fire. Kir'iakov's only action at this time, so he said, was to order up a horse battery and a Don battery and direct their fire northwards, over the heads of the Tarutinsky and Brest-sky, on to Canrobert's and Napoleon's divisions in the valley of the Alma.

---

* Bariatinsky, *Vospominaniia, 1852–55*, pp. 15–7.

The 2 Battalion of the Tarutinsky to the west of Telegraph Hill was deployed well forward and to the right of 3 and 4 Battalions of the same regiment; being on the high ground, the men could clearly see, on their right front, the approach of the red-jacketed British infantry making towards Burliuk. Meanwhile the Tarutinsky regimental priests continued to conduct the religious service, and the soldiers prayed fervently as they stood in their close columns; outside the ranks many of the officers remained on their knees until the enemy was quite close and the battalion commander Gorev gave the order 'To Arms!'. Shortly afterwards the men heard scattered rifle shots and a musket volley from the far left flank, as the Minsky battalion in Akles came under the fire of the Zouaves. A Russian non-commissioned officer continued the story:

At about midday English rifle bullets, with their characteristic ricocheting 'ping', began to fly overhead – a sound not heard before by our troops who had never been under fire and knew little of rifles. It filled most of the men with alarm so that they kept asking each other in frightened tones what the sound was, though in reality they must have known. The first to be hit was a man named Cherenov, and the news of his fall went up and down the ranks. A Russian battery on our right, just below the Commander-in-Chief's tent, engaged the English and, as the *aul* [Burliuk] was not yet aflame, we could see how its shots were falling short. Then the English guns opened up and straightaway caused havoc among our troops.

The Moskovsky Regiment marched, in accordance with Menshikov's orders, from the Russian centre across the front to reinforce the left flank, its path being behind where the Tarutinsky columns were drawn up. The Tarutinsky battalion commander, Gorev, turned his horse and hailed the Moscow men in friendly fashion, 'May God be with you!', whereupon the rank and file of the Tarutinsky, dazed and frightened, called out and echoed his words. At that moment, Menshikov, on his way back from the left flank to the centre, rode past the front of the battalion accompanied by his staff, which included many Tatar horsemen and an officer of guard cavalry, and he noted with displeasure the confusion in the Tarutinsky ranks. 'But', continued the writer, 'the men could not understand how they were being shot down by a distant enemy whom they could not even see, for the smoke had by now covered the front, and the enemy was approaching the bridge'.

The English rifle and artillery fire grew in intensity so that our commander Gorev began to move the battalion from place to place to escape it. This at least was a better way of occupying troops unaccustomed to battle, for, until he did this, many soldiers had given way to their terror and were kneeling down, huddled together in groups, calling for help on all that is holy.

Soon the Moskovsky and Minsky were being pressed back by the French and great numbers of wounded were walking or being carried along the plateau to the rear of the Tarutinsky. Many perished in the shell-fire. Gorev had moved his battalion further down the slope in the direction of the enemy, when a battery appeared on the spot just vacated by the battalion and opened fire on the village, shots going over the heads of the Tarutinsky formed up below. Our *eger* continued:

A fairly stout officer [Kishinsky] seated on a horse appeared at the gun site; I do not know whether he was a general or a colonel. But his calm, unhurried and capable manner attracted the attention of the men of the Tarutinsky, who watched him with awe. Our battalion commander Gorev, pointing him out, called to us saying: 'Men! Over there is an old fellow with a wife and family who does not give a jot for his life. What have we to lose? If any of you are afraid, then look at me; and if I as much as flinch, then you have my full permission to quit the field immediately'. These words had a great heartening effect on the men.*

An officer on the left of the main road who was able to see Burliuk and also observe the fighting on the plateau, has left the following account:

Our hearts pounded at the sight of the endless mass of [British] troops marching steadily towards us, but when our artillery, which occupied good commanding positions, opened fire, the shells fell short as the enemy was still out of range. Our [Cossack] troops then set alight the village of Burliuk and we became blinded by the smoke which drifted back on us. It would have been wiser, as those with battle experience said at the time, not to have created a smoke screen for the enemy's benefit since this enabled him to fire on us without any loss on his side; but these mistakes were not the last. As the enemy got closer our shells began to blow great holes in his ranks; but the many gaps were immediately closed up and the enemy strode on, apparently indifferent to his losses. Soon afterwards we began to feel the terrible effects of his rifle fire.

Our informant then turned to the fighting on the plateau on the far left flank.

* *Voennyi Sbornik*, 1863, No. 6.

In the space of a few minutes the Minsky were decimated, although God knows why they had been exposed so close to the sea! But the [French] rifle fire was murderous because each bullet hit its mark; anyone on a horse was an immediate target and many of the field officers became casualties in consequence. . . . Our artillery was doing marvellous execution among the enemy, whose ranks were being thinned out; but then the guns began to run out of ammunition for the two caissons for each gun had been left a verst or two to the rear where, so it was thought, they would be safe from enemy fire. And so the artillery action ceased almost as soon as it had begun.

Although Kir'iakov believed, and his opinion was accepted by Bogdanovich, that the attempt by the Moskovsky and Minsky to advance across the plateau against Bosquet's division was defeated only by the shot and shell of the ship bombardment, Enisherlov inclined to the view that a high proportion of the casualties were caused by the case-shot of the field artillery and by long range rifle fire, 'some of the bullets striking down our men at a range of over a verst [1,200 yards]'.

Meanwhile near Alma-Tamak Canrobert was across the river and coming to Bosquet's aid, moving up the ravine to the left of the Brestsky; Menshikov ordered the right hand battalion of the Moskovsky to advance down the slope and throw the enemy back into the Alma, but this Moskovsky battalion too was driven off by artillery and long range rifle fire. The Russian regiments fell back, taking up a temporary defensive line out of range of the ships' gunfire, facing west across the plateau, almost at right angles with the Brestsky and Belostoksky battalions in the Alma valley.

The Commander-in-Chief had remained unhurt, but, so far, of his aides, Captain Zholobov had lost a leg and died and *Fligel'-Adiutant* Skolkov had lost an arm. Since the enemy was by then closing in on the centre in the area of Burliuk it was necessary for Menshikov to go there, and he rode off remarking that 'if the battle continues for an hour or so, it must come to the bayonet and then what God may give'. If Kir'iakov is to be believed, Menshikov met him at the Tarutinsky at 12.30 p.m. and told him 'to ride over to the left wing which was in disorder'. Enisherlov said 'the battle on the left wing had been lost before that on the right had begun'.

* * *

The actions of Lieutenant-General Kir'iakov from noon onwards have remained unexplained over a century of Russian military history. By his own account he was with the Tarutinsky until 12.30 p.m. Chodasiewicz, with the Tarutinsky, said that Kir'iakov dismounted, having previously sent away all his aides, so that he might not attract the attention of enemy artillery or marksmen. 'In fact he appeared to me to be entirely lost and not to know where he was or what to do, while shot, shell and bullets were whistling around him; and he certainly forgot his duty as a divisional general'. When an aide galloped up and told Kir'iakov that his left was turned, he mounted his horse without a word and, according to Chodasiewicz, rode away to the rear.

Kir'iakov's own story, written two years after the battle, is confused in its timings and in its identification of enemy troops. He said that he rode over to the Minsky and Moskovsky in accordance with Menshikov's orders, had a horse shot from under him and mounted another, restored the two badly shaken regiments into good order and took them forward in attack column against the French. The enemy, said Kir'iakov, fell back 'and withdrew from the heights'. The whole outcome of the Alma battle, he hinted, was in the balance, 'but it was at this moment that matters developed badly for us on the right and centre'.*

Whether the attack for which Kir'iakov gave himself the credit ever took place is a matter of doubt. French sources do not admit to having been subjected to close infantry attack, still less to having 'withdrawn from the heights'. The French say that for an hour or more the battle on the plateau took the form of an artillery duel, Bosquet's 12 guns of calibre 12, capable of firing shell, round or case-shot, fighting it out with 40 Russian guns of mixed type and calibre, the advantage being with the French, for their guns were of better design and were admirably covered by their infantry.

The French description of the fighting on the left flank is in some measure supported by the Russian artilleryman Shcherbachev. Between twelve and one o'clock he returned to the main headquarters in the centre and was told that Menshikov and Kishinsky had gone to the left flank. When Shcherbachev arrived there he found that Kishinsky had taken under his command the left wing artillery, one light and one field battery of 17 Artillery Brigade and the horse and the Don batteries from the reserve, in all between 30 and 40 guns. These batteries, according to Shcherbachev, 'soon silenced the French artillery'. But the French infantry, approaching to within 300 paces, shot down the Russian gun crews with impunity, for the Moskovsky Regiment failed to go forward and give the artillery close protection. In such a situation, concluded Shcherbachev, a withdrawal was inevitable.

But let Lieutenant-General Kir'iakov continue his account in his own words:

* Kir'iakov, *Russkii Invalid*, 1856, No. 136.

I then withdrew the Moskovsky and Minsky [according to Kir'iakov because of the Russian failure on the centre and right] beyond the fire of the warships, and the French did not follow up. They may have been frightened by the appearance of two *diviziony* [four squadrons] of hussars under Colonel Voinilovich. . . . I halted the two infantry regiments near where the Moskovsky had been originally; the French then began to reappear on the heights and opened strong artillery fire across the Alma on the reserve battalions [Brestsky and Belostoksky] and the Tarutinsky. I could not leave the left wing so perilously exposed. There was no point in waiting to receive an order to retire, for the right wing [P.D. Gorchakov's] was already on its way back . . . I then gave the command to fall back to the Kacha, whither the right flank had already withdrawn.

Kir'iakov said that the troops to the east of the Tarutinsky were already withdrawing, and he was correct in this, for the Borodinsky, on the lower slopes of Telegraph Hill to the left of the main road in the Causeway, pressed by the British centre, were the first to quit the battlefield. But all Russian accounts are quite clear that the Borodinsky was part of Kir'iakov's 17 Infantry Division and belonged to the left flank and not to the centre or right. Kir'iakov, however, said otherwise:

On whether the right or left withdrew first depends on the interpretation of the centre – the Borodinsky. Although the regiment came in fact from the formations of the left wing, it fell back to cover the withdrawal of 2 Light Battery of 16 Artillery Brigade [belonging to Kvitsinsky] and left the battlefield together with the right flank. The Borodinsky was not under my command at the beginning of the battle nor later in the day. During the withdrawal I had occasion to see its battalions with their white markings, way out ahead. But not before 21 September was the Borodinsky returned to my command.

When Kir'iakov wrote these words he was defending himself against P.D. Gorchakov's and Kvitsinsky's view, published in the Russian press, that the left wing retired before the right. Vunsh, Menshikov's chief of staff, then took up the cudgels on Gorchakov's behalf:

But Prince Gorchakov and General Kvitsinsky do not maintain that the left flank withdrew first – they simply say that the withdrawal began to the left of them [with the Borodinsky on Telegraph Hill] and they are right. Only delicacy prevented them from saying that General Kir'iakov withdrew first.

Reasons of delicacy did not, however, inhibit Vunsh from elaborating his point or from describing the events he claimed to have witnessed.

Vunsh was with Menshikov on the left flank when news was brought to them that the British had closed on the Burliuk bridge and that a fierce battle was developing there. Together, they set off along the plateau towards the bridge.

> On our way to this bloody battle we were amazed to find that our positions to the left of the Sevastopol road [on Telegraph Hill] had been abandoned, and we were astounded all the more because even the heights [on the plateau] behind, which commanded the abandoned positions, were held by nobody. French riflemen were already running up the hill unimpeded, and these, seeing us, opened fire. . . . We rode on and, descending into a sheltered hollow, there found General Kir'iakov, alone and on foot. When the Commander-in-Chief asked him where were his troops, he merely answered 'that his horse had been shot from under him!'. [Vunsh's exclamation mark.] There was no time to be lost and the Commander-in-Chief, having sent an aide galloping after the troops who had abandoned the main position in this fashion, hurried on to the bridge.*

According to Vunsh, it was shortly after this that Kir'iakov went missing (*Kir'iakova ne okazalos' pri ego voiskakh*), so that Menshikov had to entrust the withdrawal of the left wing to the command of a Colonel Khrushchev, 'Kir'iakov not being seen again until after we had withdrawn to Sevastopol'. Vunsh's description of Kir'iakov's behaviour appears to confirm Chodasiewicz's story, published in London in 1856.† Captain Enisherlov, who produced a balanced and impartial account of the Alma battle, was in no doubt that the Borodinsky and Telegraph Hill were Kir'iakov's responsibility and concluded that if Kir'iakov did not order the withdrawal of the Borodinsky, he certainly made no effort to stop it. 'The only one', said Enisherlov, 'who can throw any light on this strange withdrawal is General Kir'iakov'.

The editor of the *Voennyi Sbornik* allowed Kir'iakov the opportunity to reply to Vunsh's narrative, and he did so, calling it 'inventions and insults', and regretting that the *Sbornik* should have given space to such a polemic wrangle as that written by Vunsh. But much of the tenor of Kir'iakov's reply was petty and hardly relevant, so that he did little to refute Vunsh's allegations. Kir'iakov simply denied that the Commander-in-Chief and Vunsh had found him in the hollow, dismounted and alone, and

---

* Vunsh, *Voennyi Sbornik*, 1858, No. 3.
† The Polish officer Chodasiewicz deserted to the British.

reaffirmed his earlier account of the meeting with Menshikov which took place at the Tarutinsky; and he said that he was in command of the withdrawal at all times, 'but forward with several Cossacks, when the Commander-in-Chief with the now dead Kornilov and several officers of his staff ordered me to take my troops back – there must be someone who was present at this interview!'. It was painful, said Kir'iakov, that Vunsh should permit himself, on the strength of a rumour, to spread a printed lie. But the Russian historians of the day, like Vunsh, judged Kir'iakov to be alone responsible for the premature and unauthorized withdrawal of the left flank.

* * *

When, at 11 a.m., the Commander-in-Chief had moved over to Kir'iakov's left flank he had left Prince P.D. Gorchakov 'as commander against the English' on the right and central sectors. Gorchakov, Kvitsinsky and Enisherlov remained at the command post on the Kurgan near the Great Redoubt from where they had an excellent view of the approach of the red-coated enemy columns. Gorchakov described the scene on the other side of the river:

> The English halted, then sent out a screen of skirmishers and opened up with their artillery, which, however, our batteries soon silenced. They then deployed from column into two extended lines with a reserve, but taking note that their left was not aligned with our right, they began to move to their left by platoons, parallel to us and about 200 sazhens [450 yards] away, as if to threaten our right flank.*

In deploying, the British troops did indeed make ground to their left because they had insufficient room to manoeuvre. But the Russians were convinced, even four years after the battle, that it had been the British intention to envelop Menshikov's right flank. Indeed Bogdanovich believed that it would have been to the British advantage to cross the river by the fords in the area of Tarkhanlar and the *traktir* further upstream, where no Russian artillery had been deployed and the Suzdal'sky stood nearly a mile from the river; he went on to conclude that this *was* the British plan, but that 'the English divisions lost direction trying to maintain contact with each other and the French, this causing them to strike the Russian line further west than had been originally intended', this accident bringing the British centre line on to the road and the Burliuk bridge opposite Menshikov's main forces. The British were certainly fated to attack at the strongest point of Menshikov's defence.

* P.D. Gorchakov, *Russkii Invalid*, 1856, No. 101.

Shortly after 1.30 p.m. the British advance, which had been slow and deliberate but made in good order (*stroino*), had brought the troops against the vineyards and gardens close to the river; there the men were ordered to lie down because of the heavy Russian artillery fire from the Causeway and Great Redoubt batteries. Meanwhile British light infantry had run on ahead and out to the flanks, occupying the gardens between Burliuk and Tarkhanlar and driving the Russian riflemen and sailors back across the river; this was done at such speed that the Russian sappers on the wooden bridge had to run for their lives, their demolition work still not done. Burliuk and Alma-Tamak had already been set aflame by Cossack incendiaries and, further downstream, Napoleon's division was across the water.

The first British attack made in the area of the wooden bridge was met by the concentrated fire of the Great Redoubt and Causeway batteries and the rifle outposts of the Borodinsky and Kazansky Regiments. According to Bogdanovich, the enemy had little support from his own artillery, 'for this was soon silenced by Russian guns'. Enisherlov reckoned that the British, and in particular Codrington's brigade that was trying to scramble over the river in the area of the bridge, 'suffered enormous casualties' that eventually forced them to fall back behind the Burliuk *traktir*. But the issue was to be decided by the riflemen they left behind who, taking cover behind the stone walls, began to shoot down the Russian gun crews, 'inflicting frightful casualties, particularly on the two [Causeway] light batteries of 16 Artillery Brigade'. These, standing in the open, soon had to withdraw, the losses among horses being so great that the guns could hardly be dragged away.

Of the four battalions of the Tarutinsky Regiment only Gorev's 2 Battalion had as yet been seriously engaged; Skal'kovsky and Chodasiewicz and officers of the other battalions had left their stationary columns, which were over the brow of the hill and still virtually unscathed, and had gone forward to the rim of the plateau to watch the fighting on the bridge below. They saw an ill-fated Borodinsky attempt to support the Causeway batteries standing to their front, when a line of their skirmishers had run forward towards the water's edge, 'only to be cut down like corn' by British rifle fire.

Enisherlov was of the opinion that if only the light battery on the Causeway opposite the bridge had been provided with an epaulement and had maintained its position, then 'not one of the English battalions, with their customary leisurely movement' would have crossed the bridge. Both batteries, however, withdrew, and with them the Borodinsky, who marched away up the hill and over the plateau having been given no orders, so thought Enisherlov, where they were to stop. The other regiment of the brigade, the

Tarutinsky, also conformed, although only one battalion had seen real action, the withdrawal being carried out, according to Skal'kovsky, 'quietly as if on manoeuvres'. Then the reserve battalions of the Brestsky and the Belostoksky followed 'at a time when the first enemy attempt to cross the bridge had in fact been repulsed'. From then onwards the Burliuk bridge was defended only by 16 Infantry Division on the east of the main road, and the only troops within range and capable of bringing fire on to the bridge were the Kazansky and the artillery in the Great Redoubt.

At about 3 p.m. the British attacked once more and Enisherlov watched the advancing redcoats 'clambering over the heaps of their dead comrades' and finally crossing the river. More British troops followed, some going over by the bridge and some fording the stream; the enemy then opened a lively fire on the Kazansky columns which stood on both sides of the Great Redoubt.

Gorchakov, watching the enemy crossing the river in great numbers 'regardless of our heavy artillery fire' and hearing that the commander of the Kazansky had been killed, ordered Kvitsinsky to go to the regiment and 'with all nearby units' counter-attack the disorganized enemy lining the river bank. Meanwhile the Uglitsky was to close up.

The enemy troops were the first to move, however. According to Enisherlov, who was watching from close by, the British brigade came steadily up the hill towards the Great Redoubt where it was met in the open by two battalion columns of the Kazansky advancing downhill towards the bridge. Enisherlov said that it was the British who broke first, for the enemy ran back down the slope to the river; 'there, however, they rapidly reformed and came back to the attack, once again engaging the Kazansky by rifle fire'. By then the Kazansky were in the line of fire of the Great Redoubt battery and the guns fell silent to avoid striking down their own countrymen. The English, 'seeing that they had nothing to fear from the musketry of the Russian column', closed in, and the exposed and unsupported Kazansky 'were soon cut down by the fire of several thousand rifles'. Colonel Seleznev, the regimental commander, was already dead and the two battalion commanders were fatally wounded.

Prince P.D. Gorchakov, however, was unable to credit Kvitsinsky and the Kazansky with even this slender success, for he said 'some mistake must have occurred and I did not see the result I had expected for our regiments were still halted'.

I considered it necessary to go personally to the threatened area in order to be at hand. Having told *Fligel'-Adiutant* Colonel Isakov of my intention and made the chief of staff responsible for the right hand sector, I went to the Kazansky, who were fighting doggedly, regardless of their huge losses. I tried to get them to advance with the bayonet, but soon saw that they were too disorganized to do this. So I moved off, leaving them exchanging musket fire with the enemy.

The Kazansky then retreated leaderless and in disorder closely pursued by fresh enemy troops, so leaving the Great Redoubt exposed to the British infantry. The field battery of 16 Artillery Brigade in the epaulement hurriedly made off, leaving two guns behind, 'and the enemy's red flag soon appeared over the deserted battery rampart'.

The Vladimirsky, standing about 1,000 yards to the rear of the Great Redoubt, were then ordered to retake the epaulement and the two guns lost to the enemy. The Vladimirsky counter-attack was subsequently held to be one of the most glorious feats of Russian arms. Yet exactly what happened and who really was in command remained in doubt, for P.D. Gorchakov and Kvitsinsky each said that he personally led the attack without the other being present.

Enisherlov was with Gorchakov and Kvitsinsky at the Lesser Redoubt when the Kazansky retreated and the guns were lost. According to Enisherlov, all three went to the Vladimirsky and Gorchakov *sent* 1 and 2 Battalions of the Vladimirsky, *under* Kvitsinsky, against the Great Redoubt. The Vladimirsky approached in column without firing while the British troops who were grouped about the epaulement 'unconcernedly watched their approach' as though they were uncertain whether the Vladimirsky were friend or foe. But then the Vladimirsky halted of its own volition. A few of the soldiers in the foremost ranks shot off their muskets, and this was the signal for the enemy to run for the shelter of the other side of the earthworks, from which they opened a ragged rifle fire on the column. The Vladimirsky then resumed its march and the British troops 'fled down the slope, abandoning the epaulement and its one remaining gun – for they had already dragged the other away'. But the enemy stopped at about 150 yards short of the river, out of musket range, and then immediately began to form up for a new attack. There were no guns to support the Vladimirsky 'since the field battery of 16 Artillery Brigade had been virtually destroyed and it was considered inadvisable to move the guns out of the Lesser Redoubt; all other artillery except the Don battery was too far away to arrive in time'. The Vladimirsky were defeated, thought Enisherlov, because they lacked the artillery support necessary to engage the English infantry near the river bed and the French guns that had already arrived on the plateau opposite. For these guns had begun to fire on the Vladimirsky from the other side of the Causeway road.

Gorchakov, the 64 year old veteran of the Napoleonic War, who, according to Tarle, 'was almost as bad a tactician as Kir'iakov', had no qualms about claiming the entire credit for leading the Vladimirsky into battle and no scruples about publicly censuring Kvitsinsky in the columns of the press for all of the failures. He wrote:

> When I arrived at the Vladimirsky battalions, which were left and forward of the epaulement, most of my staff had been wounded. My horse had been shot from under me and I had to send my unhurt aide, Major Durnov, for the first troops he came across. Meanwhile, in order to hold back the English, I took under my command a battalion of the Vladimirsky – not having met any commanders as they were all wounded. The battalion started its advance, myself in front, no shot being fired. The enemy stood waiting. We had only to cover another 150 paces to close with him when again my horse was shot down; the Vladimirsky at once opened battalion fire. . . . I certainly did not give the order to withdraw, for at the time I was fully occupied . . . and it would seem to me that General Kvitsinsky, without my permission, should not have done so. But as this measure was in reality forced upon us, following the situation on the left, I did not oppose it.

Kvitsinsky, the Commander of 16 Infantry Division, gave a different version of the same events between the Great Redoubt and the bridge. In a letter written to the *Russkii Invalid* he criticized a review in that journal of Captain Anichkov's brochure on the battle, and disagreed with the words 'then General Gorchakov, on his own initiative, ordered the Kazansky and Vladimirsky to advance with the bayonet and throw the enemy back to the river'. Kvitsinsky continued:

> The mass of English troops, notwithstanding our devastating fire of shot and shell that had made bloody furrows through their ranks, closed up once more and, with new forces, protected by swarms of skirmishing riflemen and supported by a battery firing from behind the smoking ruins of Burliuk, crossed the river and drove back the brave Kazansky, forcing our field battery to limber up and depart.*

Minutes, said Kvitsinsky, were all important, and there could no be delay. Kvitsinsky then rushed to the Vladimirsky and personally took them into

---

* Kvitsinsky, *Russkii Invalid*, 1856, No. 84.

the attack; the enemy faltered and then ran away; but having retaken the epaulement, Kvitsinsky decided against a continuation of the advance, having no nearby reserves in case of failure.

The action, to quote Kvitsinsky, 'once more began to blaze up in intensity', for the English, who had fallen back about 300 paces, opened up with rapid rifle fire and began to move up fresh masses of troops. Of the two aides whom he sent for reinforcements, one was wounded and did not arrive and the other returned to say that the Russian line had already begun to withdraw. It was at this moment, said Kvitsinsky, 'that Prince Gorchakov arrived from the left side of the epaulement and explained that his horse had been shot from under him'. Kvitsinsky continued:

> Prince Gorchakov then moved off while I stayed [with the Vladimirsky] to try and hold my ground. I felt that the critical moment of the battle had arrived. The English advanced in three columns and threatened to turn my right flank, and the French were coming up on my left; the French battery deployed against my left wing [on the other side of the Causeway] began to rake the Vladimirsky. I then decided that my aim must be to save the regiment and its colours and not [retake] the guns . . .
> I put out a screen of skirmishers under Lieutenant Bresmovsky, but then my horse was struck down and I was wounded in the leg. As I was being carried off on a stretcher made of rifles I was hit yet again by a bullet which smashed my arm and rib . . . I do not wish to detract from the part played by my respected superior Prince Gorchakov, but I consider it my duty to repeat that it was I who ordered the Vladimirsky attack, and I write this not in any sense of self-esteem, for that has no place in war, but only in the interest of truth. My actions were witnessed by many officers of the Vladimirsky, and Prince Gorchakov will confirm what I say.

Kvitsinsky, whom Bogdanovich was to call 'a true knight (*rytsar*) entirely without fear', was crippled by his wounds. But Gorchakov, instead of supporting Kvitsinsky's account, was more intent on describing what he claimed to be his own actions; his comment on Kvitsinsky was ungenerous and denigrating.

Prince Bariatinsky's horse had been wounded and lamed in crossing the plateau so that Menshikov had left him behind. Bariatinsky was, however, an observer of the Vladimirsky attack, but unfortunately only from afar. He described the scene which he saw below him:

> In the centre a huge mass of English troops in their red tunics had

already crossed the river and I could hear their blood-curdling screams as they advanced up the hill; and somewhere, far away, the sound of bagpipes. To their front and flanks their 'black [clad] riflemen' were going forward at the run. And all round the bridge were the heaps of red-uniformed English, the dead and the wounded.

Bariatinsky watched the advance of the Vladimirsky columns 'with a general officer in a grey coat at their head', and he assumed this to be 'Sibirsky' Gorchakov. Whether it was so, however, must remain in doubt.

When Gorchakov left the Vladimirsky, where he had been either on a fleeting visit or, according to his own account, leading the battalions in a final bayonet assault from below the Great Redoubt towards the river, his horse, so he said, had been shot from under him and the Vladimirsky had opened fire. Gorchakov continued:

Then seeing fresh [Russian] troops coming down the hill I went with them to the previous battery position [the Great Redoubt to the *rear* of the Vladimirsky]. There I found neither English nor Russian troops, so I arranged the men round the breastwork. I remained there with them during the fighting and then set off down the main Evpatoria-Sevastopol road, where I met Prince Menshikov, who asked where I was coming from, alone and on foot. I told him that my horse had been left near the river and my staff wounded or dismounted, and that six [*sic*] bullets had passed through my clothes. I showed these to the prince.

Gorchakov ended on a waspish note:

I am sorry that a wound prevented General Kvitsinsky from sending for reinforcements which, by my arrangement, stood on the reverse slope at 200 sazhen [450 yards] distance from the battle.

Gorchakov's account leaves unexplained why he did not himself send for the Uglitsky and what he was doing 'alone and dismounted walking away from the battle on the Sevastopol road'.

* * *

Since Kir'iakov's wing had been withdrawn down the Ulukul Valley and was already beyond Adzhi-Bulat village, the vacuum on the left had been filled by two batteries of 14 Artillery Brigade and a light horse battery, in all 24 guns under Kishinsky's command, together with the Volynsky Regiment, drawn up where the main reserve had once been to the left of the main road. To Kishinsky's right was deployed the hussar brigade in open order, with Cossacks yet further to the east. The regiments of 16

Infantry Division down in the Causeway had to retire through this rear guard line.

During the first withdrawals, Shcherbachev, Kishinsky's adjutant, had been thrown to the ground when his horse was killed; he set off on foot, together with a wounded soldier of the Moskovsky who had lost his hand; shot and shell fell all around them, a splinter wounding the soldier yet again, this time in the leg. With the aid of two walking wounded Shcherbachev managed to get the Moscow man to an ambulance where Shcherbachev witnessed scenes which he was never to forget. More than 100 wounded lay around, some in pools of blood, many asking piteously for water. But there was not a drop to be had. The dressing station had neither surgeons nor means to cope with the numbers.

Meanwhile Kornilov had been waiting anxiously in Sevastopol, but at two in the afternoon he could clearly hear the distant rumble of artillery fire and could restrain himself no longer; calling for a carriage he set off up the Sevastopol-Evpatoria road. He wrote in his diary:

> I soon met the first of the detachments withdrawing from the battlefield, and although these were all moving in good order the picture was a sad one. But God's will be done! The enemy, after a bloody error [presumably the attack on the bridge] drove us off by turning our left flank using his superiority in artillery.

Kornilov soon arrived at the field ambulance where Shcherbachev had taken the wounded Moskovsky soldier; he looked about and 'listened with compassion' to Shcherbachev's descriptions, before taking a horse from a Cossack and setting off in search of Menshikov. Kornilov commented:

> There were neither hospitals nor field dressing stations nor even sufficient stretchers, and this explains the huge numbers of wounded left on the field of battle.

Forward and further to the right, 16 Infantry Division was retiring, the Suzdal'sky linking up with the Volynsky to its left and forming a firm base on successive bounds. The Uglitsky covered the withdrawal of the remnants of the Vladimirsky and Kazansky. The British, who had dragged some guns on to the Kurgan, opened fire on the Uglitsky, causing more than a hundred casualties, and, according to Russian accounts, the withdrawing columns had to run the gauntlet of the fire of the French artillery on the plateau. Chodasiewicz spoke of disorder, of officers scarcely sober, 'of the ten minutes of fear and trembling on the second line of heights, when we saw the enemy's cavalry coming forward to cut off retreating stragglers'. The Russian officers thought themselves fortunate that the allies were not strong in cavalry, 'otherwise not more than 15,000 of us would have reached Sevastopol'. Both Vunsh and Enisherlov have described the incident when Menshikov came across the Uglitsky moving off almost at a run; the Commander-in-Chief had the regiment halted and its musicians and colours brought to the head of the column, so that it might resume its march, in slow time, with its colours flying and band playing. But then the advancing British cavalry was suddenly withdrawn, releasing its prisoners, who hurriedly rejoined the Russian lines. There was no further enemy pursuit.

Another witness, Stroganov, who was present there that evening with a field ambulance, summed up the situation:

> The enemy took the heights, yet he used them only to direct artillery fire on our troops withdrawing from the area of the bridge. He then sat there, rejoicing at his victory over what he imagined to be the advanced guard of our army; his mistake saved us and Sevastopol. For who could have thought that our handful of men *was* the Crimean Army, particularly since it was customary at that time to talk of the Russian million strong force? It is frightful to think what might have happened, had it not been for this cardinal error of the enemy's. For our defeated army set off for Sevastopol . . . hardly able to draw breath, hardly able to see reason or come to its senses and understand that this was no nightmare but bitter reality.

Stroganov's description of the plight of the Russian wounded was particularly vivid:

> The first dressing station was set up about a verst or two from Burliuk [between that village and the coast] but it never really started to function because it soon came under fire from the ships. Then, when it moved, it was engaged by French artillery. At about 8 p.m. I set off [following the mobile dressing stations] with my vehicles all loaded, on my way to the Kacha. But the situation was frightful, for hundreds of wounded had been deserted by their regiments, and these, with heart-rending cries and moans and pleading gestures begged to be lifted into the carts and carriages. But what could I do for them? We were already packed to overloading. I tried to console them by telling them that their regimental wagons were coming back for them [although of course they did not]. One man could hardly drag himself along – he was without arms and his belly was shot through; another had his leg blown off and his jaw smashed,

with his tongue torn out and his body covered with wounds – only the expression on his face pleaded for a mouthful of water. But where to get even that? In the fifteen versts from the Alma to the Kacha there was not even a rivulet!

Prince Bariatinsky was still walking his wounded horse back when he passed through the screen of Kievsky Hussars. Their commander, Major-General Khaletsky, who was known personally to Bariatinsky, offered him a regimental cavalry mount, which he refused, presumably because he wanted to save his own horse. Bariatinsky continued on his way, stopped to talk to a wounded officer whom he found lying in a ditch. Then, to his astonishment, he caught sight of a three-legged horse, for its foreleg had been partly blown away, painfully limping along the Sevastopol road; 'and on this poor beast was mounted a horsewoman, recently bereaved, one might suppose; the expression of fear and despair on her face will remain with me for the whole of my life'.

When, a little later, Bariatinsky rejoined Menshikov, Kornilov was already with him, and there Bariatinsky first became aware of the great gulf in the mentality between the two men; years afterwards, and of course with the benefit of hindsight, Bariatinsky was to comment: 'I think things would have gone differently if Kornilov had been in command in the forward area immediately after the landing'.

When Enisherlov went back to the Kacha to arrange for the reception of the withdrawing troops, he found everything in confusion. There was no *general-vagonmeister* or other officer in charge of the rear, and the transport echelons of the various regiments and the drivers of the many officers' vehicles were responsible to no one. The first news of the withdrawal was brought to the Kacha when ambulances and wounded arrived there; their appearance, said Enisherlov, had set the transport drivers 'in fearful turmoil'; teams were immediately harnessed and the wagons and carriages rushed in a disorderly mass to the Kacha for the safety of the southern bank. Enisherlov continued:

At Effendi-Koi, as on the Alma, much of the right bank was covered by gardens, broken up by walls and scattered buildings. A narrow lane led to the ford, the only crossing place, and the vehicles had jammed it so tightly that the arriving artillery could not get through. The artillery horses were already exhausted. The transport was harried off the road so that the guns could be hastened across the river, but no sooner had this been done than the transport crammed into the lane once more. The infantry, after waiting patiently and in vain for the road to be cleared again, began to file through the carts and clamber over the walls and fences in order to reach the river. With the dark, the confusion became worse. The rear was protected only by cavalry, and if the enemy had attacked all would have been up with us.

Bariatinsky, too, said that he witnessed sudden and uncontrolled panics when Cossacks were mistaken for enemy cavalry. According to Totleben the Russian troops were very dejected and in low spirits after the defeat. Many units lost their way that night, not rejoining the main force until daylight, and at least one battalion did not arrive in Sevastopol until several days later. The withdrawal route was strewn with Russian wounded left at the mercy of an unfriendly Tatar population; many of these wounded, according to a soldier of the Vladimirsky who had been left behind, were still being picked up by British stretcher-bearers days after the battle.

*   *   *

The Soviet historian Tarle summed up the battle in characteristically emphatic and categorical terms when he said that 'notwithstanding the total absence of leadership, the complete lack of even a vestige of intelligent and coherent command – not to speak of a plan of battle – officers and other ranks fought in their customary brave fashion and held on in the most impossible conditions . . . for the Russian troops suffered much from the enemy artillery and above all from the rifles of the English'. There can be no doubt of the bravery of the Russian troops for many of Tarle's conclusions are fully supported by those who fought in the battle. Yet Tarle's work contains some passages which cannot escape challenge, for by 1945 Stalin's academicians had rediscovered the military virtues and skills of the old Imperial Russian Army and had begun to paint them in the brightest of colours. The brave Vladimirsky attack, for example, could hardly justify the description of 'brilliant'; and the contemporary Russian evidence denies that it was the Borodinsky who 'drove the English back to Burliuk and who withdrew only when they had lost half their number', or that 'the Brestsky and Belostoksky maintained their positions with great determination'.

In Chodasiewicz's opinion the causes of the Russian defeat rested on a bad plan and the lack of control:

Firstly, the troops were badly deployed; secondly, nobody gave any directions what to do during the action and everyone acted as he thought fit; the battalions of the reserve [Belostoksky and Brestsky] began to retreat without orders and our [Tarutinsky] battalion followed their example. During the five hours of fighting we neither saw nor heard from our divisional general, or brigade or regimental commanders, nor did we receive any orders to advance or retire. When we withdrew, nobody knew whether we ought to go to the right or to the left. In the centre it was the same. If the men fought, it was solely because of the regimental colonels and certainly not from any orders from Prince Gorchakov. Who would have thought of ordering a regiment [the Vladimirsky] into close-quarter combat without artillery support? . . . Only on the left flank, where Prince Menshikov was present, was there some degree of order.

The non-commissioned officer of 2 Battalion of the Tarutinsky said that they 'received no order to withdraw – indeed throughout the battle we received no orders at all and everything was done by battalion commander Gorev on his own responsibility'.

Enisherlov's thoughtful analysis placed the main responsibility for the defeat on the Russian neglect of armament, and in particular on the failure to adopt the rifle as the general purpose infantry weapon. The Russian Army had not progressed since Suvorov. 'Thanks to our tactical misconceptions', said Enisherlov, 'the Alma battle was lost as soon as we had selected our positions and determined our plan of action'. Enisherlov, like Gorchakov, thought the British artillery 'pretty weak', but he was impressed by the obstinacy and skill of the British riflemen hiding in the vineyards and gardens, and with the range and stopping power of their rifles, 'for the Suzdal'sky Regiment, standing [in dead ground] at a distance of 700 sazhens [1,600 yards] from the river, started to lose men from rifle fire when the enemy was still on the right bank' and, added Enisherlov, it was 'important to note that the strike of the bullets, although at extreme range, was entirely effective'. The Uglitsky had suffered in the same way, and high-angle rifle fire had even caused casualties behind the cover of the breastworks of the redoubts. Because British infantry fought in line and not in column, they could be defeated only by riflemen or by artillery firing case-shot; round shot and shell, thought Enisherlov, was of doubtful value against such infantry tactics.

Menshikov's force held 1,700 rifles, in addition to those of 6 Rifle Battalion, but these had been distributed, ninety-six to each regiment; 'two-thirds of these rifles never fired a shot and those that were deployed were allocated to positions where they could not be used'; and the supply of rifle ammunition ran out. Enisherlov heard, too, after the battle, that the artillery ammunition echelons did not function well, although each artillery battery had a mounted officer whose duty it was to liaise with the

artillery park. Infantry companies, of course, had to rely on a dismounted
soldier. Some of the infantry battalions did not bring a case of ammunition
for each of their companies but tried to make do with one or two cases for
the battalion; only sixteen cases of small arms ammunition were taken to
the Alma for the whole force – not a quarter of the estimated requirement –
and the reason appeared to be that the case was heavy and unwieldy, more
like a crate, a load which, when broken down, required thirty pairs of men
to carry the contents slung between them in greatcoats. Each crate had a
mixed content of capsule, and rifle and musket ball and cartridge; if rifle
ammunition became short another whole mixed crate had to be sent for.
Such a makeshift arrangement could not stand the test of battle.

Russian commentators are agreed that Menshikov was at fault in not
destroying all ravine paths up the cliff and not covering them by the fire
of entrenched riflemen. Enisherlov considered that the Commander-in-
Chief's preliminary moves to the left flank were unsound, for the Moskovsky
and Minsky were brought over from the centre (the Minsky having to
march as far as two miles) when the Tarutinsky stood uncommitted barely
600 yards from where the Moskovsky went into action. All were of the
opinion that the blame for the early withdrawal belonged to Kir'iakov,
and these views were expressed publicly and bluntly. Enisherlov said:

> General Kir'iakov, having given no orders for field defences, even
> against bullets, found it inconvenient (*neudobnoiu*) to continue to occupy
> Telegraph Hill.

To which Vunsh added:

> One could, however, fully agree with General Kir'iakov that the battle
> might have cost the enemy dearer, but only provided that General
> Kir'iakov did not hand over his positions to the French without a fight.

Those regiments on the right, who were fighting against the British,
conducted themselves with determination and bravery, and lost heavily in
casualties. But, according to Enisherlov, the higher command was at fault,
for a plan should have been prepared to counter-attack the British not
merely by two battalions of the Kazansky, but by two regiments, and then
only after the enemy had been subjected to a heavy covering fire of case-shot.
Although conceding that 'Prince Gorchakov could not have done otherwise
since he did not know of General Kir'iakov's withdrawal', Enisherlov
believed that the Vladimirsky attack should never have been made, since the
battle was already lost. Nor should the Vladimirsky have gone into battle
unsupported by artillery and without an infantry reserve, with the Uglitsky

idle and close at hand. The Suzdal'sky and the artillery on the right never came into action and the large force of cavalry and Cossacks did not strike a blow.

Menshikov failed because his inadequate military education was out-moded, because he was superficial and was inclined to favour others as shallow as himself, and he was unable to assess worth in his subordinates. Menshikov was distrustful of the generals and of the general staff. And, according to de Bazancourt, who quotes as evidence 'one of the French generals', Menshikov would appear to have been so frivolous that he allowed on the plateau '*des calèches remplies de dames, et des amazones qui etaient venues assister au triomphe certain de l'armée russe*'; Bariatinsky's account certainly confirmed that Russian women were present on the battlefield. The Commander-in-Chief tried, unsuccessfully, to control the left wing in person, being unable and unwilling to decentralize responsibility. Because of the lack of co-ordinated control, the battle deteriorated into a number of localized though bloody actions, at least two general officers becoming involved in the handling of regiments and battalions while the greater part of their formations stood without orders, idle in reserve. Menshikov was a man of many failings but cowardice was not one of them; although he held his fellows and subordinates in contempt, his aides-de-camp appear to have been much attached to him. It is indicative of Men-shikov's nature and want of judgement that he should have wasted valuable time during that fateful afternoon of 20 September seeking out and visiting the badly wounded Skolkov.

It was on the Alma that Russian officers first met an enemy who fought in line, but what impressed them most was the slowness of the movement of the English troops. 'In fact', said Enisherlov, 'throughout the whole of the Crimean War they distinguished themselves by this extraordinary leisureliness in their gait; this was the cause of their high number of casualties in the Alma battle'. French infantry on the other hand 'excelled in their speed of movement and in this respect were superior to Russian as well as to English; they were also outstanding in the rapidity with which they deployed into attack columns – for we Russians sacrificed speed for good order and regular formation'. French skirmishers, too, moved with dexterity and skill, 'particularly the Zouaves who were expert in the use of cover'.

The French losses on the Alma were put at 1,351, those of the British 2,002. The Russian casualties were forty-six officers and 1,755 other ranks killed, 84 officers (including four general officers) and 3,085 other ranks wounded, seven officers and 728 men missing, totalling in all 5,709. Of these casualties 3,121 were borne by the four infantry regiments of 16 Infantry Division, the Vladimirsky 1,307, the Kazansky 1,252, the Suzdal'sky 420 and the Uglitsky 142.

* * *

On the late afternoon of 20 September when the Alma battle was almost over, Menshikov turned suddenly to his aide-de-camp Captain of Cavalry Greig, and ordered him to go to St Petersburg to report the news of the defeat to the tsar. When the surprised Greig asked what he should tell the sovereign, Menshikov replied, waving his arm in the direction of the withdrawing Russian troops: 'Tell him what you have seen!'. Greig carried out the order to the letter.

Miliutin described the scene when Greig arrived at Gatchina exactly seven days after the battle, where the whole court was agog to hear what the messenger had to say about this first battle against the Anglo-French. Until Greig was ushered into the royal presence neither Nicholas nor his court had any hint of the outcome. But Greig had neither the time nor the wit to compose himself or his despatch, and the torrent of words came tumbling out, disjointed, unbalanced and ill-considered, for, said Miliutin, 'the impressionable adjutant was so shaken by the battle that even after seven days he could not detach himself from his personal experiences, and he described the battle so clumsily and portrayed the Russian troops in so poor a light' that Nicholas sank back in a chair and shed a flood of tears. Then, as the aide-de-camp babbled on, the tsar became angry, rose and seized him by the shoulders, shaking him violently and shouting, 'Do you really understand what you are saying?'. And he ordered Greig away 'to sleep it off'.

For several days the news of the defeat was suppressed and Menshikov's couriers were ordered to leave the train from Moscow at Kolpin and go direct to Gatchina, without stopping at St Petersburg. But it was impossible to conceal the truth for any length of time. Public opinion was, however, to be prepared by an official lie, this delaying the spread of the deadly news in the capital. On 28 September the Grand Prince Mikhail wrote to his brother Constantine 'Papa permits it to be said that, after an exchange of cannonade, Menshikov was obliged by the enemy's numerical superiority to withdraw to Sevastopol'. Four days later, the defeat of the Alma was still not generally known in St Petersburg.

Menshikov, to his discredit, insinuated that the Russian troops had fought badly, a slander which was hotly denied by his own chief of staff Vunsh. At first, however, Menshikov's version was believed not only by Nicholas but even by Constantine, who could not abide Menshikov. On 28 September

Nicholas wrote to Paskevich: 'I am very upset about everything that has happened but I submit to the Lord's will and prepare myself for the worst'. The next day he wrote to General Prince M.D. Gorchakov in Bessarabia:

May the Divine Will be done. I submit to it without murmuring. But it is sorrowful and painful for me to learn that it is want of courage on the part of the troops that is the cause of our failures. I can hardly understand it, knowing from earlier reports how good they were and what spirit was in them.

Tarle believed that the impression which the Alma battle made in Russia was enormous. 'Neither Inkerman nor the Chernaia Rechka nor even the final assault and the fall of Sevastopol, though this latter event was far more important than the Alma, producing a more depressing effect'. After the Alma the worst was expected and everyone was ready for it. Aksakov wrote:

The short despatch from Menshikov about . . . the withdrawal to Sevastopol is so eloquent that no more need be said. In one night we withdrew, or better to say retreated, several tens of versts . . . It is obvious that we have few troops in the Crimea and that we were not prepared to meet the enemy. In my view we will have to lose Sevastopol and in consequence the fleet.

Another correspondent, Abramtsevo, wrote on 30 September in the same vein:

The Crimea will probably be lost, if not permanently then for some time, for we have been humbled in the greatest degree. Foul Austria is exultant.

But the Alma was not the end but only the beginning. On 5 October Prince Vasil'chikov, moving with new formations by forced marches from Bessarabia to the Crimea, wrote from Kherson to Colonel Men'kov:

Your friend Lobanov-Rostovsky talks a lot of nonsense, as is apparent. A week has passed and Sevastopol has not been taken and shows no sign of surrendering. The soldiers are marching at a miraculous pace, hurrying on from crossing place to crossing place [over the great Ukrainian rivers] and they do not know the meaning of tiredness. If they had not got the artillery with them they would be covering 50 versts [30 miles] a day. All press forward, all wondering, though they do not say it, whether they will be in time.

CHAPTER 5

*   *   *   *   *

SIEGE AND BOMBARDMENT

The promontory to the south-west of Sevastopol had originally been occupied in 500 B.C. by the Greek settlers from Heraclea who gave to it its name of Chersonese (peninsula); although the name has endured to the present day, the colony itself, after a long life in which it formed part of the Roman and Byzantine Empires and the Genoese Republic, was eventually destroyed by Tatars and Turks. In 1783 the Crimea was annexed by Russia, and the following year Catherine the Great ordered the founding of a naval base and fortress to be given the Greek name of Sevastopol, the 'celebrated city'; the Russian Rear-Admiral Mackenzie was put in charge of all planning and building.

The choice of site was an excellent one for the base was located on the south bank of the long bay which came to be known as Sevastopol Bay, four miles in length and about half a mile in width and from forty to sixty feet in depth, the water being without shoals and the bottom flat and muddy. Only in the eastern end was it shallow due to the silt brought down by the Chernaia River. The roadstead rarely froze over and its harbourage was held to be among the finest in the world; in summer the wind blew by day from the west, backing round to the east at night, this being particularly convenient for sail since vessels could arrive and leave without long delays waiting for the wind to come from the right quarter. The only disadvantage of the new waters as a port was a species of sea-worm found there harmful to ships' timbers.

The south bank of the roads was indented by a number of large bays, the most important of which, starting from the west, were the Karantinnaia (Quarantine), the Artilleriiskaia, the Iuzhnaia (South), the Korabel'naia (Shipping) Bays, and the Kilen-bukhta (the Keeling or Careening Bay or Bight). Although all of these bays were used by shipping, the finest harbourage was that of the South Bay which was over a mile long and from 35 to 55 feet in depth, having an anchorage big enough for the whole of the Black Sea Fleet; sea-going merchantmen used the Artillery Bay. Each of

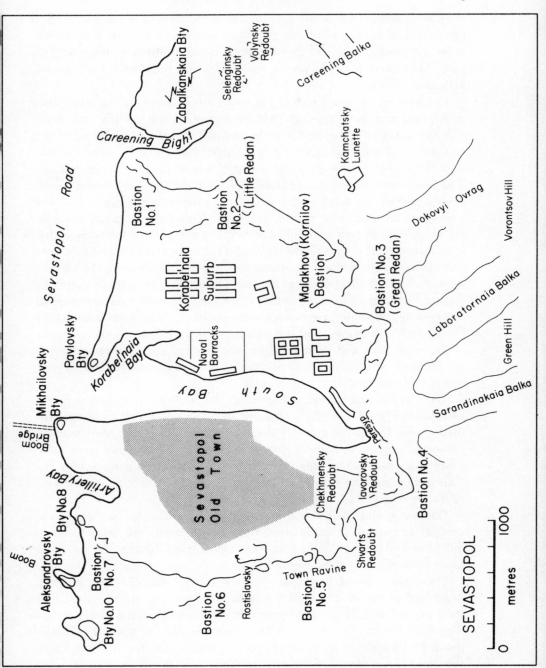

SEVASTOPOL

these bays formed the lower end of one of the deep canyons and gullies
(the *balki* and *ovragi*) which cut into the mountainous plateau to the south
of Sevastopol Bay and bore the same name as the ravine of which it formed
part. There were few bays on the north bank and these were small and of
little importance.

The base on the south side of the roads was bisected by the South Bay
which ran from north to south dividing the south bank into the main town
(the Gorodskaia) to the west and the newer Korabel'naia faubourg to the
east, the road link between the town and suburb being by a track which
skirted the south end of the bay, crossing reclaimed land called the Peresyp.
The main town was on a little tableland about 180 feet high, known as the
town mountain, its steep slopes falling eastwards into the South Bay and
westwards into the town ravine; yet, notwithstanding its raised position,
the old town was itself overlooked from the surrounding mountains so that
it lay as if in a great amphitheatre. Within the main town all the roads were
laid out in regular grid-iron pattern, only the two boulevards, the Ekaterininsky and the Morsky leading from the Theatre Square to the Nikolaevsky
Square, being macadamized; most other roads, which were narrow and
unpaved, led off from these two main thoroughfares. The town included the
old admiralty buildings, with its slipways and workshops on the west side
of the South Bay, and the arsenal and the artillery and engineer stores; at
the northern extremity of the main town a ferry ran from the Grafsky jetty
across the roadstead to the north side.

The Korabel'naia suburb to the east of the South Bay was a more recent
extension of the base and it housed the new admiralty buildings, the
marine stores, and the new dry docks at the mouth of the Dock Ravine.
Although much of the drinking water in Sevastopol was drawn from wells,
a large quantity was brought into the base by aqueducts coming from the
Chorgon springs and from the Chernaia River, this source also being used
to fill the dry docks.

The north bank of the roadstead, usually known as the Severnaia, was
sparsely developed in comparison with the old town and suburb, but it
did have a number of industrial buildings, mainly biscuit and provision
factories producing ships' supplies.

The population of Sevastopol was principally Russian and, in 1854,
numbered 45,000 of whom all but 7,000 were naval or army personnel or
their dependents. There were some Armenian and Jewish traders but few
Tatars or Greeks in the town. The Tatar peoples, who comprised two
distinct nationalities, were mainly in the rural areas; the Mongol Tatar,
the direct descendants of the original horde, inhabited the steppe, while

the Turkish Tatar cultivated the uplands. The Greeks in the Crimea usually kept to their own villages. Whereas Tatars and Jews were well disposed to the invaders, the Greeks, antipathetic to the Turk and allied to the Russian by religious ties, were usually hostile.

* * *

In the time of Catherine the Great permanent coast batteries had been installed on both sides of the roads, and, over the decades, these were steadily increased in number until, by 1852, they comprised eight batteries, five mounted in stone casemates and three (Nos 4, 8 and 10) in earthworks. The coast batteries bore either a name or a number and were so sited that enemy vessels approaching Sevastopol would first come under the fire of No. 10 Battery at a range of 2,400 yards when they were still outside the bay; on entering the roadstead, the enemy would be engaged successively by the Aleksandrovsky Battery and the Konstantinovsky (on the north side), and then by the guns of No. 8 Battery; shortly afterwards the Niko-laevsky Battery (north side) and the Mikhailovsky would be within range, and finally, as the enemy vessels reached the entrance to the South Bay, No. 4 Battery (north side) and the Pavlovsky Battery would come into action. Three of the coast batteries at the entrance to the roads, No. 10 Battery, the Aleksandrovsky and the Konstantinovsky, were originally manned by army artillery although they were later to be reinforced by sailors; all other coastal guns inside the roadstead belonged to the navy. The number of guns to a coast battery varied from 34 (the Pavlovsky) to 105 (the Nikolaevsky); each battery manned several types of armament, the cannon ranging from 12-pounder to 36-pounder, but including also howitzers, bombards and mortars. In 1852 there was a total of 533 guns mounted for coastal defence.

During the spring of 1854 the seaward defence of the roads was strengthened by the building of three new batteries to the east of the Pavlovsky. Two were constructed on the north shore, the Twelve Apostles facing the Careening Bay with the Paris Battery to its left, the third battery, the Sviatoslavsky, being sited on the south bank near the Careening Bay, these batteries taking their names from the ships' crews that built them. In the middle of April a new No. 12 Battery was begun to the north of the Konstantinovsky, built by and called the Kartashevsky (known to the allies as the Telegraph), while, yet further to the north, a high stone tower was erected on the rock and this, No. 13 Battery, took the name of the Volokhov in honour of the merchant lieutenant of reserve who paid the cost of it. This was called the Wasp Battery by the allies. The last to be built was No. 11 Coast Battery, sited about 120 yards from the Konstantinovsky and armed with five 220-pounder mortars.

By 1 May the 14 coast batteries consisted of 28 long-range bombards, 344 guns of varying calibres from 12-pounder to 36-pounder, 200 howitzers, both 18-pounder and 36-pounder, nine carronades and 29 mortars, mostly 180-pounders, in all 610 guns not including the guns of the fleet. For, from the middle of March, the Black Sea Fleet inside the port was brought to action readiness, being anchored in the roads in two lines, Kornilov's squadron of four men-of-war, a frigate and four steamers at the entrance of the South Bay, while Nakhimov's squadron of eight men-of-war and several smaller craft were in the depth of the roads. Kornilov's squadron added a broadside fire of 230 guns, and Nakhimov's squadron 300 guns, to that of the coast artillery. To safeguard against a surprise attack from the sea two floating booms had been constructed of spare masts and bowsprits, chained and roped together, and these lay at anchor ready to be towed into place, linking the Nikolaevsky and the Mikhailovsky Batteries and blocking the roads' entrance. Two transports were converted into fireships and a rowboat squadron had been formed to grapple with enemy fireships.

The Russian Navy had few steamships and there was little understanding in St Petersburg or in the Crimea of the extent to which steam and the screw had revolutionized naval warfare and the landing of ground forces from the sea. The disembarkation of a large enemy expeditionary force was thought to be so difficult and hazardous as to be an almost impossible enterprise. Although Menshikov may have discounted an invasion, he did, however, fear that the enemy might use landing parties to destroy the coast batteries from the seaward side, and he regarded No. 10 Coast Battery as particularly vulnerable. In the spring of 1854 this fort was provided with caponiers, covered passages across the ditches, facing on the Quarantine Bay to protect its left flank.

The Sevastopol base had always been open to attack from the land. There was an isolated and partially disused octagonal fort (the Star Fort) built on the Severnaia in Alexander's reign, at which time it had been intended to construct further forts of a similar type south of the roads; but this idea was subsequently discarded in favour of fortifying the whole of the main town and suburb by a continuous ditch and wall linking projecting bastions of irregular pentagon shape, each with its base in the line of the main works. According to the 1834 project, subsequently modified by Nicholas during his 1837 tour of inspection, the land defence on the south side was to have consisted of this continuous semi-circular line of defences around the Korabel'naia joining up with those on the town side running from the Ushakov to No. 8 Coast Battery, covering in all a length of 9,000 yards and made up of eight earthwork bastions linked with trenches and connected by crenellated and loop-holed walled ramparts. All the bastions (except the Malakhov) were to be numbered starting from the east, No. 1 Bastion in Careening Bay, No. 2 being 600 yards to its right, then the Malakhov on the steep Kurgan with No. 3 Bastion close by between the Dock and the Laboratornaia Ravines, No. 4 being opposite South Bay, No. 5 on the crater between the town and the town ravine, No. 6 being a further 1,000 yards to the right and No. 7 near the shore, adjacent to No. 8 Coast Battery. But little was done to implement the project, except for the construction of defensive obstacles between 5, 6 and 7 Bastions and some work on No. 7 Bastion and the landward defence of No. 8 Coast Battery. The length of the perimeter defences actually completed, totalled only 1,600 yards, not a fifth of the distance round the town. On the north side there was nothing but the old octagonal fort.

During the summer of 1854 some additional work was put in hand on the land fortifications, the Black Sea Fleet having been made responsible for building and manning the defence of the whole of the land perimeter of the base, except for that sector in the west considered by Menshikov to be particularly vulnerable to attack by enemy landing parties – between No. 7 Bastion and the town ravine. There the army was put in charge. Some 18-pounder howitzer batteries were sited between No. 5 and No. 7 Bastions and a new field-work, known as the Shvarts Redoubt, was begun to the left of No. 5 Bastion. But little was actually achieved before the allies landed, for there was a lack of money, labour and resources. Admittedly, there was a plentiful local supply of a hard and durable lime-stone known as steppe stone, but this was difficult and costly to work and transport; in some rocky areas there was a shortage of soil for earthworks. But, in spite of these difficulties, formidable defences might have been constructed, as the events between 20 September and 17 October were to prove, if the will had been there; the main reason for the lack of progress lay in the absence of any sense of urgency at Menshikov's headquarters.

In the middle of April, 6 Corps sapper battalion had arrived in Sevastopol and immediately began the construction of a road from the Korabel'naia suburb across the mouth of the Careening Ravine, mounting the ridge and then running near the coast before dropping down the St Georgievsky gully to the Inkerman bridge. This new road, which cut the travelling distance between Sevastopol and Inkerman by three miles in avoiding the main Sapun plateau, was to prove Sevastopol's main lifeline to the rest of the Crimea.

On the day of the enemy landing not one of the bastions had been completed, nor were they linked to each other even by earthworks.

* * *

When Menshikov had departed for the Alma he had left in Sevastopol only four reserve battalions of the Litovsky and Vilensky and four battalions of marines; these were reinforced by four battalions of sailors formed, at Kornilov's orders, from ships' crews. Meanwhile the fleet was ordered to be ready to sail. Totleben, who up to this time had been unemployed, made a number of recommendations to Kornilov asking for labour, materials and resources to make tools; he also wanted to start work immediately on a system of field-works on both flanks of the Severnaia fort and to throw up hasty fortifications covering the road from Balaclava in case of an allied landing in the south. Kornilov approved these measures and began to remove guns from the warships in order to thicken up the artillery defences.

Just before midnight on 20 September, the day of the Alma, Kornilov and Bariatinsky arrived at the Severnaia shore and crossed the roads in a cutter. All that night, first the wounded and then parties of troops arrived at the shore of the roadstead and were ferried across into the main town. Meanwhile the main body of the defeated Army of the Crimea retreated by the march route down the old post road across the Inkerman causeway, entering Sevastopol from the east along the sapper road. By the evening of 21 September they had arrived at their bivouac area on the Kulikovo field to the south-west of the city.

Menshikov had arrived back on the south bank early in the morning of 21 September and there he gave out his preliminary orders. He had decided against holding the Kacha or the Belbek, nor did he intend to use the army to defend the Severnaia. The sailors would have to do the best they could there. An infantry regiment would be sent northwards to cover the withdrawal, but only as a temporary measure. The Tarutinsky were thereupon paraded that same morning, together with Kondrat'ev's light battery, ready to be transported across the harbour to the north side where they were to form an outpost line on the Belbek and then fall back on the Severnaia fort; from there they would return to the south side. Before moving out of Sevastopol the regiment was inspected by Menshikov who, according to Chodasiewicz, 'looked downcast and bad-tempered', his condition not being improved when Kondrat'ev told him that his battery had lost too heavily in casualties to be fit for any action. From Menshikov downwards, said Chodasiewicz, not one of the leaders knew what to do, for they were all at their wits' end; the troops were without spirits, and nobody wanted to think or speak about the previous day's battle, except for one other rank veteran of thirty years' service who ventured his own opinion on the high command when he told Chodasiewicz that 'the fence was good but the posts were rotten'.

Menshikov had ordered the Chief of Staff of the Black Sea Fleet to prepare a number of the older men-of-war for scuttling across the entrance to the roads, and he was deaf to Kornilov's many objections. On that morning of 21 September Kornilov convened a naval council of war attended by the senior staff officers and captains commanding warships. Menshikov was not invited. Kornilov, who acted as chairman, told the council nothing about the order he had just received from the Commander-in-Chief to sink the Russian warships. Instead he outlined the battle situation and gave warning that if the enemy took the Inkerman heights their artillery would force Nakhimov's squadron to move from its anchorage, so reducing the number of guns for the defence; the enemy fleet might then try to enter the roads. Alternatively, the allied army might close up to the Severnaia shore, in which case Kornilov regarded the Russian fleet as lost. Still concealing Menshikov's orders, Kornilov put the motion to the council that the Black Sea squadrons should put to sea immediately and attack the allied fleet. Kornilov argued that the enemy was not really as strong as might be supposed, and that the allies were disorganized and in confusion. In support of these views he cited two incidents: the *Sviatoslav* had stood off-shore outside the range of the coast batteries for a whole day and had not been attacked, while the steamer *Taman'* under Captain-Lieutenant Popov had crossed the Black Sea to Nikolaev without meeting a single enemy vessel except for a Turkish merchant brig which it sank.

The council heard Kornilov out in silence, and very few of those present supported him. Then Captain Zorin proposed the contrary view, that all the sailors of the Black Sea Fleet should be used to man the land defences, and that part of the fleet should be sunk as blockships across the entry of the roads. This was music which Kornilov did not want to hear, and he was not prepared even to discuss the motion; he abruptly closed the meeting telling all present to prepare to put to sea; 'they would receive the necessary signal in due course'.

Kornilov returned immediately to Menshikov, and, saying nothing about the council of war which he had just left, he bluntly informed the Commander-in-Chief that he would not carry out his orders regarding the scuttling but proposed to take the fleet out to sea. Menshikov coolly instructed him to fetch Vice-Admiral Staniukovich, who would henceforth be in charge of the sinkings. 'And as for the Chief of Staff, he could quit the Crimea and take himself off to the Nikolaev headquarters'. Kornilov had to obey or go, and he chose to obey. But even then he deliberately delayed giving out the necessary orders, hoping for a reprieve; and he did not order the dismantling of guns or the removal of stores from the ships, so that when the scuttling order was finally given after 6 p.m. on 22 September, it was too late and everything, including the guns, went to the bottom. Of the four men-of-war, two frigates and a port ship to be sunk, three ships were scuttled before dawn and three more at 8 a.m. on the morning of 23 September; the last, *The Three Bishops*, proved almost unsinkable and did not go down until the early afternoon. These sunken blockships formed a wreck boom across the fairway connecting the Konstantinovsky and the Aleksandrovsky Batteries. The remaining 10 men-of-war were drawn up in line along the south shore from the Artillery to the Careening Bays where they could bring their guns to bear on the north side; all other vessels, except the steamers, were moored in the South Bay ready to be scuttled should the base fall into enemy hands. The crews of the sunken craft were reformed into artillery batteries and naval infantry battalions.

Whether or not Menshikov should have sunk these ships or have put to sea was subsequently argued at length in the Russian press. The allied fleet had an overwhelming superiority in numbers and in material since it was believed to number 89 warships of all types, of which 50 were screw-propelled steamers; the Russian had 45 vessels in all, many of them corvettes and brigantines, of which 11 were paddle steamers. If the Russian Fleet had left Sevastopol it could have been maintained by no other Black Sea base. The military theorist Moshnin, by quoting precedents of the American Civil War, argued that wooden sail could engage ironclads with every hope of success; others thought that the wreck boom across the roads served no purpose since events were to prove that the coast artillery batteries were themselves sufficiently strong to keep the allies out of the roads. But, in general, military opinion inclined to the belief that Menshikov's order to scuttle part of the fleet and use his naval resources for the defence of the base was the correct course to have taken. If he had not done so, Sevastopol might have been lost on 17 October.

Yet Menshikov's immediate purpose does not appear to have been the defence of the base or the security of the fleet, for, on the night of 23 September, the Commander-in-Chief told Kornilov that he intended to withdraw the field force eastwards out of Sevastopol. Menshikov reasoned that, since there were no Russian troops north of the roadstead, the victorious allies could easily extend their hold eastwards to Bakchisarai, gaining control of the centre of the road network which provided Menshikov's communications with Perekop and the mainland of Russia: this network was vital to him for supplies and reinforcements, the divisions which were coming

1 Nicholas I, Tsar of Russia 1825–55

2 Field-Marshal Paskevich, The Prince of Warsaw, Commander-in-Chief of the Active Army

3 Alexander II, Tsar of Russia 1855–81

4 His Highness Prince A.S. Menshikov, General-Adjutant and Admiral, Commander-in-Chief, Crimea

5 Admiral P.S. Nakhimov (killed at Sevastopol, 1855)

6 Vice-Admiral V.A. Kornilov (killed at Sevastopol, 1854)

7 Vice-Admiral A.I. Panfilov. Commanded Sevastopol sector

8 Rear-Admiral V.I. Istomin (killed at Sevastopol, 1855)

9 Naval-Lieutenant V.A. Stetsenko, ADC to Menshikov

10 Lieutenant G.D. Shcherbachev, Artillery of the Guard

11 Captain of Cuirassiers A.I. Zholobov (killed at Alma), ADC to Menshikov

12 Colonel E.I. Totleben, Commander of Sevastopol Engineers

13 General-of-Infantry Prince P.D. Gorchakov, Commander 6 Corps at the Alma

14 Lieutenant-General V.Ia. Kir'iakov, Commander 17 Infantry Division at the Alma

15 Lieutenant-General O.A. Kvitsinsky, Commander 16 Infantry Division (wounded at the Alma)

16 Major-General L.S. Kishinsky, Commander of Artillery at the Alma

17 Captain-Lieutenant Prince V.I. Bariatinsky, Flag Officer to Kornilov and ADC to Menshikov at the Alma

18 Vice-Admiral M.N. Stavinkovich, Commander of the Sevastopol Port and Dockyard 1854

19 Colonel V.F. Vunsh, Chief of Staff on the Alma

20 Colonel A.P. Khrushchev, Commanded Alma withdrawal

21 Vice-Admiral F.M. Novosil'sky, Commander of Naval Infantry at Sevastopol

22 Colonel N.B. Gersevanov, Chief of Operations, Crimea

23 Lieutenant-General F.F. von Moller, Commander Sevastopol Garrison

24 Major-General A.K. Baumgarten, Brigade Commander 10 Infantry Division and Commander Sevastopol Sector

25 Alexandra Stakhovich, Matron of Sevastopol hospitals

26 Nina Grabarichi Nursing Sister (wounded at Sevastopol)

27 Lieutenant-General P.P. Liprandi, Commander of 12 Infantry Division at Balaclava and 6 Corps at Chernaia Rechka

28 Major-General K.R. Semiakin, Brigade Commander at Balaclava

29 Major-General F.G. Levutsky, Brigade Commander at Balaclava

30 Colonel Prince A.V. Obolensky, Commander of the Don Battery taken by the Light Brigade at Balaclava

31 Major-General A.O. Sabashinsky commanded the Selenginsky at Inkerman and 5 Sector at Sevastopol

32 General-Adjutant Baron D.E. Osten-Saken, Commander of the Sevastopol Garrison 1855

33 General of Infantry P.A. Dannenberg, Commander of 4 Corps at Inkerman

34 Lieutenant-General F.I. Soimonov, Commander 10 Infantry Division (killed at Inkerman)

35 Lieutenant-General P.Ia. Pavlov,
Commander 11 Infantry Division

36 Major-General N.D. Timofeev, Force
Commander at Inkerman

37 Grand Prince Nikolai Nikolaevich

38 Grand Prince Mikhail Nikolaevich

39 Colonel Prince V.I. Vasil'chikov, Staff
Officer to the Commander-in-Chief

40 Lieutenant-General S.A. Khrulev,
Commander of Korabel'naia suburb

41 General-Adjutant N.A. Read,
Commander of 3 Corps, killed at Chernaia
Rechka

42 Major-General K-M.A. Martinau
commanded 12 Infantry Division at the
Chernaia Rechka where he lost his arm

43 General-Adjutant Baron P.A. Vrevsky,
confidant and representative of the tsar,
killed at Chernaia Rechka

44 Major-General P.V. Veimarn, chief of
staff of 3 Corps, killed at Chernaia Rechka

45 General of Artillery Prince M.D.
Gorchakov, Commander-in-Chief Danube
and subsequently Commander-in-Chief
Crimea

from Bessarabia. At the moment, however, his vedettes told him that the allies were still closely grouped near the sea and were moving very slowly south on Sevastopol. Menshikov had therefore resolved to seize the opportunity, while it still existed, of escaping from the naval base and trying to outflank the allies from the east so that he might put his troops between the enemy and Perekop. This, at least, is what he said. When Kornilov protested that the seamen remaining in the base could not hold Sevastopol unaided, Menshikov remained inflexible, being certain that 'the enemy would not undertake an attack of any vigour, even on the Severnaia, if it had an army on its flank and rear'.

This is the version expounded by Kinglake, based on information drawn from Totleben's quasi-official account. But Totleben's narrative was written years after the event, and he introduced into Menshikov's appreciation certain key factors, such as the dilatoriness and lack of purpose of the enemy, about which the Commander-in-Chief must at the time have been completely unaware. And Menshikov's subsequent actions showed that, whatever he may have said at the time, he had no intention of 'menacing the enemy flanks and rear'.

There was, however, another consideration which may have influenced Menshikov in coming to his decision. The morale and discipline of the Russian troops was fast breaking down and mutiny was in the air. The force on Kulikovo field was being kept in idleness, with time on its hands to ventilate its grievances, and even Panaev, Menshikov's aide and supporter, was obliged to admit that wild scenes of disorder occurred on 23 and 24 September, with drunken soldiers and sailors roaming the Sevastopol streets, shouting that 'Menshikov has sold Sevastopol to the English'.* For as Chodasiewicz said, 'Whereas Kornilov was very popular, officers and men were much dissatisfied with Menshikov and his commanders'. The gendarmerie and police were ordered to confiscate or destroy all alcohol, and all inns and hotels were closed. Menshikov may have reasoned that discipline could only be restored by removing the Russian solder from shelter and inactivity and making him march in the presence of the enemy. But Menshikov was a very suspicious and mistrustful person who communicated his inner thoughts neither to his staff not to paper.

The Russian field force was to leave Sevastopol after dusk on 24 September, organized as an advanced guard of 13,000 troops, under Major-General Zhabokritsky, and a main body consisting of 6 Corps, under Prince P.D. Gorchakov, with Kir'iakov's 17 Infantry Division in the lead following on Zhabokritsky's heels. Marching eastwards out of Sevastopol

* Panaev, *Russkaia Starina*, 1877, T.XVIII, p. 499.

by way of the Inkerman causeway, the main body was then to halt near the Bakchisarai road on the Mackenzie heights, while Zhabokritsky moved on to Otarkoi, so forming a flank guard between the main body and the enemy. The subsequent movement northwards of Gorchakov's force was to be regulated by Menshikov's later orders. Most of the wheeled transport was to be left in Sevastopol.

At sunset on 24 September, just before Menshikov's force marched out of the base, Russian seamen on the top of the Severnaia fort could discern the allies still bivouaced on the banks of the upper reaches of the Belbek. Later that night the enemy was believed to be in the same position, for his camp fires three miles to the north-west were plainly visible to the Russian troops crossing the Mackenzie heights. Much of Menshikov's route was on a single track through woodland scrub and forest, and no flank guards were put out because of the difficulty in moving and controlling them in the darkness; the security of the force thus depended on its ability to outflank and get to the north of the allies by an undetected and rapid night march.

Zhabokritsky's advanced guard carried out its orders, and, after a brief halt, moved on from the Mackenzie heights to Otarkoi. Kir'iakov on the other hand appears to have misunderstood the plan, for, instead of waiting the arrival of Gorchakov, he followed Zhabokritsky blindly on towards Otarkoi, where he lost his way, so managing to pass the advanced guard and leave it miles behind, until he finally arrived at the Kacha. According to Chodasiewicz who marched with Kir'iakov's column, the night was pitch black and some of the exhausted men wandered from the track, falling to their deaths over the precipices; all knew they were in the presence of the enemy and all feared being taken prisoner, fright giving them speed and endurance. So they continued to march although completely beaten, for the men were too demoralized to fight and there existed 'the most un-bounded licence, as the officers were afraid to curb their men'. Kir'iakov himself was to come under suspicion of wanting to put as great a distance as possible between himself and the enemy.

Since Kir'iakov's force could not be found on the Mackenzie heights, Gorchakov halted there, and this caused the delay which was to result in the loss to the enemy of artillery park baggage vehicles at the tail of the Russian column. For, unknown to Menshikov, before that night was out the allied armies were on the move southwards over the Mackenzie heights, intent on outflanking Sevastopol and getting to the south of the Russian forces.

* * *

The Anglo-French army had remained on the battlefield of the Alma on the night of 20 September and had made no effort to pursue Menshikov's withdrawing army or keep it under observation, for during the next two days the allies were fully occupied in burying their dead and embarking their wounded. At last, on the morning of 23 September, the invading troops started to move to the south, across routes littered with Russian military equipment, until they arrived in the valley of the Kacha a few miles away. There they seemed likely to stay, for first the French and then the British requested postponements; instead of a concerted plan there was frequent disagreement between the Commanders-in-Chief, Lord Raglan and Marshal St Arnaud, as to how Sevastopol should be taken.

After some deliberation the allies decided to close up on the Belbek during 24 September without, however, definitely committing themselves to an attack on the Severnaia, the north bank of the roadstead. But in order to avoid being pinned by what they believed to be new defences at the mouth of the Belbek, they began to move south-eastwards, away from the coast, to the upper stretches of the river. There they found 'the ground was so thickly strewn with the marks of hasty [Russian] flight and confusion, as to show that defeat had been lapsing into ruin, and that the enemy force that entered Sevastopol was a hurried and fugitive crowd; but the allies failed to read these signs and take action upon them'.

Many months before, when the allies were at Varna, they had been faced with the choice either of landing on the west coast of the Crimea and march-ing directly southwards on the Severnaia and Sevastopol, or of seizing a southern port, such as Balaclava, and attacking northwards on the naval base; and they had decided on the first of these alternatives. But now doubts began to assail them. Although the allies were aware of the existence of the octagonal Star Fort, they also knew that it was in disrepair and overlooked from the surrounding heights: but now they had come to suppose that there were other defences to be overcome on the Severnaia before they could close up to the waterline and capture the coast artillery batteries. To these difficulties they added others. They had been informed, on 23 September, that the roads had been closed by blockships, and they came to the conclusion that they could not cross the water to the south side without the support of their own warships operating inside the roads. In truth, on 25 September, the Severnaia defences were manned by a reserve battalion, a company of sappers and an ill-armed and disorganized body of sailors.

The autumn storms were likely to interrupt reinforcement and supply over the beaches of the west coast, with the further possibility of heavy losses to shipping; the allies soon began to wish that they had landed on the south coast where there were sheltered ports. Moreover Lord Raglan knew that there *had been* no landward defences to the south of Sevastopol when the area was seen by a British traveller, a Mr Oliphant, a year or so before. So Raglan came to the conclusion, which was shared by St Arnaud, that unless the Severnaia was to be attacked without delay, the only other course was to make a long flank march, skirting Sevastopol from the east, and to set up new support bases in the ports on the southern coast of the Crimea. Sevastopol could then be attacked from the landward side to its south.

It was resolved that the allied armies should move south and set up a base at Balaclava, and that the British, being on the left, should lead the march. Raglan set off early in the morning of 25 September towards the Mackenzie heights to join the roadway between Sevastopol and Bakchisarai before turning south, following immediately behind the advanced guard, Lucan's cavalry division; this, however, lost its way in the thick woodlands, and so it came about that Raglan and his staff were the first to arrive on the main road near the Mackenzie Farm. There Raglan came upon the artillery park baggage vehicles forming the rear of the huge Russian column which had already passed by on its way from Sevastopol towards Bakchisarai. Among those captured by the British cavalry were some foot soldiers of the Black Sea Cossacks and a drunken Russian artillery officer, but, since no action was taken by Raglan's staff to interrogate the prisoners, Raglan remained ignorant of the Russian aim. The British force then turned southwards while Menshikov's army continued to march northwards along the same road. Thus it was that the Anglo-French and Russian Armies exchanged positions almost simultaneously, remaining ignorant of each other's movements and intentions, in a march and counter-march that Nakhimov, when he learned the truth, called 'blind man's buff'.

The loss of the artillery park baggage vehicles was not reported to Menshikov until after midday on the 25 September, nor did the Commander-in-Chief know that the Russian rearguard, a battalion of the Tarutinsky and four guns marching behind the artillery park, had been cut off from the main column by the British cavalry and had retreated pell mell back to Sevastopol. But Menshikov had received a report from P.D. Gorchakov that there had been a sighting early that morning of English columns on the march as if in the direction of Inkerman. Menshikov viewed the information with amazement and disbelief. During the night he had already sent one officer back to Kornilov asking for news about the enemy and he now decided to send a second aide to Sevastopol, this time to Staniukovich, telling him to deploy a battery covering the Inkerman bridge and dam the

Chernaia and 'fortify the Malakhov Kurgan and the Careening Ravine'. For Menshikov concluded that if there was any truth in Gorchakov's report, 'this development would make our communications with Sevastopol most difficult' for 'the enemy was probably about to probe the approaches to the base from the east'. These approaches were in fact easily accessible to the allies. Yet when they were reconnoitred by two squadrons of Cardigan's cavalry brigade, presumably after Staniukovich had taken action on Menshikov's order, the British said that they found the river estuary near the causeway 'very marshy' and covered by a battery of heavy guns, a strong force of infantry and some cavalry. The light cavalry reported to Cardigan that this approach to Sevastopol from the east was 'impractical for the allied force'.

At 1 p.m., when Menshikov heard of the loss of the baggage vehicles, he angrily blamed Kir'iakov and sent to him an order to return from the Kacha to Otarkoi immediately. So it came about that 17 Infantry Division was to march fifty miles in two days to little purpose, for no sooner had it reached Otarkoi than it was passed *en route* by Menshikov's main force on its way to the Kacha, whence it, too, was ordered to return. From 26 September onwards, the whole of the Russian field force, except for Zhabokritsky's Otarkoi detachment, remained on the Kacha waiting to receive supplies from Simferopol. There, however, the town was in turmoil, for the Tatar population had heard the previous day of the Russian movements and believed that they heralded the withdrawal of Russian power from the Crimea. In the uprising that followed, the Russian governor and gendarmerie fled their posts.

During his long wait Menshikov took no action to regain contact with the main enemy forces.

*   *   *

Before Menshikov quitted Sevastopol he had reorganized the military command of the base so that Kornilov was to control all ground and seaward defences of the Severnaia, while Nakhimov, the senior of the two vice-admirals, was to command all forces in the main town and the Korabel'naia suburb. This arrangement resulted in the establishment of two virtually independent commands responsible to no one. Yet a further complication arose in that Menshikov nominated Lieutenant-General Moller, the Commander of 14 Infantry Division, as garrison commander in the base 'to command the army troops there'. Moller was the senior of all the lieutenant-generals and Menshikov had such a poor opinion of his capabilities that he once wrote to Prince M.D. Gorchakov in Bessarabia 'I do not know what to do with him . . . I would be most grateful if you could write and ask me for him so that I can hide the fact that he is not wanted here'.

Nakhimov had objected to Menshikov's reorganization, telling the Commander-in-Chief that he was 'happy to stay and die in Sevastopol but he did not feel fitted to command ground troops' there. Menshikov, however, would not be moved and insisted on leaving three independent commanders without proper division of responsibilities, while continuing to send orders to a fourth, Vice-Admiral Staniukovich.

When Menshikov left Sevastopol on the night of 24 September there remained in the base only four reserve infantry battalions and four depot battalions of 13 Infantry Division (the Brestsky, Belostoksky, Litovsky and Vilensky), a rifle battalion, a battalion of sappers and 17 battalions of sailors, in all 17,800 men. To this force was to be added the battalion cut off by the British advanced guard, the Tarutinsky men, who, on returning to Sevastopol in the early hours of the morning, caused great alarm to the defenders who mistook them for the enemy. On 25 September Sevastopol was virtually undefended and only twelve guns were in place on the north shore.

On 24 September six enemy steamers had approached the roads and exchanged shots with the Volokhov tower and the Konstantinovsky Battery, and this was the signal for Kornilov to man his scanty defences and set up his north bank headquarters, consisting of Rear-Admiral Istomin as his chief of staff and Lieutenant-Colonel Totleben as his ground forces aide. All of Kornilov's 12,000 men on the north side were sailors except for the gun crews of the army Konstantinovsky Coast Battery and a battalion of the Vilensky held in reserve. Kornilov deployed 6,000 sailors under Captain Bartenev to hold the Severnaia octagonal fort, a force of 2,200 men under Captain Varnitsky to dig and man the trench system eastwards from the fort and 3,200 sailors under Vice-Admiral Novosil'sky to construct the trenchworks on the left flank.

Meanwhile the digging continued by day and night, for an attack was expected hourly, the tools used during the day being taken over by those sailors who arrived for the night work. The trench system grew rapidly on both sides of the fort and a further three batteries were dug in. None could leave his place of duty, for Kornilov would permit no relaxation of effort; even the priests had to hold their daily services on the earthworks, moving along the line from company to company. And this stern and religious patriot stressed to the clergy the nature of their duty when he said: 'Let the troops first be reminded of the word of God; then I will give them the word of the tsar'. Faultlessly attired in his general-adjutant's uniform and accompanied by a numerous staff, Kornilov rode all day up and down the defence works, haranguing the working parties and talking to anyone he met on the way. The Chief of Staff was a man of education and culture, polished, courteous, taciturn and reserved. But his frank and simple speech struck home to the heart of the Russian sailor and soldier, and his talks, so often recounted, were to make him immortal in both Russian and Soviet history, for no leader since Suvorov became more popular with the rank and file. Kornilov told his men to kill anyone who spoke of surrender, to kill even himself if he should order a withdrawal. 'Your business', he said to the infantry, 'is to keep the enemy away from the guns; and if they succeed in getting into the batteries then you must give them a Russian welcome – with the bayonet!'. In another of his speeches he said:

Men! The tsar relies on us to hold Sevastopol. There is no retreat – in front is the enemy and behind us is the sea. Prince Menshikov has out-flanked the allied army, and as soon as we are attacked he will take the enemy in the rear.

Kornilov's real opinion of Menshikov and his strategy was, however, very different.

General of Cavalry Khomutov, the Commander in East Crimea, said in his reminiscences that Menshikov's authority over his subordinates was badly shaken after his failure on the Alma, so that his orders, however peremptory or urgent, were no longer regarded as binding: 'Instead his juniors would consult amongst themselves and deliberate, and execute his orders or not according to their own discretion'. From 24 September, when Menshikov quitted Sevastopol, the Commander-in-Chief was re-garded as of little account and this was no better illustrated than at the military council meeting which took place on the south bank on the morning of 25 September.

During the night march over the Mackenzie heights Menshikov had detailed a Captain Lebedev to go back to Sevastopol for news, and when Lebedev arrived in the base he was admitted to the military council which was in session. Lebedev asked Kornilov if the Commander-in-Chief might be informed of the intentions of the military council, to which Kornilov replied that the council 'intended to discuss what to do now that Sevastopol had been wilfully deserted and left to its fate by Prince Menshikov'. Nak-himov, blunt in his speech but milder in his manner, questioned Lebedev closely about the Commander-in-Chief's intentions and the state of the army. Lebedev, encouraged by Nakhimov's courtesy, asked the admiral what he should tell His Highness, the Commander-in-Chief, they were doing in Sevastopol. Nakhimov replied:

> Tell him that we are all having a meeting and that there was present
> here our military leader, senior to us all in rank, Lieutenant-General
> Moller, whose value and usefulness I would rate as less than that of any
> midshipman!

Moller, hearing his name mentioned, stood up, but, as soon as he understood
the drift of the conversation he sat down again, only to get to his feet once
more to protest that he would willingly put himself under the command
of Kornilov, his subordinate in rank. Lebedev was obliged to return, the
bearer of insults to the Commander-in-Chief.

Prince P.D. Gorchakov's intelligence to the Commander-in-Chief that
an English column was on the move towards Inkerman, sent by Menshikov
to Staniukovich that same morning, does not appear to have been relayed
to Kornilov or Nakhimov, for they were not aware of the enemy movement
until later that day when the look-out on the top of the naval library building
on the south bank reported that he could see red-jacketed columns on the
Mackenzie heights marching away to the south. Then, at dawn on 26
September, French troops appeared on the Sapun heights immediately
to the south of Sevastopol.

From the time of the allied landings until 26 September, the defences
of the south bank had been strengthened by only 27 guns, and these of only
small calibre. Only the western sector, between No. 5 and No. 7 Bastions,
was ready for battle, for the remaining three miles of line was unfinished and
open, being without ditches and having only scattered defences 'with a
low field profile'. The garrison of the south side consisted of only five and
a half battalions, in all 3,500 men.

Nakhimov's immediate reaction, when he heard that the enemy was
outside the town, was to issue an order at 7 a.m. to prepare the remaining
ships of the Black Sea Fleet for scuttling and muster the crews on the
Theatre Square. But when Kornilov arrived shortly afterwards the Chief of
Staff had the order cancelled. Kornilov then brought over his own headquarters to join Nakhimov's and, leaving Bartenev in command on the
Severnaia, he ordered 11 naval battalions (6,000 men) to be ferried by
steamer across the roads to the south side. Another military council meeting
was then called, attended by Kornilov, Nakhimov, Moller and Totleben.

Nakhimov had no faith that Sevastopol would hold out and had no wish
to survive its fall and he did not conceal his forebodings, fears and depression
from Kornilov. He felt himself unfitted by experience and by temperament
to command the defence – wrongly as it transpired, for after Kornilov's

death the main burden of the siege was to fall on Nakhimov; and while Totleben's engineering genius gave the Sevastopol defence a body in the shape of fortifications, Nakhimov's leadership and presence on the gun platforms and in the trenches was to give the garrison its spirit and morale. During the military council meeting of 26 September, however, Nakhimov asked Kornilov to take over the responsibility for the defence of the whole of Sevastopol and willingly put himself under Kornilov's command.

If Moller lacked ability, he had understanding enough to realize his own limitations; following Nakhimov's lead, he ceded the command to Kornilov. But since Kornilov doubted that he had authority to command army troops it was decided that Kornilov should command but that Moller should act as Kornilov's chief of staff on all army matters and issue orders over his own signature but in Kornilov's name. The Commander-in-Chief and the field army was no longer taken into account and the defenders worked out their own salvation 'though this was rarely in harmony with seniority and military precedents'. On 26 September Kornilov entered in his diary the news that Balaclava had been occupied by the allies 'but not a single word (*ni slukhu ni dukhu*)' had been received from the prince. The next day he wrote:

> The prince ought to be made accountable to Russia for the loss of Sevastopol. If he had not gone – God knows where – we would have been able to defend it. If only I had known that he was capable of such a treacherous act then I never would have agreed to have sunk the ships [in the roads] but would have given battle.

Kornilov had stressed to his military council that the need was for quick action to strengthen *the appearance* of the defences and deter the enemy from an immediate attack and so gain time. The burden of the defence during the next month was to be borne by the Black Sea Fleet, for not only were naval officers in command but sailors provided most of the artillery, the infantry and the working parties; many of the senior officers, some of them rear-admirals, were pleased to serve in any capacity, often commanding a battery of eight guns. Since there was no naval field organization above the level of battalion and battery, Kornilov reorganized the ground defence of the south side into territorial sectors, each having a commander and staff responsible for operations and defence works with its own chief of artillery. The west of the town side, from No. 10 Battery to the Shvarts Redoubt formed No. 1 Sector, commanded by Major-General Aslanovich with Ivanov, a naval captain, as chief of artillery; Aslanovich disposed of only six battalions and 12 guns. The south from the Shvarts Redoubt to No. 3

Bastion comprised No. 2 Sector under Vice-Admiral Novosil'sky with Rear-Admiral Iukharin as chief of artillery; No. 2 sector deployed eight naval battalions and eight guns. The Korabel'naia suburb formed Rear-Admiral Istomin's sector with six naval battalions and eight guns of the fleet battery, under Rear-Admiral Bukotich (junior) as artillery chief. Istomin's sector was originally No. 3, but when a new No. 3 Sector under Rear-Admiral Panfilov was later added and interposed between the Peresyp and the Dock Ravine, Istomin's command was renumbered as No. 4 Sector.

Immediately after the battle of the Alma the people of Sevastopol had been seized with panic and a group of Russian merchants had sent a deputation to Kornilov pleading that *parlementaires* should be sent to the French to ask that the civil population be evacuated to Odessa 'in French ships'. Kornilov had told them simply that he would bear their request in mind but that 'now was not the time'. By the morning of 27 September after the army troops had left the naval base, the mood of the remaining defenders and of the civilian population had entirely changed. All feeling of panic had disappeared. The actual bayonet strength of the defenders was steadily increasing because Kornilov was drawing further men from ships' crews and was enlisting a considerable number of volunteers from the local population. Civilians, men and women, even whole families, flocked to the fortifications asking to be enrolled in the labour force; convicts in the prisons petitioned to be allowed to join the defenders and were accepted by Kornilov. Since there was a shortage of tools, wooden shovels were made locally and officers were sent to Odessa to make a collection of the iron shovels in the merchants' stores. There were more Russian women volunteering for hospital and munition work than could be employed. Bariatinsky has told how, just before the siege began, he was riding through the Ekaterininsky with a message from Kornilov for No. 4 Bastion, when he was called by two sisters, the wives of Admirals Novosil'sky and Panfilov, who wanted his advice as to whether they should shore up their basement or an upper storey as a shelter against bombardment. Day and night the streets rumbled to the sound of heavy guns as they were dragged by marching sailors on their way to the bastions.

Kornilov and Nakhimov, according to Bariatinsky, inspired all, military and civilian, by their presence everywhere in the base and on the defensive works. For they were indefatigable. Their subordinates took their cue from them and spent all their waking hours with the men on the rapidly growing defence line. One Rear-Admiral Bukotich, the father of the rear-admiral in No. 3 Sector, a long retired pensioner who had distinguished himself in the campaigns against the Turks in 1828 and 1829 and who now lived in

Sevastopol, appeared on horseback at the bastions each day, dressed in full parade uniform, talking endlessly to officers and troops. But as the old gentleman had lost his reason his presence sometimes embarrassed and delayed the workers. But although the officers in charge of the working parties complained to Kornilov about him, Kornilov refused to stop Bukotich's daily rides round the perimeter; indeed whenever Kornilov met the old admiral during his rounds he would bow to him and sometimes engage him in conversation, listening politely and with sympathy to his disjointed talk.

Tolstoy, who was a battery commander in No. 4 Bastion, wrote a letter to his brother, a few days after his arrival in the base, describing a scene he had witnessed of Kornilov making his rounds. Instead of hailing the men with the traditional greeting, 'Health to you!', the admiral called to them 'If you must die, lads, will you die?'. 'And', continued Tolstoy, 'the men shouted "We will die, Your Excellency, Hurrah!". And they do not say it for effect, for in every face I saw not jesting but earnestness'.

On the morning of 27 September there were five battalions (3,500 bayonets) on the Severnaia and 23 (16,000 bayonets) on the south side, together with 32 field guns, in addition to 3,000 sailors still on board the warships. In the next few days the bastions and trenchworks grew rapidly under Totleben's direction, new lunettes were constructed and further field batteries installed all along the perimeter, these being designated both by a number and by the name of their commander. Many were subsequently to become famous: No. 2 (Gribok), No. 3 (Budishchev), No. 5 (Nikonov), No. 6 (Zherve), No. 21 (Ianovsky) and No. 26 (Shemiakin). The 84 gun man-of-war *Iagudiil* (Captain Kislinsky) was brought into South Bay to cover the defence of the Peresyp, but, as its guns could not cover the southeast approaches, three new batteries were sited there: No. 14 (Alekseev), No. 15 (Perekomsky) and No. 16 (Kriakin); and a bridge was set up over the South Bay in case the Peresyp should become unusable.

On 28 September Stetsenko, Menshikov's naval aide, came trotting into the city asking for news about the enemy, for the Commander-in-Chief still had none. Menshikov's field army was about to be increased, on 1 and 2 October, by a further 10,000 men, Lieutenant-General Ryzhov's cavalry force of 1 Uhlan and 2 Hussar Composite March Regiments, and a further reinforcement sent by Khomutov – the Butyrsky Regiment, six reserve battalions of the Volynsky and Minsky, a reserve Black Sea Cossack battalion and two *sotni* of Don Cossacks. But Menshikov still declined to spare any troops for the beleaguered base. Menshikov, according to Tarle, 'was in a state of complete apathy and indifference and was content to joke and sneer at his own stupid and drunken generals, while he prepared the tsar for the fall of Sevastopol'.

By the morning of 30 September the enemy had not yet appeared in force to the south of the city when Menshikov himself came down to the water's edge on the Severnaia, escorted by part of Zhabokritsky's force, to have a conference with Kornilov. The meeting proved to be a stormy one. The Commander-in-Chief was still stressing the weakness of his field force and told Kornilov that Sevastopol must stand or fall on its own resources: he might, however, he grudgingly said, use 'some of his formations to divert the enemy's attention'. Kornilov made it clear that he had no faith in these half-promises and, angry at the refusal to give him troops, he asked for a council of war to be assembled, in the expectation that other opinions would be added to his own, so forcing Menshikov to reconsider his decision. Kornilov had even contemplated making an appeal direct to the tsar, and his treatment of the Commander-in-Chief was such, thought Panaev, one of Menshikov's aides, as to make it abundantly clear that 'not only did he think that His Highness's strategic ideas were worthless but, in addition, he considered the Commander-in-Chief to be a deserter or a returned runaway'. Menshikov finally gave way without assembling the council, and ordered three regiments of Kir'iakov's 17 Infantry Division, the Tarutinsky, Borodinsky and Moskovsky with two battalions of sailors to be ferried across the roadstead. On 2 October Kornilov wrote to his wife in Nikolaev, 'Menshikov has returned to his troops on the Belbek and has left us here to sweat it out (*otduvat'sia*)'.

Even at the end of September both Menshikov and M.D. Gorchakov believed that a new allied landing was likely between Odessa and the Crimea, possibly near the mouth of the Dniester. But although this belief could explain Menshikov's fear that the enemy might cut his land communication with Russia, it could hardly justify leaving Sevastopol and the fleet exposed to enemy attack, particularly since Prince M.D. Gorchakov had willingly accepted the responsibility for all coastal defence from Odessa to Perekop.

From 24 September there was in Sevastopol a feeling of grim determination: from 3 October, a newly found initiative: for Menshikov began to send Cossack and Russian cavalry squadrons from the field army, firstly to the Mackenzie heights and then down the Chernaia River to the area of Chorgun, hardly two or three miles from Balaclava, thus uncovering the enemy right flank and keeping open Sevastopol's communications with the rest of the Crimea. The enemy allowed this to happen without challenge. On 3 October Kornilov noted in his diary that the Sevastopol defences 'were becoming more and more imposing to look at, and some of the forts were mounting 68-pounder armament'. Three days afterwards, with the arrival of the Butyrsky, the strength of the defenders stood at 25,000 men, and a few days later Menshikov himself returned to the north side bringing with him the remainder of the field force. There, however, he remained until the middle of October, with 30 army infantry battalions (27,000 men) and 27 field guns standing idle on the Severnaia, presumably so that he might escape northwards and save part of his force should the Gorodskaia and Korabel'naia be taken by the enemy. When, on 10 October, the many enemy trenches and saps became visible to the garrison on the south side, it was obvious that the allies intended a siege rather than a direct assault. This intelligence was greeted with relief in Sevastopol.

During the next week the allies brought up a large number of field guns and siege artillery. The first bombardment could not be long delayed.

* * *

On 16 October Kornilov wrote what was to be his last letter to his wife, saying that the tempo of work on the defences continued uninterrupted and that the enemy had allowed them a quiet day. Later that evening when Captain-Lieutenant Popov made his report, Kornilov told him:

> Tomorrow will be a hot day, for the English at any rate will make their presence felt. I fear a big loss [among our men] because they are untrained to meet a bombardment. It is a great pity, but there it is! Many of us will not be alive tomorrow night.

Popov reminded him of the tsar's instructions that he (Kornilov) should not expose himself unnecessarily to danger, to which Kornilov is said to have replied: 'If I am not seen everywhere out there tomorrow, just what will they think of me?'.

According to the Russian reconstruction of the events of 17 October, the French, who occupied the sector to the west and south-west of the old town, were to have opened fire on No. 5 Bastion as a signal for the opening of the bombardment; the action was then to be taken up by the British batteries to the south and south-east of the Korabel'naia. Shortly afterwards the allied fleets would come up the mouth of the roads of Sevastopol Bay and bombard the coast batteries. Although Kornilov was of opinion that the allies were likely to confine the action to a bombardment, he did not rule out the possibility that they might use the cover of the heavy artillery fire to throw in their infantry and storm the fortifications.

At dawn on 17 October, as soon as the mist had cleared, the Russian defenders saw that the embrasures of the enemy siege guns had been opened.

At 6.30 a.m. the Russian artillery began a heavy harassing and counter-bombardment without waiting for the enemy to open fire. Twenty minutes afterwards the bombardment and counter-bombardment had already reached their height all along the line, so that Sevastopol was, said Zhandr, encircled by a double ring of stabbing fire and flash, and a thick pall of smoke hung heavily over the battlefield blotting out the sky so that the sun could be seen only faintly as a pale and wan moon. With the roar of the guns and the whistle of shot and the explosion of shell, the noise was so deafening that the call of bugle and drum could no longer be heard. Guns became overheated, however much water was poured over the barrels; the earthen breastworks were continually blown apart and almost as rapidly built up again by the quick hands of the defenders; blocked or broken down embrasures were cleared and repaired with frantic haste so that the guns might be ready to engage enemy infantry with canister. Within an hour of the opening of the bombardment heavy damage was reported to the infantry shelters, with many casualties to the Russian columns drawn up there waiting to repel the enemy assault. Only 118 guns were in action on the Russian side, 64 against the French and the remainder against the British, since the other pieces, because of their siting, could not be brought to bear on the enemy artillery.

At the first sound of gunfire, at about 6.30 a.m., Kornilov's staff had saddled up their horses and reported to the Volokhov house. Kornilov, together with Totleben and Bariatinsky, set out for No. 4 Bastion 'where the hottest fire was falling', since this was being engaged by both French and British artillery. Arriving there, they dismounted and continued on foot, leading their horses by the bridle. Prince Bariatinsky continued:

> I was following the admiral, with my own aide, Midshipman Prince Espor Ukhtomsky, coming behind me, when a bomb fell between us. No one was hurt but my frightened horse tore itself from my grasp and galloped away, leaving the bridle in my hands; and I recall that, for no reason at all, I continued the rounds of the bastions holding on to that bridle. Inside No. 4 Bastion the scene was frightful for the destruction was enormous, whole gun teams having been struck down by shellfire; the wounded and dead were being removed by stretcher-bearers, but they were still lying around in heaps. In particular the naval infantry battalion under Alexander Petrovich Spitsyn had been formed up in close order inside the bastion awaiting the enemy assault, but, as there had been no time to build the protecting traverses, the men were exposed to the enemy fire and had suffered great losses; yet they still stood stoutly waiting,

motionless and silent. Admiral Kornilov, accompanied by the [acting] sector commander, Rear-Admiral Novosil'sky, went round the guns and encouraged the crews, having a few cheerful words with everyone.*

Kornilov, already bespattered with mud and blood, then moved on to No. 5 Bastion where he met Nakhimov, dressed as usual in frock coat and epaulettes. This bastion had been under no less heavy a fire than No. 4, 'with shot and shell striking home; and there were many dead lying about and severed limbs everywhere'. The admirals, said Bariatinsky, conversed quietly while they watched the gun crews at work. Nakhimov had been slightly wounded in the face but he did not seem to notice it, and Bariatinsky watched the blood trickling down his neck and staining completely red the white ribbon of the George Cross which he had won at Sinope. Bariatinsky, between times, was scanning the sky for enemy shot or bomb, and, seeing a projectile coming straight at them, he 'seized both admirals by the coats and hurled them aside'. The shell burst beyond them. Bariatinsky continued:

> At that moment, Captain-Lieutenant Likhachev, whom I could recognize only by his dark grey coat and his voice, came up to me. But he had no eyes or face, for his features had completely disappeared: instead there was a mass of bloody flesh.

Likhachev was dazed but otherwise his behaviour appeared normal, so that Bariatinsky was at first at a loss to know what had happened to him. Then, taking the skirt of Likhachev's coat he began to wipe his face, to discover that Likhachev was completely unharmed and that his face had been covered by the bloody remains of some poor sailor, blown to pieces at that position.

> I thought at first that Likhachev was going to be ill, but he merely asked me for a cigarette which he lit from the slow match burning at the gun; and he continued to smoke quietly, leaning against the parapet.

Kornilov then started off for No. 3 Bastion and the Malakhov, but was stopped on the way by Flag-Officer Kriudner with a message from Istomin, asking that the admiral should not, in any circumstances, go to the Malakhov at that moment. Since the intensity of the fire against No. 4 Bastion seemed to be increasing, Kornilov began to fear that the French were about to attack with the bayonet, and he hurried back there once more; and when Zhandr reminded him that No. 3 Bastion was faring no better than No. 4, he decided that he would, Istomin notwithstanding, go there next.

Kornilov first returned to his quarters in the town at about 10 a.m. to

* Bariatinsky, *Vospominaniia 1852–55*, p. 39 *et seq.*

eat and to check on the ammunition resources, for, he told Popov, he 'feared that such a cannonade could not be maintained for long'. There, according to Bogdanovich, Kornilov met Menshikov, who had been inspecting the bastions in the Korabel'naia, and together they went to the Grafsky jetty, from which the Commander-in-Chief took a boat to the north side. Before Kornilov had taken his leave he had given his gold watch to Captain Khristoforov, who was about to journey to Nikolaev, with instructions that it should be given to his (Kornilov's) eldest son. Kornilov then went down to the Peresyp to meet Totleben preparatory to going out to No. 3 Bastion.

By then the French batteries were silent for they had suffered many casualties in the counter-bombardment, but the fire on the left continued unabated; the British not only had a superiority of 73 guns to 54, and these of greater calibre, but, according to Bogdanovich, they deployed their artillery and controlled their fire with much greater skill than did the French. For the British practice was true to the artilleryman's axiom of dispersion of guns and concentration of control and fire. The French had done the contrary and had paid the penalty.

No. 3 Bastion, commanded by Captain Popandopul, had suffered grievously from the British bombardment, the damage and casualties being heavy; during that day five bastion commanders were to succeed Popandopul, each in his turn being killed or severely wounded. Lieutenant Zhandr, who was with Totleben and Likhachev on the Peresyp, attempted unsuccessfully to dissuade Kornilov from going there, and Kornilov's staff were amazed when the admiral said that he would go by way of the trenches and not by the safer rearward approach through the hospital quarter. The party started off down a narrow path towards the earthworks where they were met by Captain Ergomyshev, commanding 3 Sector artillery, and by the bastion commander Popandopul, who had only just before lost his son, a battery commander within 3 Bastion. Both officers begged Kornilov not to visit the bastion. Then, seeing that he was determined to do so, they led the way along the trench system in the direction of the Malakhov Kurgan.

On the way Kornilov caught sight of the Moskovsky drawn up ready to repel the assault by enemy infantry, and, seeing that they were suffering many casualties in the enemy gun fire, he had them withdrawn behind the Lazarevsky shelter. Having crossed the bridge over the Dock Ravine, Kornilov started to climb towards the Korabel'naia along the west slope of the Malakhov, where he was greeted by the cheering of 44 Naval Infantry Battalion. But he sternly reprimanded them, telling them to save their hurrahs until the English had been beaten. Then, dismounting, he strode on to the Malakhov tower. There all the guns on the upper platforms had been silenced and only some small calibre pieces outside were attempting to reply to the enemy, but, as their range was too short, the admiral told them to cease fire. Kornilov entered the tower and talked to the wounded, but was prevented by Istomin from visiting the upper tower with the argument that the guns were silent and the platform partially destroyed, although Istomin had himself been up there shortly before. Heedless of the protests of his staff, Kornilov said that he must visit the Butyrsky and Borodinsky in the Ushakov Ravine before starting back, and he set off with Zhandr along the breastwork which sheltered their horses. He had not gone six paces when he was hit by a round shot which smashed his leg and wounded him in the body; he was removed insensible to the naval hospital.

When Kornilov had recovered consciousness, he was visited by Istomin 'with the hope that the wound was not serious'. But Kornilov knew that death was at hand, and he told the surgeons not to waste time on him, and he sent Istomin back to his duty in the bastions. And so he died, according to Likhachev, 'his stern face wearing in death the same slight courteous smile it had in life'. Wrapped in a St Andrew's flag, he was buried on the hill next to his former chief Lazarev, in the plot he was soon to share with Nakhimov and Istomin.

* * *

Early in the day there had been much nervousness that the enemy might close in under cover of the smoke; but the Russian army and naval infantry waiting to withstand the assault had suffered so many casualties from the enemy's gun fire, that it became necessary to withdraw the columns to the rear, relying on mounted liaison officers to recall them should they be required. In No. 5 and No. 6 Bastions and in the Malakhov, the barrack shelters for the infantry had been destroyed.

At No. 5 Bastion much of the defensive masonry was flattened by the French fire, the five guns behind the parapet being put out of action; of the 39 gun crew, 19 became casualties, flying stones and brickwork causing more injuries than splinters. Two French batteries between Nos 5 and 6 Bastions appear to have blown up when their magazines were hit, and, from about 10.30 a.m., the French artillery was silent and not a man could be seen. The Russian commanders began to think that the enemy had deserted his guns, but when a patrol of sailors tried to approach they were driven off by musketry and case-shot. The French took no further part in the battle for another 44 hours.

Meanwhile the British guns continued their day long bombardment; the upper storey of the Malakhov was in ruins, and red hot shot falling in the town started several fires. The English artillery on the Green Hill caused much damage since it was firing directly into the left side of No. 4 Bastion, and could, at the same time, enfilade its right face; the battery also engaged No. 3 Bastion, some of its shots, ricocheting on the slope on the right of the town ravine, raking the area behind. It was No. 3 Bastion, manned by sailors and sappers and by then under the command of Ergo-myshev, that suffered most, since it came under fire of heavy calibre guns not only from the Green Hill but also from the Vorontsov. By 3 p.m. all the embrasures had been destroyed, a third of the guns of the bastion were out of action and a third of the crews were dead; all the officers were dead or wounded and all the crews had been replaced twice over. Shortly after-wards, a bomb ignited the powder magazine, blowing out the front of the bastion and reducing much of it to a heap of rubble; over 100 men were killed, many disappearing without trace. Of the 75 men of the *Iagudiil* who marched into the bastion that morning, only 25 returned to their quarters the next day. Volunteers had been used to carry supplies from the hospital jetty to the bastion, but many of the carrying parties perished in the heavy artillery fire.

As the dust settled from the debris of No. 3 Bastion, prolonged cheering could be heard from the British lines and this was taken to mean that their infantry were about to leave the trenches and storm the bastion. Naval gunners were rushed into the ruins of the bastion to man such guns that were still serviceable and the Budishchev Battery took up the fire defence of the smitten area. No enemy attack followed. An hour later a powder locker blew up in the Malakhov, without, however, causing much damage. And so the artillery battle against the British continued without respite until nightfall.

*   *   *

The allied fleet had been anchored off the Kacha and in Kamyshev Bay and its approach to the mouth of the roads had been delayed by a calm. Towards midday the warships appeared, approaching slowly as all the sail were under tow, and they eventually came into line about 1,500 yards from the entrance to the roads. On the right wing, against No. 10 Coast Battery and the Aleksandrovsky, stood fourteen French line ships, mostly sail, and some smaller craft, while to the north, on the left, there were eleven British men-of-war lying off the Konstantinovsky; between the French and British squadrons were two Turkish vessels. The whole of the enemy fleet was extended over a distance of two miles between the Chersonese Bay and the Volokhov fort and was in fact too far out to sea to use its fire to good effect. The Russians subsequently considered the sea bombardment to be only a sub-

sidiary operation designed by the allies to divert attention away from the
land side.

The first enemy salvo came just after midday and was immediately
answered by the coast batteries. The French and Turkish vessels, with
a joint broadside of 745 guns, engaged the town side at a range of about
1,700 yards, and themselves came under fire from 33 guns of No. 10 Battery
and 17 of the Aleksandrovsky on the south side, and also of 23 guns of the
Konstantinovsky on the north side – in all 73 coast guns. The British
squadron, on the other hand, split itself into various task forces which
attacked individual coast batteries from defiladed waters, so that the
Arethusa, with a broadside of 25, engaged the Kartashevsky, which could
reply with only three guns, while the *Albion*, with a broadside of 45, bom-
barded the Volokhov which answered with only five guns. Six other British
warships with a total broadside of 304 guns attacked the Konstantinovsky
from a range of 1,900 yards and could be answered by only 18 guns of the
Konstantinovsky, but the British also came under the cross-fire of 36 guns
from No. 10 Coast Battery and the Aleksandrovsky on the south side.
Another three enemy men-of-war, with a broadside of 124 guns, managed
to approach within 1,000 yards of the Konstantinovsky from the north-
west to a position where they could be engaged by only two guns of that
battery, but these vessels, too, were enfiladed by 13 guns of No. 10 Battery
and the Aleksandrovsky firing from across the bay at a range of 1,900 yards.
The total allied broadside of 1,240 guns was to engage in a fire fight with
150 coast artillery guns, of which 47 were in embrasured casemates, the
remainder being protected by breastworks. But due to the defects in the
arcs of fire in the Russian guns, and because of the enemy's skill in exploiting
such weaknesses, many of the coast guns had to engage targets across the
other side of the roads by indirect fire and at extreme range.

By 1.30 p.m. the firing of the allied fleets was so heavy that many ships
had become lost to sight, enshrouded in a heavy pall of smoke. Some of the
guns of No. 7 Bastion tried to engage the enemy ships, and No. 8 Coast
Battery nearby took up the firing, but the bastion and battery ceased when
it became obvious that the enemy was out of range. The Nikolaevsky, the
Mikhailovsky, the Pavlovsky and No. 4 Coast Battery, all well inside the
roads, fired a few shots blindly into the wall of smoke at the entrance to the
waterway, fearing that the enemy was about to emerge. The visibility was
so poor that even the gunners of No. 10 Battery at the mouth of the roads
could not observe the targets or the strike of their shots and were obliged
to sight on the gun flashes of the enemy ships.

The fire of most of the French warships, concentrated on No. 10 Battery, was so fierce that it became impossible to approach the gun site from the land side; the observers from No. 7 Bastion, seeing the strike of shot and shell and the torn up earth all around, assumed that the battery must have suffered very heavy casualties. But since, as far as could be observed and heard from No. 7 Bastion, the battery guns still appeared to be firing, Nakhimov would not permit anyone to go out and report on its condition; finally, however, at about 4 p.m. when it became certain that all its guns were silent, Nakhimov ordered a volunteer relief party of 40 naval gunners under Lieutenant Troitsky to double out from No. 7 Bastion to bring the guns into action again. But Troitsky returned with the astonishing news that the battery was still in good fighting order and had suffered only minor damage and comparatively few casualties; it had ceased fire only on the orders of its commander, Captain-Lieutenant Andreev, as the guns were so overheated that he feared a premature explosion. Early in the bombardment a grenade store had ignited and a shell caisson had blown up, without, however, causing any casualties, and Troitsky returned with what was in effect a list of grumbles unconnected with the fury of the French bombardment: the battery was short of men so had set the infantry guard to work to crew the unmanned mortar; there were not enough magazines and these were too small and indifferently sited; and the stoves for heating the shot were so badly made that they had been discarded after only half an hour's use.

Most of the other coast batteries suffered few casualties and little damage in spite of the intensity of the enemy bombardment. The Konstantinovsky however was not so fortunate, for the British warships brought rearward and flanking fire to bear, and, in spite of having several vessels holed and set on fire, they closed up all but three of their men-of-war directly against the Konstantinovsky, the Kartashevsky and the Volokhov, the Konstantinovsky standing the main brunt of the attack. The British vessels suffered considerable damage so that some had to withdraw or be towed off: the *Rodney* ran aground, right under the guns of the Konstantinovsky, and it took two hours for steamers to refloat it; but meanwhile its guns continued to batter the fort and, said Bogdanovich, 'not without success'. At the end of the action the Volokhov had suffered 23 casualties, but the Kartashevsky none. In the Konstaninovsky all but five of the 27 guns were out of action, five men were dead and 50 wounded and the battery was silent, for the remaining crews had been forced to take cover. The Kartashevsky and Volokhov, disposing in all only eight guns which could be brought into action against the ships, had inflicted damage on the enemy out of all proportion with that caused by the powerful two-tiered casemated Konstantinovsky.

At 6.30 in the evening the allied warships weighed anchor and withdrew, having suffered 520 casualties from the fire of the coast guns and having fired off, so it was believed, about 50,000 rounds. The coast artillery had fired 16,000 shot and shell. The total coast artillery casualties were 138 men, the Konstantinovsky losing 55, No. 10 Battery 35, and the Aleksandrovsky and Volokhov 25 men each. The naval fight had unexpectedly proved 'the undoubted superiority of the earthwork defended battery over that set in stonework at sea level, for earthworks were found to be more efficient for working and less dangerous for the gun crews'. In the casemated forts, shot or shell striking the masonry caused many injuries by splinters or stones, and bombs exploding in the confined space of a chamber were invariably fatal to the occupants; smoke and fumes in the casemates made firing, even breathing, difficult.

The day of the first bombardment had shown the British gunners, both on land and sea, to be superior to those of their French allies. But in all they had achieved very little. The Russian ground casualties, in addition to those among the coast artillerymen, had been just over 1,100; yet the allied losses, including those at sea, had totalled 860, and the damage to allied ships and guns had not been light. In all, the allies had failed in their main aim to crumble away the Sevastopol defences.

When it was taken into account that the Russian field army was avoiding battle and that the fleet was idle in the roads, it became clear that it was within the Russian capability to hold off superior enemy ground and naval forces using, for the most part, grounded ships' companies; for the enemy had already lost their opportunity to seize Sevastopol at little cost to themselves. Totleben later told Canrobert, the French Commander-in-Chief, that if the allies had thrown all their forces at Sevastopol before the defences had taken shape, 'they would have taken it easily'; Osten-Saken believed that 'this mistake, one of many made by the allies, was undoubtedly the greatest'; and Nakhimov, when he heard of the enemy movement to the south, being a man of few words, and those expressive and to the point, said that 'Raglan and Canrobert were donkeys'.

* * *

The whole of the night of 17/18 October was taken up with the repair of fortifications and the moving up of artillery ready to renew the battle with the enemy on the Green Hill. More guns were allotted to 5 (Nikonov) Battery, to the right face of No. 3 Bastion and to the left of No. 4 Bastion. By dawn, No. 3 Bastion had 19 guns of its former 23 repaired or replaced and ready for action.

Shortly after first light the British batteries opened fire once more on

3 and 4 Bastions and on the Malakhov. The bombardment lasted all day, and, as the French artillery was still silent, all Russian guns within range were brought to bear on the British. About 10,000 rounds were fired during the day, and the Russian losses, mainly in No. 3 Bastion, totalled 83 dead and 460 wounded, the casualties being so heavy that thereafter traverses were built over each gun in 3 and 4 Bastions. The cross-fire of Russian artillery from the Malakhov and the ships in Sevastopol Bay had forced 'the English right hand Lancaster battery', known to the Russians as 'the five eyed', to direct the fire of two of its five guns on to the roads; several days later four of these guns were removed, and only the fifth, 'the Cyclops', continued to harass the shipping.

At 6.30 a.m. on 19 October the allied bombardment began once more, by French as well as by British artillery. But whereas the British guns fired all day, the French suffered again in the counter-bombardment and were silent by the early afternoon. This day's fighting cost the Sevastopol defenders 516 men and 14,000 rounds of artillery ammunition. The Russians in Sevastopol continued to rely on the stout-heartedness of its seamen gunners and army artillery, the defenders introducing their own techniques which could be learned from no text book. Gun drills were not observed because trained gun numbers were no longer available, and gun crews acted as they thought fit. There was no order of dress and crews often smoked short pipes – in defiance of regulations – as they served their guns. Yet, according to Totleben, naval traditions died so hard that gun crews continued to fire broadsides, so that all guns were 'instinctively reloaded and fired' irrespective of the nature of the target.

So the bombardment continued day by day, the weather becoming increasingly severe as winter approached. The daily ammunition expenditure varied from 10,000 to 12,000 shot and shell, but after the first three days' bombardment there was a significant drop in Russian casualties, although they continued to average as many as 250 a day. The reason for the fall was to be found in the improved cover – and in particular in the construction of traverses – and in the newly introduced signal system of watchmen who scanned the sky and followed the trajectory of shot and bomb, by night as well as by day for the burning fuses were clearly visible and made the projectiles appear like shooting stars. The cry of 'Pushka!' denoted shot or shell and was the signal to take immediate cover; 'Martella!' was the warning that an enemy mortar bomb had been fired and that listeners should be prepared to take cover; meanwhile the sentinel watched the slow flight of the projectile and would follow his first warning by the second shout of 'Gone over!' or 'Bomba!', the order to take cover. During a heavy cannonade by guns, however, the watchmen served little purpose 'and you were in the hands of God for survival'.

On 19 October the French were observed to be digging a parallel and trenches on Rudolf Hill, about 700 yards distant from No. 4 Bastion: from this it was deduced that the enemy would probably launch his major attack from that area; yet it was also apparent that the storming of the bastion was still some little time away. No. 4 Bastion stood on a height between two broad steep-sided ravines but was clearly overlooked from the Green and Rudolf Hills. The bastion had a three-sided front, and, because of the ravines, it could not be strengthened significantly by extending it in area; in consequence the bastion was forced to rely on the flanking fire provided by the distant batteries behind Nos 3 and 5 Bastions. When the allied intention became clearer these two flanking bastions were provided with additional batteries and traverses, and an epaulement for four mortars was put in on the right face of No. 4 Bastion. The allies meanwhile tried to conceal their intention by bombarding subsidiary targets, the British concentrating their attacks on No. 3 Bastion and the *Iagudiil*. By the seventh day of the bombardment the *Iagudiil* had been holed seventy-two times, and red-hot shot, bombs and rockets had set it and two nearby blockships on fire, so that Menshikov ordered that the 84 gun man-of-war be removed by day to the area of the naval hospital. Even there it was not safe, for a bomb, though it failed to explode, dropped through the deck and penetrated the crowded wardroom.

On the night of 20 October two fighting patrols of company strength, under the naval officers Lieutenant Troitsky and Midshipman Prince Putiatin, went out on to the Rudolf Hill to harass the diggers of the French trenches, and, at the cost of four dead, one of whom was Troitsky, and fifteen wounded, succeeded in spiking a number of enemy guns. The French were undeterred, however, and made surprisingly fast progress, for by the night of 22 October their trenches were only 500 yards from No. 4 Bastion and the Shvarts Redoubt and they had begun on the second parallel. This new parallel was well within case-shot range, but since most of the forward digging was done under cover of darkness, it became necessary to put out twenty men strong listening patrols, usually Black Sea Cossack infantry. On hearing the enemy at work at the top of the town ravine, the patrols were withdrawn and the area of the parallel was sprayed with canister. A quarter of an hour later the *plastun* patrols were put out once more.

The enemy bombardment was causing enormous damage within the town, for the buildings and houses were devastated by high-explosive shell and incendiary red-hot shot. Readers of Tolstoy will recall the harrowing circumstances under which troops and civilians lived and the appalling conditions and heavy death toll in the hospitals. Yet in those early days of October 1854 there was a mood of patriotic exaltation, which was probably at its peak when Kornilov was alive. And, rightly or wrongly, Bogdanovich gives Menshikov the credit for insisting that each soldier was to have a pound of meat and two cups of vodka a day, and for arranging that all wounded and sick be evacuated to the Severnaia.

The months of stalemate and heavy bombardments were to lead to conditions close to those known to later generations as trench warfare. The numbers of unburied dead and untended wounded obliged both sides to agree short truces so that dead and wounded could be recovered, and this resulted in contact, even fraternization, with the enemy. The French were generally popular since, according to the Russian view, there were many national characteristics common to both peoples; the Frenchmen were cheerful and loquacious, 'a quick witted people (*poniatlivyi narod*)', one Russian soldier called them, and, in fraternizing, appear to have experienced little difficulty in making themselves understood. The British soldier, on the other hand, was not so well liked, for he was either silent and indifferent or he treated the Russian as he treated all foreigners, with good-tempered condescension or amused contempt. According to the Russian soldier memoirist in *Souvenirs de Sébastopol*, some British infantrymen's idea of social intercourse was to take off their jackets and offer their guests a bout of fisticuffs.

In the first of Tolstoy's tales from Sevastopol, written in December 1854, the officer, like the men, is animated by ideals, by patriotism and noble incentives; when the writings were brought to the attention of Alexander II, the story is said to have filled him with such emotion that he ordered its publication in Russian and in French. But the latter tales were different, for Kornilov, Istomin and Nakhimov were dead. A note of realism, of truth and disillusion was apparent. Part of these latter writings were suppressed by the tsarist authorities.

* * *

When Nicholas heard of the first bombardment of Sevastopol and the enemy's lack of success he wrote to Menshikov in jubilant tones, praising God and the heroic defenders of Sevastopol. The Malakhov was to be renamed the Kornilov, and the tsar marvelled 'how No. 10 Battery had escaped unscathed'. Nicholas continued:

I think that the battery commander should have a George Cross, Fourth

Class, and to each man in No. 10 Battery should go a gift of three rubles, and for all others present in the action, two. Five crosses should be allocated to each battery.

But although the tsar, making much of Kornilov's successes, tried to dispel Menshikov's doubts and fears, he made it clear to his Commander-in-Chief Crimea that, with the arrival of 10 and 11 Infantry Divisions from Bessarabia, he hoped that the Menshikov 'would find it possible *to attack* – and maintain the honour of Russian arms'.

The next day Nicholas wrote to his confidant Prince M.D. Gorchakov, referring to the heroic and Herculean (*bogatyrskaia*) defence of Sevastopol. He continued: 'Menshikov will guarantee nothing, but he does not despair of prolonging the defence until after the arrival of 10 and 11 Infantry Divisions'. Menshikov's indecisiveness was already affecting the tsar, for he said that, although he regarded failure as too dreadful to contemplate, he still remained 'prepared for anything'.

Nicholas ordered that Kornilov's widow was to have a pension of 5,000 rubles and that Kornilov's debts up to a limit of 27,000 rubles should be paid off, these costs being borne by his privy purse, outside any award made by the Pensions Board. The widow was to become a Dame (Second Class) of the Order of St Catherine the Martyr. To Kornilov's wife, Nicholas wrote a personal letter of condolence.

Elizabeth Vasilevna. The glorious death of your husband has deprived our fleet of one of its most distinguished admirals and me of one of my dear colleagues, who has continued the excellent tradition of Mikhail Petrovich Lazarev. The whole fleet grieves deeply with you in all your sorrow . . . Russia will not forget his [dying] words and your children will bear a name distinguished in the history of the Russian Fleet.

* * * * *

CHAPTER 6

BALACLAVA

During the first three weeks in October Menshikov's force had been rein-forced by the arrival of Lieutenant-General Liprandi's 12 Infantry Division from 4 Corps, coming by forced marches from Bessarabia, comprising the Azovsky, Dneprovsky, Ukrainsky and Odessky Regiments with one field and three light batteries, and by the Butyrsky (from 17 Infantry Division) and one battery, a rifle battalion, a Black Sea Cossack infantry battalion and six reserve battalions of the Minsky and Volynsky. In all this reinforcement totalled 24 battalions. In addition, the cavalry force under Lieutenant-General Ryzhov had been further augmented, so that he now had two hussar and two uhlan march regiments, 53 Don Cossack Regiment and the Ural Cossack Regiment. Menshikov entrusted to this cavalry general the horse artillery and all cavalry already in the West Crimea, that is to say the hussar brigade of 6 Cavalry Division and a reserve guard *sotnia* of Crimean Tatars; Ryzhov's command did not, however, include Lieutenant-General Korf's Reserve Uhlan Division with two horse batteries, all of which had been detached to the area of Evpatoria.

Menshikov's force already stood at 65,000 and with the arrival of 10 and 11 Infantry Divisions, the two remaining divisions of 4 Corps, would have risen to between 85,000 and 90,000 men, giving Menshikov an advantage in strength which might have enabled him to force the enemy to raise the siege of Sevastopol; for, although the French had landed yet more troops in the Crimea, the allied total was put at not higher than 75,000–80,000 men. All allied troops were to the south of Sevastopol. Since it had been arranged between Raglan and Canrobert, the new French Commander-in-Chief (St Arnaud had died of cholera), that the French would relinquish their share of Balaclava and use instead two small ports further to the west, the British were committed to holding the exposed eastern flank between Balaclava and the Baidar Valley, that area which was patrolled by Russian cavalry and Cossacks.

Menshikov, however, had no faith in victory, and it seemed unimportant to him whether or not he awaited reinforcements. Miliutin said of him at this time:

> From the stories brought back by visitors to the Crimea and from Menshikov's own letters it was apparent that the Commander-in-Chief regarded the situation with the greatest of pessimism and despaired of holding on to Sevastopol. But the sovereign would not entertain the thought of giving it up.

Continually goaded by the tsar, Menshikov decided against waiting for the two additional divisions and proposed to attack the extended and thinly held British flank and to strike against the enemy base and port of Balaclava.

The Russian horse patrolling the Baidar Valley reported to Menshikov that Raglan had confided the forward defence of his flank to the Turks, for the British Commander-in-Chief presumably believed that the Turk, when entrenched and supported by artillery, was a match for the Russian; 'and', said Tarle, 'so the Turk might have been, if the defence had been undertaken by a first line Anatolian force'. But the Turks deployed by the British were second line colonial troops, mostly Tunisians, who had been lately used by the French as porters, poorly trained and indifferently led. So Menshikov decided that an attack in this quarter offered the best chance of success since it would enable him to outflank the main allied force on the Sapun and get between the British and their base.

Balaclava was protected by two defence lines, the inner, no more than 600 yards from the port, being formed by a number of batteries connected by a continuous line of earthworks running in a semi-circle from the Spiliia Mountain, on the coast, north-westwards to the Simferopol road beyond Kadikioi. The outer defence line lay a further 1,500 yards to the north-east and was based on six redoubts sited laterally on a long and exposed hogback ridge known to British troops as 'the Causeway', since the Vorontsovsky road ran along its shoulder. This ridge separated the Balaclava South Valley from the Chernaia Rechka North Valley. The redoubts were numbered from the right, the right hand No. 1 Redoubt standing 2,000 yards north-west of the Komary village and about 1,000 yards from No. 2; 2 and 3 Redoubts were only 500 yards apart, but No. 4 was somewhat isolated, being 800 yards from No. 3 and having no redoubt on its left, for Nos 5 and 6 Redoubts were still in the course of construction and were not yet manned. Three of the redoubts had been armed with two British 12-pounder guns (three in No. 1 Redoubt), and a British artillery non-commissioned officer had been assigned to each. The guns and each of the redoubt garrisons were manned by about 250 Turkish colonial troops,

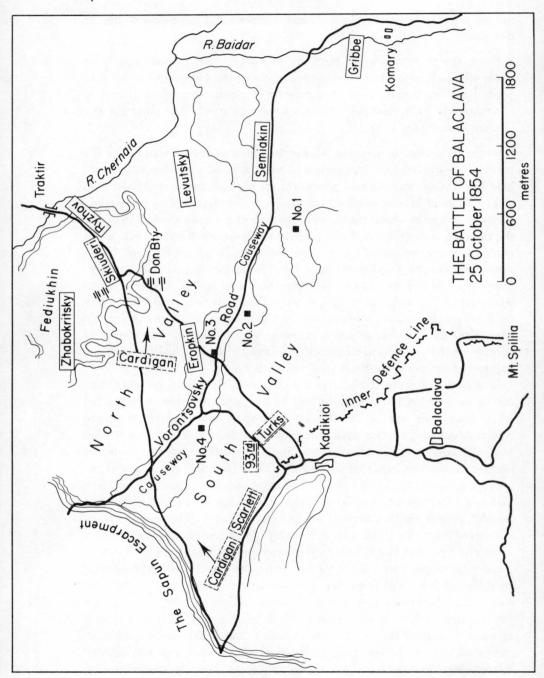

R. Baidar

Gribbe

Komary

THE BATTLE OF BALACLAVA
25 October 1854

metres

0   600   1200   1800

Traktir

R. Chernaia

Levutsky

Semiakin

Ryzhov

Skiuderi

Don Bty

No.1

Fediukhin

Zhabokritsky

North   Valley

Eropkin

No.3

Causeway   Road

No.2

Cardigan

Vorontsovsky

South   Valley

Inner Defence Line

Kadikioi

Mt. Spiliia

No4

93rd

Turks

Balaclava

Causeway

Scarlett

Cardigan

The Sapun Escarpment

but these 'had sat there quietly for several weeks and had done little to prepare the positions'. In the Russian view the redoubts were isolated and without depth and were entirely unsuitable for a co-ordinated defence.

The greater part of the allied field force was on the Sapun plateau to the south of Sevastopol at some distance from the lower lying area of Balaclava; only Lucan's cavalry division was stationed below the plateau about a mile and a half north-west of Kadikioi. The defence of the port and the base had been entrusted to Colin Campbell, a British brigade commander, and its garrison, including the troops manning both of the defence lines, was estimated at 2,800; of these about 1,000 were Turks and 1,100 were British sailors and marines. The only regular foot at Campbell's disposal were 650 men of 93rd Highlanders.

* * *

Eropkin's composite uhlans, one of the march regiments which had entered the Crimea with Ryzhov, had been formed from the reserves intended for the six light cavalry divisions, but such was the dearth of cavalry, outside Bessarabia, that all reinforcement units were gathered up to form new regiments. Eropkin had few trained horses or soldiers, since most were recruits of only a year's service; many of the horses had been fitted with curbs for the first time. The training of riders and horses had been continued during the march southwards to Nikolaev, but as soon as the regiment entered the Crimea the march tempo became forced, without any rest, 50 versts (35 miles) being covered a day. Yet riders and horses, far from being exhausted, were remarkably fit, 'for Russian troops would rather march than be in barracks, as a relief from boredom'. The regiment knew that further reinforcements were awaited from Bessarabia, after which the Crimean Army would go over to the offensive, and, according to one squadron commander in memoirs which he wrote *after* Balaclava, 'the regiment yearned for action – we wished particularly to engage English cavalry, known so well for the ferocity of its attacks and its cold-blooded slashing'. Meanwhile uhlan squadrons were edging forward west of the Chernaia River across the Baidar Valley, less than three miles from Balaclava, in order to keep a watch on the Tatar population and prevent it from taking provisions to the enemy.

On 3 October, a force of three battalions, two *sotni* and four guns, under Lieutenant-Colonel Rakovich, left Mackenzie Farm for Chorgun, crossing the Chernaia two days later and gaining contact with Eropkin's uhlans in the valley of the Baidar. This Baidarsky group was reinforced by the arrival of Major-General Semiakin's brigade of 12 Infantry Division and 1 Ural Cossack Regiment, and, on 18 and 19 October, it carried out a close reconnaissance of the Turkish positions, providing information on which Menshikov based his plan. On 23 October, the Baidarsky group became the Chorgun force under Liprandi, and, with the arrival of the remainder of the division, it was quickly brought up to a strength of 17 battalions, 20 squadrons, 10 *sotni* and 64 guns. There is little doubt that Menshikov's intention, according to the widely accepted Russian view at the time, was the capture of Balaclava.*

Ryzhov had concentrated his cavalry force on the Kacha, about three miles from Bakchisarai when, on 23 October, he received a written order from Menshikov instructing him to send a hussar march regiment westwards to the mouth of the river to keep the enemy fleet under observation. All other cavalry and horse artillery, together with an infantry regiment and four rifle battalions, were to be assembled on the Mackenzie heights at nine o'clock that night, ready to move southwards to Chorgun, where they were to come under the command of Liprandi's 12 Infantry Division. After the taking of the redoubts, the Russian cavalry, said Ryzhov, 'was to move at speed and attack the English horse occupying the fortified positions adjacent to Kadikioi and Balaclava'.†

The advance against the outer defence line started before dawn on 25 October. On the left Major-General Gribbe with the Dneprovsky and the Composite Uhlan Regiment, some Don Cossacks and a few guns, advanced along a gorge leading to the Baidar Valley, the infantry taking Komary while the uhlans and Cossacks drove enemy picquets out of the monastery on the hill to the south. Nearly a mile to the north, a centre force under Semiakin advanced westwards from Chorgun towards Kadikioi on two routes; the left hand column under Semiakin's personal command consisted of the Azovsky and a battalion of the Dneprovsky and supporting artillery, the right hand column under Major-General Levutsky being made up of the Ukrainsky and eight guns. To the north of Semiakin's force marched a separate group under Colonel Skiuderi, consisting of the Odessky, 53 Don Cossack Regiment and artillery; this was to dislodge an enemy picquet on the *traktir* bridge and move along the main road on to Redoubt No. 3, being followed by Ryzhov's cavalry force in column of attack, made up of the eight squadrons of the Kievsky and six of the Ingermanlandsky Hussars and the Ural Cossack Regiment, together with a Don and a light horse battery. Except for this cavalry, Liprandi's reserve consisted of only

---

* Cf. Bogdanovich, *Vostochnaia Voina*, Vol. 3, p. 110; Tarle, *Krymskaia Voina*, Vol. 2, pp. 73–4.

† Ryzhov, *Russkii Vestnik*, 1870, No. 4.

a Ukrainsky battalion and one battery, this diminutive force being posted at the *traktir* bridge.

In order to safeguard the right flank of the advance against interference by Bosquet's troops on the Sapun plateau to the north, yet another Russian column of 5,000 men under Major-General Zhabokritsky, based on a brigade of 16 Infantry Division and including the Vladimirsky, Suzdal'sky, 6 Rifle Battalion, two squadrons of the Ingermanlandsky and two *sotni* of Popov's 60 Don Cossacks and fourteen guns, was to march southwards from near the mouth of the Chernaia River, skirt the Sapun escarpment and take possession of the Fediukhin heights forming the northern edge of the North Valley.

The Russian approach march went according to plan, Liprandi taking energetic measures both to co-ordinate the movement and to be seen by the rank and file. He stood by the roadside near the *traktir* bridge so that Skiuderi's and Ryzhov's men passed by him as if on review, answering his traditional greeting of '*Zdorovo!*' with a chorus of '*Zdraviia zhelaem!*'; he then visited the troops to the south before they attacked the redoubts, telling the men that he 'hoped they would fight as well as they had done on the Danube'; his few words, according to the uhlan officer Kubitovich, 'electrified the units and they cheered him heartily'.

At 6 a.m. Levutsky's guns began a cannonade against Nos 2 and 3 Redoubts, while on the extreme left Gribbe brought his artillery on to the heights forward of the monastery and opened fire on No. 1 Redoubt.

The Turks had apparently been warned by Tatar spies of the imminence of an attack, and the forward picquets driven off the *traktir* bridge and out of Komary village by the Russian advance should have sounded the alarm. Yet the opening of the bombardment appears to have surprised the garrisons of the redoubts and thrown them into confusion. Ushanov, one of Liprandi's staff officers, has told of the Turkish failure to clear the thorn scrub and bushes around the redoubts, cover which was well used by Russian riflemen and infantry during the final approach. No. 1 Redoubt was attacked by Kridener's Azovsky Regiment 'under the personal direction of General Semiakin', moving, according to Liprandi's official report, 'in two lines in company column, not more than 100 paces between the lines, with a battalion of the Azovsky and one of the Dneprovsky in battalion attack formation in the third line'. Arriving at 150 paces from the foot of the hill, Semiakin ordered the assault. With a shout of 'hurrah' the companies climbed quickly up the slope, and, at half past seven, the Azovsky raised its colours over the redoubt. According to Liprandi, three guns were taken there and 170 of the enemy killed. If true, this large number of killed could indicate a very stubborn defence, but Ryzhov said that the Turks there 'did not show much determination'; since Tarle believed that No. 1 Redoubt was surprised and trapped, it could also point to a wanton killing of prisoners. The Turks abandoned Nos 2 and 3 Redoubts; the garrison of No. 4 waited for Skiuderi to deploy the Odessky Regiment against it, but then streamed away to the south before the attack was launched.

Meanwhile the British and French commands had hurriedly sent for infantry divisions, although it appeared that several hours might elapse before these were deployed. During the fighting on the outer line, 'six English field guns had attempted to come forward between Nos 1 and 2 Redoubts to engage the advancing columns in the flank, but these had been forced back by Ukrainsky riflemen and Lieutenant-Colonel Afanasev's 6 Light Battery and some guns of 4 Field Battery under Lieutenant Postnikov; but, seeing that the redoubts had already been taken, the enemy artillery made no further attempt to aid the Turks, but began to withdraw on Kadikioi'. Having dismantled the guns in No. 4 Redoubt, so the Russian story has it, the wheels and mountings were broken up and the artillery pieces were toppled down the hill; the Russian troops then evacuated the strong point and withdrew on to the nearby No. 3 Redoubt.

Liprandi was already in undisputed possession of the outer ring of the allies' defences, when, at 10 a.m. he ordered Ryzhov to take his cavalry force of the hussar brigade, together with 1 Ural Cossacks and three *sotni* of 53 Don Cossack Regiment, 'against the enemy camp'. Ushanov, an artillery officer at Liprandi's headquarters, believed that Ryzhov's mission was 'to attack the English transport lines (*vagenburg*) drawn up in laager formation; Bogdanovich and Totleben thought the objective to be an artillery park. Ryzhov himself was clear that he had 'the particularly difficult task of attacking infantry and all the English cavalry in a fortified position with an understrength hussar brigade'.

The British cavalry division had meanwhile stood to at the western extremity of the South Valley facing north-east towards the Causeway, with Cardigan's light brigade on the left and Scarlett's heavy dragoon brigade on the right, awaiting the arrival of the two infantry divisions which had been called for. Further to the right the 93rd (Sutherland) Highlanders were deployed in line, facing north, on a hillock on the southern slopes of the South Valley, covering the approaches to Kadikioi; to the Highlanders' right stood the equivalent of a Turkish battalion formed largely from stragglers who had deserted the redoubts. Both the Highlanders and Lucan's cavalry division were supported by horse, field and naval artillery.

Scarlett was moving his squadrons eastwards along the South Valley in order to support the Turks fleeing from the redoubts, some of whom were being hunted down by Cossack lancers; meanwhile Ryzhov's cavalry was advancing steadily westwards along the North Valley, preparatory to wheeling left and crossing the Causeway and the Vorontsovsky road in the area of No. 4 Redoubt. The British and Russian cavalry could not see each other because of the ridge of the Causeway between them, and might indeed have passed each other, had not the British dragoons caught sight of the forest of flashing Cossack lanceheads on the other side of the ridge; this caused Scarlett to change front rapidly in order to meet the oncoming Russian cavalry.

Meanwhile Ryzhov had ordered four squadrons of the Ingermanlandsky to attack the 93rd Highlanders and Turks, who stood on the British right. The hussars moved over the Causeway and advanced across the South Valley, the Cossacks on each wing cantering on ahead in order to envelop the enemy flanks. At first the kilted and red-coated infantry were not visible, as they had been withdrawn down the reverse slopes of the hillock and ordered to lie down so that they might escape the Russian artillery fire; many of the Turks, however, were seen to flee. Then, on the word of command, the Scottish infantry stood up and came steadily up the hill in line, advancing on the moving enemy cavalry. Kubitovich, whose uhlan squadron was standing in reserve, watched the scene; as the hussars approached, he said, the British artillery was bespattering them with case-shot, while the enemy infantry still came clambering up the slope, 'coolly coming to close quarters and then opening a murderous fire (*gubitel'nyi ogon'*) against the oncoming cavalry'. According to Kubitovich, the Ingermanlandsky withdrew, reformed and advanced yet again, before finally being driven back.

Liprandi, in his despatch to Menshikov on the following day, regarded the unsuccessful attack on the Highlanders and the advance against Scarlett's heavy dragoon brigade as a single operation, for he said:

I then directed the cavalry [two hussar regiments] with three *sotni* of 53 Don Cossacks and 1 Ural Cossacks on to the enemy camp, which they soon reached [*sic*], but they were met by enemy rifle fire from the flank and English cavalry from the front, which forced them to stop and withdraw.

Liprandi's version is not borne out by Kubitovich and Bogdanovich, who were of the opinion that the hussars were forced to retire by the rifle and artillery fire rather than by the threat of Scarlett's flank approach. Ryzhov, too, said that he withdrew the whole of the hussar brigade after attacking the Highlanders and reformed into attack column in the North Valley, beyond the right flank of Liprandi's infantry.

The Russian accounts of the cavalry actions which were to follow differ much, even between eye-witnesses. When Ryzhov wrote his account he was elderly, for he was a veteran of the Napoleonic Wars, and nearly 14 years had elapsed since the battle, and, although not vaunting his own bravery, he made extravagant claims for the cavalry he commanded. Ryzhov said that he moved into the attack against Scarlett with the hussar brigade in columns of *divizion* with the Kievsky forward and the Ingermanlandsky following. The uhlan Kubitovich, who watched the attack, said that it was the Ingermanlandsky who were out in front in open order, with the Kievsky in the second line in attack column. The two hussar regiments were supported by Don Cossacks on the flanks, and Ryzhov's only uncommited reserve was the Ural Cossack Regiment, for Liprandi had kept the Composite Uhlan Regiment under his own control.

The accounts of the cavalry engagement are confused. Kubitovich saw the hussar brigade begin its advance in good order with 'Ryzhov, like Murat, riding out in front and not deigning even to draw his sabre'; at some time during the engagement, it is not clear when, Ryzhov's horse was killed and he was rescued and remounted by an Ingermanlandsky non-commissioned officer. Ryzhov said that he had ordered the brigade to advance at the trot, for the enemy was over a mile away. But, said Ryzhov, the approach was marred by Liprandi, who sent an officer direct to the Ural Cossacks, Ryzhov's sole reserve, ordering them to advance with the hussars, 'and these set off after the hussars at full gallop, my [Ryzhov's] aide being unable to stop them in their headlong career'. Ryzhov continued:

> In front of me was all the English cavalry, not more than 200 sazhens [450 yards] away, deployed in single line, the . . . [Russian] right being raked by a fairly strong battery near Kadikioi. On the [Russian] left at 100 sazhens distance stood infantry in columns. The Ural Cossacks, with a great hurrahing, galloped on, still in six-deep column, moving far to the right of the enemy but did not close with him. Meanwhile the hussars came close in on the English.

Scarlett's brigade, still not fully deployed into line, awaited the hussar attack. Russian sources are generally agreed that the hussar brigade appeared to falter at some 100 or so yards from the British line and came to a halt, and that it was at this moment that Scarlett, with that part of his brigade which stood ready, delivered his impetuous charge against Ryzhov's stationary cavalry. Ryzhov's description, however, was somewhat different, in that he has said that he brought his forces to a halt short of the British cavalry, in order that he might redeploy them.

I ordered Voinilovich's Kievsky to take the left so that they should engage the English red guard dragoons [*sic* – presumably Ryzhov's confusion between Scarlett and 'red'] and, because of the extended line, I was obliged to use both hussar regiments together side by side, without any reserve. It was surprising how the enemy, superior to us in numbers, allowed us to come up the hill and deploy at our leisure. He awaited us, however, with great composure; only the Cossacks continued their everlasting screaming, and they, anyhow, were some distance away.

This account might explain the halt of the hussar brigade, but, thereafter, Ryzhov's narrative, as published in the *Russkii Vestnik*, was no longer based on established fact, for he continued:

Then an enemy battery from the area of Kadikioi opened fire and our line quickly went into the attack. I held my breath for I had no reserves and I knew that I could not stop the enemy if the battle went badly for the hussars . . . I have served for forty-two years, having taken part in ten campaigns, among them Kulm, Leipzig and Paris, but never before have I seen such action where both sides slashed away at each other for so long . . . But the hussars forced the stubborn enemy to turn tail and shelter behind his infantry. The hussars hurled themselves after them, but at this moment I judged it opportune to call a halt and reform.

The slashing hand-to-hand combat described by Ryzhov did indeed take place, except that Scarlett's force, outnumbered by the Russian, made the initial attack; and the outcome was different from Ryzhov's version in that, as other of Scarlett's squadrons came up, it was the Russian light horse that turned away, until it was eventually driven headlong from the field with a loss of 270 men, the British casualties being not a third of that figure. Seeing that the hussars were breaking, Liprandi sent an officer to his last cavalry reserve, the Reserve Composite Uhlan Regiment standing on the Vorontsovsky road almost opposite the Kadikioi heights. Kubitovich said:

This officer, not understanding General Liprandi's intention, told the regimental commander that we were to go forward to support the hussars. We were astounded, for we well understood that in carrying out such an order we would have to meet the withdrawing hussars who might throw us into disorder before we could meet the enemy. But an order is an order. We deployed the squadrons into line and went forward at a smart trot. An enemy battery, hitherto hidden, actually came forward to meet us and, turning, opened fire with case-shot. But General Liprandi, who was watching from No. 1 Redoubt sent an aide after us to tell us to return to our original positions. We were indeed lucky to have received the order before the hussars threw us into confusion. We then wheeled to our left and returned.*

Ushanov, none too reliable a witness, developed the theme of Liprandi's report to Menshikov, when he said that 'the English cavalry following up were drawn by General Ryzhov into the fire of Levutsky's and Skiuderi's guns'.† Bogdanovich, however, was surprised that Cardigan did not complete the rout begun by Scarlett: he summed up the action by saying that the hussars, not expecting such an attack, were crushed (*smiaty*), 'while the Cossacks had an even worse time'; Major-General Khaletsky was wounded and Colonel Voinilovich was killed and 'our four regiments galloped back in disorder to the Chorgun gorge, the English holding on in pursuit until they came under fire from our batteries; the heavy casualties they suffered there then caused them to withdraw'. Menshikov, for his part, told the tsar only what he wanted him to know, and in his despatch informing Nicholas of the capture of the redoubts and the charge of Cardigan's light brigade, he chose to omit any mention of Ryzhov's advance and rout before Kadikioi.

Ryzhov's cavalry, after its flight from Kadikioi, was reformed at the end of the North Valley, behind the shelter of Zhabokritsky's force on the Fediukhin and behind Liprandi's infantry on the line of the high ground between No. 3 Redoubt and the Komary village. Since the hussar brigade was well to the rear, the only connecting links between Liprandi and Zhabokritsky were 3 Don Field Battery in the well of the valley and Eropkin's uhlan regiment higher up on the Simferopol road between No. 2 and No. 3 Redoubts. The Don field battery was therefore in a forward and exposed position. Some way behind it lay the Ural Cossacks and two squadrons of the Ingermanlandsky; well to the rear were the other four Ingermanlandsky squadrons and beyond them the Kievsky.

* * *

The British Commander-in-Chief, Lord Raglan, had thought of sending the British cavalry division forward to the line of the redoubts, but its commander, Lord Lucan, had been reluctant to move until the arrival of the supporting infantry. There was little sign of movement from the Russian side and the battle appeared to have been finished for that day. But then

---

* Kubitovich, *Voennyi Sbornik*, 1859, No. 5.
† Ushanov, *Artilleriiskii Zhurnal*, 1858, No. 2.

Raglan, looking through his telescope from his commanding position on the Sapun escarpment, observed that the Russians were removing the British 12-pounder guns from the captured redoubts, and he decided to try and prevent the enemy from making off with these trophies.

The subsequent chain of errors which culminated in the charge of the light brigade is, of course, well known. An aide, Captain Nolan, was sent by Raglan to Lucan with a scribbled note, unclear in its content, and, so Raglan subsequently said, with a qualifying verbal message. Since Lucan was in the valley and unable to see the removal of the guns from the redoubts, the only guns that might have been visible were those of the Don Cossack field battery at the far end of the North Valley. The astounded Lucan asked Nolan whether he really understood what was being ordered – an advance between two features (the Fediukhin and the Causeway) held by enemy guns. When Cardigan in his turn received the order, he too remonstrated, but was told by Lucan 'that there was no choice but to obey'. The light brigade, made up of a number of very much understrength regiments, probably in all no more than 700 sabres, consisted of the long service soldiers called by Tarle 'crack troops', and these deployed for battle. Captain Nolan, who accompanied the brigade, was killed by Russian artillery fire as soon as the advance began, attempting, so it was subsequently believed, to point out to Cardigan that the brigade was advancing on the wrong guns.

Ryzhov said that, as far as he could recall, ninety minutes went by from the time of Scarlett's heavy brigade action, there being no further movement on the enemy's part, so that he, too, began to think that the battle was finished for that day. He went forward to the Don battery, which was covering the approach from the west along the North Valley, to speak to its commander Colonel Prince Obolensky. While he was talking there, 'the sharp eyes of the Don gunners' noted the far distant cloud of dust raised by enemy cavalry coming down from the slopes into the valley. Two minutes later, said Ryzhov, it was clear that the enemy was coming along the valley in to the attack. The Don field battery opened fire, firstly with shot and shell and then, as the range closed, with case-shot.

On the flanks, a light battery on the Causeway and a field battery from Zhabokritsky's sector on the Fediukhin heights, together with riflemen from 4 Rifle Battalion, were firing on the oncoming cavalry; the Odessky, holding the high ground on the southern heights, as soon as they sighted the enemy, hurriedly fell back over the ridge of the Causeway on to No. 2 Redoubt and formed square.

Cardigan's light brigade continued its rapid advance, watched by uhlan officers from the ridge just vacated by the Odessky; and it was clear to these observers that neither case-shot nor rifle fire could stop the British horse. At this point Lieutenant-General Ryzhov ordered his cavalry forward to protect the Don battery, but, said one of the uhlan officers, 'the Cossacks, frightened by the disciplined order of the mass of cavalry bearing down on them, did not hold, but, wheeling to their left, began to fire on their own troops in their efforts to clear a route of escape; the Ingermanlandsky, who were covering the guns, were put into a fearful turmoil, being thrown back on the Kievsky; the whole of the Russian cavalry force in the valley made off, the good officers trying in vain to hold their men – some threw themselves forward against the enemy only to be cut down – General Ryzhov being one of the last to withdraw, seeking death, for he knew that he would be held responsible'; and, concluded Kubitovich, 'the fault was indeed Ryzhov's for he should not have sent Cossacks ahead to meet the charge of line cavalry'. Kubitovich continued:

> The English then rode down the Don battery sabring a number of gunners as they passed through; but the majority of the gun crews made off, mounted on horse teams and limbers. The enemy spiked some of the guns, hoping to drag them off on his return, but most of the cavalry continued the headlong chase after the hussars, slashing at them without mercy. The horse teams and limbers of the Don battery together with 12 Horse Battery and all the cavalry were soon milling about at the river, all trying to get over the bridge, while the English chased them almost as far as the transport lines.

Boganovich accepts these eye-witness accounts, for he concludes that 'the Russian cavalry, crowded together, rushed for the bridge, so that it was with great difficulty that the withdrawing guns could be got over'.

Kozhukhov, a subaltern officer of a light battery of 12 Artillery Brigade, was present with the guns and a battalion of the Ukrainsky covering the gorge near the *traktir* bridge, from where he had good observation of the enemy approach all the way along the North Valley. According to him, the two cavalry and two Cossack regiments in the valley went forward to protect the guns. Watching the action from the rear, when the British light brigade was still some distance away, Kozhukhov was under the impression that the hussars, not the Cossacks, were in the van and that the hussars broke first; the Cossacks joined the rout, and then all four regiments pressed back on the artillery they were supposed to be covering. A moment later all four regiments were galloping back in disorder to the bridge (above which Kozhukhov stood), pursued by an enemy that Kozhukhov reckoned to be outnumbered by five to one. The Ukrainsky and the battery covering the

Chorgun ravine could do nothing to bar the withdrawal.
Kozhukhov continued:

There, in a small area at the exit of the gorge, were four Russian horse regiments stampeding around, and inside this mass, in small isolated patches (*kak redkie piatna*), were the red-coated English, probably no less surprised than ourselves how unexpectedly this had happened. The enemy soon came to the conclusion that they had nothing to fear from hussars or Cossacks and, tired of slashing, they decided to return the way they had come through another cannonade of artillery and rifle fire. It is difficult, if not impossible, to do justice to the feat of these mad cavalry, for, having lost a quarter of their number and being apparently impervious to new dangers and further losses, they quickly reformed their squadrons to return over the same ground littered with their dead and dying. With such desperate courage (*otvagoi otchaianiia*) these valiant lunatics (*bezumnye khrabretsy*) set off again, and not one of the living – even the wounded – surrendered.*

The hussars and Cossacks, said Kozhukhov, did not come to their senses for a long time. They were convinced that the whole of the enemy cavalry were still in pursuit and they did not want to understand that they had been crushed by a comparatively insignificant handful of desperadoes (*nichtozhnoiu sravnitel'no gorst'iu smel'chakov*). 'The first to recover were the Cossacks and, true to their nature, they set themselves to the task in hand – rounding up English horses and offering them for sale. Expensive blood horses were sold for three or four half-imperials – or even less. Many of these fine horses did not survive the winter, but those that did were later to change hands for 400 rubles or even more.'

Liprandi had ordered Eropkin's uhlans at Redoubts Nos 2 and 3, to attack the enemy horse in the flank down the shoulder of the valley as they made their way back to their own lines, this order being received among the lancer ranks, according to Kubitovich, with much satisfaction. The squadrons moved off at a fast trot towards the brow of the hill, passing one of the Odessky battalions still formed up in square. The battalion commander was nervous and, because the uhlan squadron mounts were not of a uniform colour since they were composite units formed from various detachments, he came to the conclusion that he was about to be attacked by enemy cavalry. He ordered his square to open fire. This caused casualties and cries of treachery from the ranks of the uhlans. After some delay, the lancers

---

* Kozhukhov, *Russkii Arkhiv*, 1869, No. 2.

reached the road leading to the *traktir* bridge and the Mackenzie heights, and there, when still on the high ground, the lancers deployed from column into line. Uhlan squadron commander Kubitovich continued:

We saw the enemy coming back down the valley at a trot, and we marvelled how they came along steadily in faultless style as if on manoeuvres. No. 1 Squadron under *Rotmistr* Verkhkitsky, moving first to the right and then to the front, was the first to close. This left ample room for my squadron and I led it straight at the foe. No. 3 Squadron under Major Labrenius turned left and followed after us. Brave cornet Astafev, a troop commander in my squadron, started racing ahead, rushing headlong at the enemy, and this was in fact a breach of discipline. But his example fired our recruits.

According to Kubitovich the appearance of the uhlans was entirely unexpected by the enemy, and the mounted flank attack, 'usually disastrous for the cavalry who receive it', was, thought Kubitovich, most effective. But the real sabre work had not yet begun.

For then the desperate slashing started. Our artillery and infantry reopened fire, but I must say they caused as many casualties to us as to the enemy, particularly to our horses. The English fought with amazing bravery, even the dismounted and wounded fighting on until they dropped.

But few of the enemy, or so said Kubitovich, got back, 'and we pursued them almost as far as No. 4 Redoubt'. The uhlans made their way back to the road to the Mackenzie height and awaited the order to dismount.

We then saw more dust coming down the valley and we could make out that they were hussars in a black dolman edged with gold, mounted on dark horses, very much like out Leichtenbergers [Kievsky]; indeed a general staff officer told us that these newly arriving troops were the Kievsky Hussars coming up to reinforce us. When they came nearer, however, we saw that they were in fact more of the withdrawing enemy and we rode down into the valley to bar their passage.

A short engagement ensued during which Kubitovich claimed to have seen 'Lord Cardigan, who only evaded capture due to his spurs and his very fine horse'. British accounts do not credit Eropkin's uhlans with quite the same determination as described by Kubitovich; but since this is a Russian chronicle, let the Russians themselves tell their story, for in the main they tell it very well.

Ryzhov, like other of the senior commanders, tends to touch lightly on his failures. When the Don battery was first attacked, he said, he ordered forward the first line of cavalry to meet the enemy, but 'the best officers had already become casualties'; he described how the Kievsky went forward with a great cheer, but he did not follow with what happened thereafter. Ryzhov again warmed to the task, however, when he described the valour of Eropkin's uhlans:

> The uhlans had been directed to take the withdrawing enemy in the rear, so that the enemy cavalry – who had been made drunk to give them the necessary courage after the defeat that they had suffered earlier that day [a reference to Scarlett's brigade] – was taken between the lances [of the uhlans] and the sabres [of the hussars]. From this moment the battle might have been compared to the coursing of hares. Even the enemy reserve, seeing how matters stood, turned back, not being able to save their fellows. This is how the battle finished. The pure truth flows from my pen, as I was a personal witness; I do not brag and nothing is added – if anything, the facts are understated. It remains a matter of regret to me only that Count Lucan [sic] did not fall into our hands, for he owed his life to the speed of his excellent horse. *I saw with my own eyes how, fleeing from his pursuers, he drunkenly swung his sabre to the right and to the left* [author's italics].

Lieutenant-General Ryzhov's article in the *Russkii Vestnik* brought an immediate answer in the *Russkii Arkhiv* from another eye-witness, Kozhukhov, the artillery officer who had been near the *traktir* bridge:

> General Ryzhov censures General Liprandi for not giving proper due to the exploits of the hussars, which 'ought to be written in the pages of military history as one of the most brilliant cavalry exploits'.*

But, in fact, continued Kozhukhov, Ryzhov's description of the action of the hussars was entirely similar to that already given by Kozhukhov himself and published in earlier articles. It was only the presentation and conclusions that were different. For Ryzhov contrived to frame his narratives in such a way as to make blame read like praise, rather, said Kozhukhov, in this fashion:

> All our cavalry, attacked by an enemy much inferior in numbers, became confused and with a great cheer of 'hurrah' – ran away.

At the end of the battle no one had much sympathy for the Russian

* Kozhukhov, *Russkii Arkhiv*, 1870, No. 9.

hussars. Yet it was commonly felt, continued Kozhukhov, not only by the officers but also among the men, that the fault lay not with the cavalry but with the senior cavalry leaders.

How else could one explain Ryzhov's own words, that he sent the hussars out to meet the enemy cavalry charge which was almost on them. There was no time to have formed up, and to do this was, in any case, a gross tactical blunder.

Nor could Kozhukhov accept Ryzhov's description of the attack by Eropkin's Reserve Composite Uhlan Regiment.

General Ryzhov said that the uhlan attack was brilliant. Well, we watched the uhlans go into the attack and we saw no brilliance. Indeed no real attack, as such, took place and the fighting which did occur was not pressed home. If what Ryzhov has said is in fact true, how can one explain how the 'disorganized groups of enemy cavalry, already defeated, without leaders or direction', could fight their way through a mass of fresh cavalry [uhlans], leaving in our hands only the dead and wounded.

Kozhukhov had some comment on Ryzhov's claim to have stopped the withdrawal of the hussars.

Ryzhov says that the hussars were stopped by him, reformed and sent back in pursuit of the withdrawing enemy, who was thus caught on two sides [between uhlans and hussars] so that the battle took on the aspect of hare coursing. I saw no hare coursing, but I did see the hussars, mixed with Cossacks, fleeing on their way to Chorgun, leaving only the Ukrainsky and my battery in the field. As for drunkenness [among the enemy cavalry], there was some talk of it at the time but no one seriously believed it. I, at any rate, saw most of the enemy wounded, and I saw none drunk. It is indeed difficult to imagine that drunken cavalry could have achieved what those English horse actually did.

*   *   *

Liprandi's report to Menshikov of 26 October claimed the capture of eight guns, not including those destroyed in No. 4 Redoubt; this, too, made no mention of Ryzhov's defeat by Scarlett's heavy brigade. Cardigan's light brigade was described by Liprandi as a force of more than 2,000 cavalry, 'which forced General Ryzhov to withdraw along the road to Chorgun in order to decoy the enemy away'. The attack by the uhlans, according to Liprandi, was made with determination and in good order and had most brilliant success, 'for all the enemy fled in disorder'. In this attack, said

Liprandi, the enemy lost 400 dead, 60 wounded and left behind 22 prisoners. Attached to his report was a list of officers and a few other ranks whom he wished to recommend for awards.*

Menshikov's despatch to the sovereign claimed the capture of 11 guns, no mention being made of the Scarlett engagement. Menshikov continued:

> The English cavalry under Lord Cardigan attacked the hussar brigade of 6 Cavalry Division with unexpected impetuousity but was taken in the flank by two *diviziony* [four squadrons] of the Reserve Composite Uhlan Regiment and the cross-fire of riflemen and the artillery of 12 and 16 Infantry Divisions. . . . At the same time as attacking our hussars the English cavalry charged 3 Don Field Battery, sabring some of the gunners. Our losses in infantry would appear to be not exceeding 300 dead and wounded – losses in other arms are not yet known; enemy losses are reckoned to be heavy.†

Menshikov selected the name of only one officer from Liprandi's list of those to be commended to the sovereign, that of his own naval aide accredited to Liprandi's headquarters, Captain-Lieutenant Villebrant.

Such was the effect of this mendacious despatch to the sovereign that Nicholas went to the tsarina to tell her of this feat of arms, and according to Tiutcheva, threw himself down before the sacred icons, sobbing with emotion.

* * *

Bogdanovich summed up the Russian view of the battle when he said that Cardigan's attack lasted only twenty minutes and that, of the 700 British cavalry involved, 300 became casualties. The loss, thought Bogdanovich, might have been greater had not the French cavalry leader General Morris sent d'Allonville with 4 Regiment Chasseurs à Cheval to create a diversion by attacking Zhabokritsky's artillery on the Fediukhin heights.

This attack, by colonial African light horse, was made by two squadrons under Abd el Al against a field battery, while a further two squadrons under the personal command of d'Allonville attacked the two infantry battalions covering the guns. The French cavalry broke in and sabred the gunners and were only driven off, according to the Russian account, when Zhabokritsky managed to restore order amongst the two Vladimirsky battalions and threw off the cavalry at the point of the bayonet. The French cavalry were successful, in that they succeeded in their main aim, the silencing of Zhabokritsky's 14 guns.

* Liprandi, *Russkii Invalid*, 1854, No. 235.
† Menshikov, *Russkii Invalid*, 1854, No. 234.

When the allied infantry formations arrived, Cathcart's division and
Espinasse's brigade were sent against Zhabokritsky, while Cambridge's
division moved against Liprandi's troops occupying the redoubts. But the
infantry never came to close quarters, although there was some exchange of
fire between Cathcart's division and a battalion of the Odessky. The
artillery cannonade continued until after midday.

The allies decided to leave the outer defence line in the Russian hands,
and, to this extent at least, the battle must be regarded as a tactical success
for Menshikov; the allies were obliged to restrict their sphere of operations,
confining themselves in large measure to the covering of the Balaclava flank.
The final Russian losses were put at 238 killed and 312 wounded, that is to
say 550 in all. The Russian estimated the British losses at 360 and the
French at 38; the Turkish casualties were put at 260. The attack by the
light brigade was regarded by Bogdanovich as 'a brilliant exploit of self-
sacrifice, but all condemned the British leaders for exposing such a large body
of cavalry to certain destruction'.

Menshikov had undertaken the offensive because he had been pressed by
Nicholas to do so, but he did not escape the censure of future historians
for refusing to await the arrival of 10 and 11 Infantry Divisions, which might
have given him the necessary strength to seize Balaclava. According to
Tarle, Liprandi waited in vain for hours at Chorgun for formations, pro-
mised by Menshikov, in order to push home his attack. For, concluded
Bogdanovich, the loss of the base would have put the enemy into a difficult,
almost impossible, position; as it was, the attack of 25 October merely
demonstrated to the enemy the weakness of his own position and permitted
him to remedy it.

Inside Sevastopol the troops knew that English hussars had broken
Russian line cavalry and Cossacks, and henceforth Russian commanders,
officers and men regarded British cavalry as unpredictable – even mad.
But Menshikov's Army of the Crimea had taken to the field once more, and
not entirely without success, and this provided the Sevastopol garrison with
some comfort, which, said Tarle, was shared even by such stable and
level-headed people as the sombre Totleben.

CHAPTER 7

*   *   *   *   *

INKERMAN

The ground to the south of Sevastopol is in the form of an equilateral triangle, each side being about 10 miles long, with the city near its apex; the left side and the base are bounded by the sea while the right is lined by the Balaclava heights and the rivers of the Balaclava and the Chernaia. The peninsula thus formed, known as the Chersonese, is a tableland which rises steadily towards the south-east to terminate abruptly in the steep escarpment of the Sapun; this escarpment stretches from the Balaclava heights in the south to the area of the Careening Ravine just outside Sevastopol, a line of almost sheer cliffs seven miles long and standing between 500 and 700 feet above sea level. Most of the Chersonese plateau to the south of Sevastopol as far east as the Sapun escarpment was held by the allies.

During October the enemy had reorganized their armies into two separate bodies of troops, each named according to its function. The primary task, that of besieging Sevastopol, had been entrusted to a siege corps, its left being formed by 32 French battalions (18,500 men) and its right by 28 British battalions (16,500 men); but the British right was more than 4,000 yards from Sevastopol Bay to the east of the city, so that Menshikov could still move his troops in and out of the besieged area along the sapper-built coast road. The enemy troops not engaged in the siege formed a corps of observation facing east to guard the long allied right flank running north to south along the line of the Sapun escarpment, that flank which had already been attacked by Liprandi. On the extreme left of the observation line stood Bentinck's brigade of guards; in the centre were Bosquet's 24 French and eight Turkish battalions, totalling in all 23,000 men; on the right was Colin Campbell's infantry brigade of 2,000 men near Balaclava. Twelve French and 20 British squadrons of cavalry, all much understrength, were concentrated behind the corps of observation. In all, the strength of the allied siege and observation corps was reckoned to be between 60,000 and 70,000 men.

On 30 October Menshikov had moved his army headquarters to Chorgun,

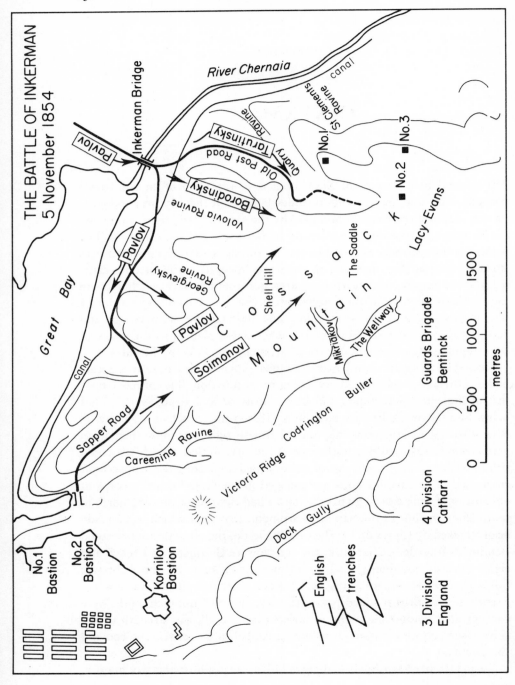

THE BATTLE OF INKERMAN
5 November 1854

River Chernaia

Inkerman Bridge

Pavlov

canal

St Clements Ravine

No.1

No.3

No.2

Tarutinsky Ravine

Old Post Road

Quarry

Borodinsky

Volovia Ravine

Lacy-Evans

Great   Bay

Pavlov

Georgievsky Ravine

Pavlov

Soimonov

Shell Hill

The Saddle

Mountain

Cossa

canal

Miriakov

The Wellway

Sapper Road

Buller

Guards Brigade
Bentinck

1500

Careening   Ravine

Victoria Ridge

Codrington

1000

metres

No.1
Bastion

No.2
Bastion

Kornilov Bastion

500

4 Division
Cathart

Dock   Gully

English

trenches

0

3 Division
England

but a few days later, on 3 November, he shifted it yet again to Inkerman, where it was more centrally situated. On 3 and 4 November two divisions of Dannenberg's 4 Corps arrived in the theatre from Bessarabia, Soimonov's 10 Infantry Division being marched into Sevastopol while Pavlov's 11 Infantry Division was held back on the heights of Inkerman. The strength of the Russian force, which was made up of three groupings, Sevastopol, Inkerman-Mackenzie and Chorgun, was raised by this reinforcement to 107,000 men, not including the sailors or Khomutov's 20,000 men in the Tavrichesky peninsula. Menshikov had, therefore, a thirty per cent numerical superiority over the allies and was stronger than them in artillery.

Nicholas knew of the Emperor Napoleon's intention to send a further three divisions to the theatre, and appreciated that the allies could move their troops from Western Europe to the Crimea by sea more quickly than Russian forces could be marched from North or Central Russia. The news from Sevastopol was still disquieting for the French siege troops were pressing hard on No. 4 Bastion, to the south-west of the base, having constructed saps to within 150 yards of the salient; a deserter had already brought news to the besieged garrison that the French would soon storm the defences. The tsar was therefore convinced that Menshikov must at all costs exploit his superiority in numbers before the enemy should redress the balance, and he believed it to be imperative that the Russian should attack before the French broke into Sevastopol.

Menshikov's troops were already in positions from which they might have enveloped and destroyed the besiegers; on the other hand, the dispersal of the Russian forces on exterior lines brought with it serious difficulties of control and co-ordination. The advantages of terrain lay with the allies, since the ground held by them was broken and suitable for defence; it was, moreover, unknown to the Russians, nearly all of whom were new to the Crimea.

The line of the sheer Sapun cliffs bordering the Chersonese plateau was virtually inaccessible except by a few difficult routes. The least steep were the two in the far south, using the Balaclava-Kadikioi or the Vorontsovsky roads to Sevastopol, along the axes already tried by Liprandi; successful thrusts in these areas would have cut the British troops from their base, but such success would have been conditional on overcoming the recently strengthened enemy fortifications, and would have risked being taken in the flank by a British counter-stroke from Balaclava. In the event of Russian failure Menshikov's own communications with Bakchisarai and Perekop might have been broken. Another possible path was that leading from the ford across the Chernaia below the *traktir* bridge; this ran directly west-

wards across the aqueduct, climbing the Sapun cliff, eventually to join the
Vorontsovsky road on the plateau. This route was, however, barely more
than a track and very difficult for the passage of large bodies of troops.
Bogdanovich has said that Menshikov well understood that a main attack
on any of these three routes offered little prospect of success.

There remained only the routes ascending the north-east corner of the
Sapun range, between Sevastopol and the lower Chernaia Valley where
there was a mile and a half long ridge, running north to south, bounded on
the east by the Sapun escarpment but separated from the main Chersonese
plateau on the west by the deep and steep-sided Careening Ravine. This
ridge, called by Kinglake Inkerman mount but known to the Russians as
the Cossack Mountain, was about 1,200 yards across from west to east at
its northern end near Sevastopol Bay, but narrowed in the south to a 400
yard wide saddle which led on to the Sapun plateau. The steep northern
and eastern slopes of the Cossack Mountain were indented by small *balki*,
affording difficult, though possible, access for large bodies of troops to the
top of the ridge; the most important of these entrants were the St Georgievsky, the Volovia and the Quarry, and these could be approached either from
Sevastopol or from across the mouth of the Chernaia River. The Chernaia
estuary was a great marsh, covered with high reeds and crossed by a 700
yard long causeway leading to a partially demolished bridge. Whereas the
Mackenzie and Inkerman heights to the east of the estuary were overgrown
with forests, the Chersonese plateau and Cossack Mountain to its west were
open and bare, arid and dry in the summer and muddy and desolate in the
winter. The ravines, however, were often covered with stunted oak and thorn.

Menshikov had little confidence in his own ability and no faith in the
Russian troops under his command; he had no wish to resume the offensive
but was under continual pressure from Nicholas to do so. According to
Tarle, Menshikov regarded the British force as being less formidable than
the French, and so he resolved to attack the British besiegers entrenched on
the upper stretches of the Careening Ravine and at the southern end of the
Cossack Mountain. The occupation of the Cossack Mountain by Russian
troops could have given Menshikov a foothold on the heights on both sides
of the Careening Ravine and entry on to the Chersonese plateau, so taking
the pressure of the siege away from the north-east corner of Sevastopol, and
ensuring that the allies should not cut the east-west sapper road into the
fortress. Whether Menshikov was motivated by such strategic considerations
is, however, open to doubt.

The approaches to the Cossack Mountain were admittedly difficult, but
the British forces there were believed to be neither strong nor alert. For, on

26 October, the day after the battle of Balaclava, a sortie had been made
from Sevastopol on to the Sapun, with the double aim of reconnoitring the
British positions and at the same time distracting the enemy attention from
Liprandi's formations near Chorgun. This sally was made by the Butyrsky
and Borodinsky, with four guns, all under the command of Fedorov, the
Colonel of the Butyrsky, the force crossing the Careening Ravine near the
estuary and ascending the ridge from the north. The daylight approach
march was so well concealed by the broken country and the scrub in the
ravines, that Fedorov was able to ascend the plateau and close in on the
enemy positions before his movement was brought to a halt by British
artillery fire. Many men of the Butyrsky, Fedorov among them, were struck
down. The price of this intelligence to the Russians was 270 casualties, of
whom 25 were officers.

At the time of Fedorov's attack, Menshikov had become aware of the
movement of French troops towards the centre in order to support the British
salient, from which he concluded that he could achieve no permanent
success against the British unless he also attacked both the French besieging
force near Sevastopol and the corps of observation along the extended Sapun
ridge, in order to pin the enemy reserves. So he decided to mount his main
offensive on the British centre on the Cossack Mountain, using Soimonov's
and Pavlov's forces to make concentric attacks, the one from the Korabel'naia
suburb of Sevastopol and the other from the area of the Chernaia estuary.
At the same time strong subsidiary attacks were to be made on the flanks of
the allied line, on the French siege positions to the west of Sevastopol and
on Bosquet's observation corps on the Sapun escarpment far to the south.
By these tactics Menshikov hoped to surprise and overwhelm Lacy-Evans's
troops and possibly also Cathcart's division, before England's 3 Infantry
Division or the French could come to their assistance.

Dannenberg's 4 Corps did not arrive in the forward area until 3 and 4
November, but Menshikov allowed it little time for rest and none for
reconnaissance and preparation; on the afternoon of 4 November, he issued
his written orders for the new offensive which was to take place during the
same night. Although these orders were received by Dannenberg at 1700
hours that day, they were not issued to the troops until the small hours of
the morning.

*   *   *

Menshikov's written orders were brief, quaintly worded and lacking in
clarity, for once again he broke up tactical formations to fight under commanders other than their own. Lieutenant-General Soimonov, the Commander of 10 Infantry Division, with three of his own regiments under

Major-General Vil'boi, three regiments of 16 Infantry Division and one of
17 Infantry Division under Major-General Zhabokritsky, in all 19,000 men
and 38 guns, 'would begin his attack from the Careening Ravine at 0600
hours'. Lieutenant-General Pavlov with his own 11 Infantry Division and
a brigade of 17 Infantry Division, 16,000 men and 96 guns, 'would at
0600 hours repair the Inkerman bridge and make haste to join Soimonov,
while General of Infantry Dannenberg would accompany Pavlov, taking
command of the two columns after they had joined up'. On the far left flank,
the Chorgun force, based on Liprandi's 12 Infantry Division together with
52 cavalry squadrons and 10 Cossack *sotni* totalling 22,000 men and 88 guns,
all under the command of General of Infantry P.D. Gorchakov, was 'to
support the general attack, distracting the enemy forces and drawing them
on itself, trying to secure the approach to the Sapun, the dragoons being
ready to scale the heights at the first opportunity'. Lieutenant-General
Moller, the Commander of the Sevastopol garrison, was 'to go over to the
attack, covering with his batteries the right flank of the attacking force and,
in the event of interference by the enemy's batteries, to capture them'.
This task of Moller's was to be additional to the foray from No. 6 Bastion
on the extreme right flank.

In all 60,000 men and 234 guns had been detailed for the offensive, not
including a further six battalions (4,000 men) and 36 guns left on the
Mackenzie heights to cover the road to Bakchisarai.

Soimonov's orders, written as soon as he had received Menshikov's
directive, were clear, and he stated in the first paragraph his intention *to
cross* the Careening Ravine and attack south-eastwards along the ridge of
the Cossack Mountain. In accordance with Menshikov's instructions he
sent a copy of his own orders to Menshikov and to Dannenberg.

Dannenberg was a veteran of the Napoleonic War and had once been
regarded as a most distinguished, well educated and able military leader. Yet
the earlier campaign on the Danube had shown a lack of decisiveness in his
character, for it was generally believed in St Petersburg that the failure at
Oltenitsa had been caused more by a lack of foresight than by ill fortune.
According to Bogdanovich, Menshikov had originally wanted to attack on
4 November, but had put off the offensive by one day, 'partly to give the
troops a day's rest and partly, so it is said, at the request of Dannenberg,
so that he should not have to go into battle on the anniversary of Oltenitsa'.*
At Inkerman Dannenberg had been given a much more difficult operation
than at Oltenitsa, and his orders and correspondence, written on the night

* Bogdanovich, *Vostochnaia Voina*, Vol. 3, pp. 132–3.

of 4 November, show that he was unfitted for the task.

Apparently ignoring Menshikov's directive that the Commander-in-Chief intended to retain control until Soimonov and Pavlov joined forces, Dannenberg, late that night, began to replan the whole of the movement and battle plan. But first he wrote a letter to Menshikov saying that 'the long and deep Kilen-balka [Careening Ravine] separates Soimonov from me [and Pavlov] at the beginning of the attack, yet it seems to me indispensible that we should attack on both sides of the ravine'. This letter, although it admitted of no answer or conclusion, should have sounded a note of warning at Menshikov's headquarters, since Soimonov had already made it clear in the copies of the order that he had sent to Menshikov and to Dannenberg that he intended *to cross* the Careening Ravine.

Dannenberg then wrote a battle order covering the movement and approach march, phases for which he was not of course responsible, changing Menshikov's, Soimonov's and Pavlov's plans and ordering action contrary to that which he had recommended earlier that evening to Menshikov. For Dannenberg decided that Soimonov should first cross the Careening Ravine and march as far east as the Inkerman bridge, in order to cover Pavlov's bridging of the Chernaia. Dannenberg's orders contained the following paragraphs:

> Lieutenant-General Soimonov will depart from the Grafsky Dock at 0200 hours, under the guidance of Captain of the General Staff Iakovlev, to the place from where it will be possible to cover the crossing of the Chernaia by [Pavlov's] troops . . . As soon as 10 Infantry Division have covered the crossing places, then Lieutenant-General Pavlov's troops will cross the Chernaia by a bridge to be put in place by the navy, and should continue by the road recently constructed along the bay [the sapper road] under the guidance of Shtabs-Kapitan Cherniaev of the General Staff.

Dannenberg then set out in detail how the operation should be executed: the Kolyvansky and the Tomsky with a field battery, and the Ekaterinburgsky in reserve, all part of Soimonov's command, would cross the Careening Ravine and march to the area of the Inkerman crossing; the remainder of Soimonov's column would 'then follow', presumably by the same route. When Pavlov had crossed the Chernaia his column was to fan out on three routes, the three regiments on the right moving along the sapper road 'in the interval left free between 10 and 16 Infantry Division of Soimonov's column'. In other words, three of Pavlov's regiments, having passed through 10 Infantry Division which was holding the bridgehead, would henceforth be sandwiched between Soimonov's two divisions. Dannenberg's plan was involved and confused and, in view of what was yet to follow, almost entirely incomprehensible.

There are some points of similarity in Dannenberg's and Soimonov's orders, mainly in the order of movement of regiments across the Careening Ravine; but there is no indication of the timing of the signing and of the despatch, and it is uncertain whether Soimonov's orders were issued before Dannenberg's. But since Soimonov took no action to cover Pavlov's crossing, it appears likely that Dannenberg merely wrote his own instruction, having a copy of Soimonov's order at his elbow, introducing his own variations at will. According to Gersevanov, the acting chief of staff at the Commander-in-Chief's headquarters, Menshikov, when he saw Dannenberg's written orders, forbade their distribution; yet Pavlov did in fact receive his copy, or so said Alabin, but this is not improbable for Dannenberg marched with Pavlov's column.

The sequel was even more bizarre. In the early hours of the next morning Soimonov's column, under the guidance of Lieutenant-Colonel Zalesky and Captains Iakovlev and Andreianov – who were presumably aware of the Commander-in-Chief's plan since they belonged to Menshikov's staff – had already crossed over the Careening Ravine from west to east. There, as the column was making its way through the darkness up the steep slopes of the Cossack Mountain, Soimonov received a message from Dannenberg ordering him to attack *to the west* of the Careening Ravine. Soimonov concluded that any attempt to conform with this sudden change of plan would put not only his force but the whole operation in jeopardy. He therefore deliberately disregarded Dannenberg's order. From such auspices did the Inkerman battle begin.

* * *

From morning till night on 4 November there had been heavy rain, turning the clay soil around Sevastopol into a quagmire and breaking up the roads and tracks. The enemy outposts, sheltering from the rain and cold winds, paid little attention to the unusual activity in the city area.

Soimonov, who wanted to get into battle quickly and close with the enemy before first light, had concentrated his troops near No. 2 Bastion even before the appointed time. At 2 a.m. he moved out from Sevastopol, his force crossing the bridge at the mouth of the Careening Ravine, then climbing the steep and miry approach to the sapper road. The leading brigade of 10 Infantry Division, which formed the advanced guard for the whole force, deployed into No. 1 Order of Combat without halting, with the skirmishers of 6 Rifle Battalion out in front. The Kolyvansky and the Tomsky, the two regiments in the van, were each accompanied by a battery, and the third regiment, the Ekaterinburgsky, followed behind; the remainder of Soimonov's artillery travelled right at the rear of the infantry column of the main body, behind the Uglitsky, Butyrsky, Suzdal'sky and Vladimirsky, marching in that order. Soimonov's column followed the sapper road for about half a mile, then moved off to the south-east along the ridge, arriving at a point about a thousand yards from Lacy-Evans's camp. There, in the misty darkness, Soimonov silently deployed the first three regiments, the Tomsky on the right and the Kolyvansky on the left with the 22 field guns of the two batteries sited between them; the two first line battalions of each regiment were in company column, the remaining two battalions of each regiment in the second line being in battalion column of attack; the Ekaterinburgsky remained in reserve. The other four regiments of Soimonov's column were still on the march route. Soimonov had had no news of Pavlov's progress.

It was at this point that musketry fire was heard from the direction of the Careening Ravine, and it was assumed that the skirmishers from 6 Rifle Battalion had come under fire from an outpost. The alarm had been given and the British picquets were soon at the ready, with reinforcements turning out from the camp; Pennefather, the British commander in the area, began to draw up his troops on the high ground athwart the ridge, with his right on No. 1 Redoubt (the Sandbag Battery) and his left near the top of the Careening Ravine. Movement and noise on the other side of that ravine gave warning to Soimonov that the other British brigades on the Victoria Ridge were standing to.

The first brigade of 10 Infantry Division moved steadily towards the enemy through the fog and darkness and immediately came under fire. In spite of the heavy casualties caused by the enemy riflemen, and the difficulties of the ground, so runs the Russian account, the leading battalions of the Tomsky and the Kolyvansky 'overran Pennefather's brigade, taking No. 2 Redoubt, capturing two guns and breaking up the carriages'. According to Bogdanovich, Buller's brigade, on Pennefather's left, was also forced back and '1 and 3 Battalions of Ekaterinburgsky, having crossed the upper slope of the Careening Ravine, threw themselves on Codrington's brigade, taking and spiking four guns, until they were driven off by superior forces'. The casualties were said to be very heavy, and whatever initial success the Russian troops might have had, they were soon in retreat. During the course of minutes, Soimonov was killed; Vil'boi took his place and was immediately wounded; he was succeeded in turn, firstly by Colonel Pristovoitov, who was himself wounded, and then by Colonel Uvazhnov-Aleksandrov, who was shortly afterwards killed. Colonel Zagoskin, the artillery commander of 10 Infantry Division, was also fatally wounded.

The three forward infantry regiments began to fall back on to the Butyrsky and Uglitsky, who had the support of a further 16 guns of 17 Artillery Brigade which had been moved up by Zhabokritsky; meanwhile the Vladimirsky and Suzdal'sky were deployed in reserve on the right flank. The Russian infantry owed their salvation to the thirty-eight guns in the forward area, since the artillery enabled them to break contact and withdraw out of range of enemy rifle fire. By then it was 8 a.m. and still nothing had been heard from Pavlov.

* * *

Pavlov's troops had left their bivouacs at 2.30 a.m., arriving at the Inkerman bridge two and a half hours later. All was quiet in the area, but Lieutenant Tveritinov and the naval detachment had not managed to complete the repair of the causeway bridge; Pavlov had to wait until 7 a.m., when it was already light, before the crossing could be made. Hardly had the head of the Okhotsky's six rank column arrived on the wooden approaches to the bridge, when the cannonade was heard from the area of Sevastopol. Pavlov's column, having crossed the Chernaia, continued on three divergent routes, the Okhotsky, Iakutsky and Selenginsky and the artillery going by the northern coast route along the sapper road, the Borodinsky taking the centre route along the Volovia Ravine, while the Tarutinsky continued on the old post road up the Quarry Ravine. Shortly before 0800 hours Pavlov's men began to climb the Cossack Mountain.

One of the Tarutinsky battalions was met by rifle fire from the right flank of the enemy position (Adams's brigade), but continued to climb the steep and rocky slopes. A quarter of an hour later the men were on the plateau where they deployed into company column, attacking Adams's right under the cover of some of Soimonov's guns. The other two Tarutinsky battalions and the Borodinsky were moving further to the right, the Tarutinsky overrunning 'a battery where the English had two guns'. The British, however, immediately retook the position. The Tarutinsky and Borodinsky, according to Bogdanovich, were taken into the attack once more, 'only to be met by the fire of fresh troops from Bentinck's brigade of guards, afterwards joined by Pennefather's brigade'. The two Russian regiments, disorganized by their two attacks, had suffered such losses that they fell back to the Quarry, from which they were withdrawn to the Inkerman bridge.

The account of a non-commissioned officer of the Tarutinsky, subsequently published in the *Voennyi Sbornik*, has described how, on the night of 4 November, the battalion had already bedded down in the huts of a little village on the Mackenzie heights, when a Cossack and a mounted field gendarme arrived, bringing the commander his orders. Two hours later the battalion was on the move, 'each man wrapped in his own thoughts and many feeling that this day would be their last'. No one knew why and where they were going, 'although the good night meal, the cup of vodka and the march towards the enemy lines caused some comment'. Many of the men were nervous and, said our informant, even the battalion commander's horse was neighing and restless.*

As the Tarutinsky approached the bridge it was already getting light, a steamer could be seen in the bay, and foot and horse batteries already over the river were climbing the road on the other side. Having crossed the bridge the Tarutinsky reformed into company column, 2 Battalion, to which the non-commissioned officer belonged, being ordered to remain near the river while the other battalions moved off up the hill 'in different directions' through the blackthorn and Cornelian cherry scrub. The foot artillery still in the valley then opened fire, the shot passing over the heads of the stationary battalion; the steamer's guns joined in, and soon came the burst of the answering shells, not only on the ridge but down in the valley near the bridge; shell and shot began to fall nearby, causing the first casualties to the Tarutinsky men.

At this moment, 'an angry general [Dannenberg], who was unknown to us, arrived with our new regimental commander, Colonel Gordeev'; he wanted to know why the battalion was waiting there and he had some hard things to say about the commander. The battalion started to climb the slope, numbers of the men already beginning to fall; on the way up they passed empty ammunition boxes, dead horses and little heaps of dead and maimed gunners.

The Tarutinsky battalion was halted once more immediately behind one of Soimonov's gun positions, the mounted commander, wrapped in a cloak, quietly directing the fire, while the gun crews, 'unmindful of the fate of their comrades, continued to obey him'. 'But', said our informant, 'shells were knocking out our guns, for the enemy, apparently firing from a single epaulement, although economical with his fire, used it with great effect'. The Russian guns were silenced, however, when Soimonov's men began withdrawing in disorder across their front.

The Tarutinsky prepared to advance once more, the battalion commander Gorev warning his men against losing their place and ranks as Soimonov's

* *Voennyi Sbornik*, 1861, No. 9.

regiments had done. The battalion then turned to its left down the hill
again, from where the Tarutinsky could see 'the red jackets of the English
guards' on the opposite slope across the Quarry Ravine. On being given the
word of command, the company columns moved off down the slope,
hurrahing as they went. One of the first casualties was the mounted Gorev,
hit in the head by a bullet, a wound which covered his tunic with blood; the
men immediately began to waver. But Gorev called out in his booming voice:
'And that is the way you will perish!'. Gorev was last seen waving his troops
on, calling after them 'God be with you!'. He was never seen again. Thereafter all control and order was lost in the confusion and the shouting, the
firing of muskets and the groans of the wounded as they fell.

It is possible that the Tarutinsky non-commissioned officer repeated not
what he had seen, but what he had heard from other companies, for he was
convinced that there were British guns up on the ridge. In other respects
however, his account is closely borne out by Chodasiewicz, an officer in
another battalion of the Tarutinsky. The non-commissioned officer continued:

> We ran forward with our company columns broken, hurrying across the
> lower stretch of the Quarry, shouting and cheering, clambering up the
> steep slope, panting in our exertion and fear. On this slope to our right
> was an English battery, visible to us only by the puffs of smoke coming
> from the guns. They took no notice of us, however, but continued to
> fire in the direction of the Sevastopol road, but no sooner had some of
> our companies neared the top than they were liberally dosed with case-
> shot . . . [When we reached the summit] some of the English rushed out
> of the epaulement and attacked our men with the bayonet, throwing them
> over the ledges.

The No. 1 Redoubt (the Sandbag Battery) was taken, 'but the enemy
dare-devils (*udaltsy*) hardly withdrew sixty paces and, seeing that they
were not followed, calmly opened up a steady fire, picking us off, one by
one'. Meanwhile the Russian infantry down on the road and on the opposite
heights in the rear, began to fire on their own troops, many of the Borodinsky
and Tarutinsky being struck down, 'for on the steep sides of the mountain
those who were hit by the enemy fell on their backs and rolled headlong
down the hill, while those who had a bullet in the back fell flat on their faces;
and there they stayed'.

All this occurred because of a lack of officers and leadership – what our
battalion commander had said came true. Some soldiers forgot their duty

and wandered about in search of booty, took the wounded off to the dressing stations, indeed some dragged off corpses in order to escape the battle . . . Because of this disorder the English had no difficulty in driving our men off . . . The officers were gone and the men took no notice of the non-commissioned officers. The distant noise of [what were thought to be] French drums beating caused panic. There were shouts on all sides of 'Where is the reserve?'. That is how it was.

The task of the Tarutinsky, according to Chodasiewicz, had been to take the eastern side of the Cossack Mountain, providing cover for other of Pavlov's men to bring up gabions and fascines and throw up a trench work. But its 4 Battalion became mixed with some of Soimonov's troops that were retiring from the enemy near the top of the Careening Ravine; 4 Battalion descended once more into the Quarry and the other battalions lost direction and followed. When the Tarutinsky attacked the British positions on the other side of the Quarry Ravine, Soimonov's broken troops, mainly Ekaterin-burgers, having, according to Chodasiewicz, shot down many of their own officers, opened fire on the Tarutinsky and the Borodinsky. Nor could the officers of other regiments restrain them from doing so.*

Having already repulsed the leading regiments of 10 and 17 Infantry Divisions, the British began to advance, Bentinck's brigade of guards on the enemy right flank moving into the Quarry, while Pennefather's and Adams's brigades came up in the centre. Buller was present on the left flank while Codrington remained firm on the Victoria Ridge beyond the Careening Ravine. Bogdanovich estimated that about 30 British 9-pounder guns opened a concentric fire on the 38 field guns standing on the Cossack Mountain. When Dannenberg reached the heights from the sapper road he had already had two horses shot from under him.

Soimonov's advanced guard and Pavlov's left wing had been defeated. It was now the turn of Pavlov's right wing to take up the attack.

Most of Pavlov's artillery was still stretched along the sapper road down in the bay, and those guns that were being brought up over the difficult ground of the Georgievsky Ravine had to be broken down into several loads. Eventually, 32 of Pavlov's field guns were brought up on the mountain, but the leading regiments of Pavlov's right wing had to advance against the enemy without waiting for this artillery support. The Okhotsky led the attack in two lines, the first in company and the second in battalion column, the Iakutsky and the Selenginsky following behind, also in two lines. The Okhotsky came under the cross-fire of the British batteries standing beyond

* Chodasiewicz, *Within the Walls of Sevastopol*, pp. 182–95.

the Quarry, but they succeeded in crossing the Quarry Ravine to attack the feature earlier occupied by the Tarutinsky. After what was described as 'fearful hand to hand fighting', the Okhotsky claimed 'to have thrown the enemy [Coldstream] out of the position, inflicting on them about 200 casualties and capturing nine guns, of which three were thrown into the ravine and the remainder spiked'. The Okhotsky losses were admitted to have been enormous, and included Bibikov, the regimental commander.

The British began to reinforce their threatened right wing, but when Cathcart and Torrens arrived with detachments to try to turn the disorganized Okhotsky, they came under close range fire from the Iakutsky on the one side and the Selenginsky on the other, losing heavily in casualties. The situation of the British was subsequently judged by Russian commentators to have been serious, and among those killed or wounded were Cathcart, Seymour, Torrens, Goldie, Brown, Adams, Codrington, Bentinck and Buller. Raglan, the British Commander-in-Chief, had already sent to Bosquet for aid.

The first French reinforcement, judged by the Russians to be 'a mere handful', consisted of 1/7 Light and 2/6 Line Regiments and four companies of 3 Chasseurs and 12 guns. These were met by heavy fire from the Okhotsky, Iakutsky and Selenginsky, and they fell back covered by their own artillery fire, suffering heavy losses as they did so.

It was already 9.30 a.m. and the critical moment of the battle had been reached. Victory, thought Bogdanovich, should have gone to the Russians if only the attacks from Sevastopol and the Chorgun could have pinned the French troops on the flanks.

Just before 10 a.m. Major-General Timofeev, an old artilleryman who had served in the Turkish War of 1828, made his sally from the defensive wall to the right of No. 6 Bastion, with four battalions of the Minsky and four light guns of 14 Artillery Brigade. The Russians crossed the Quarantine Ravine, to the right of the cemetery, and moved on the left flank of the enemy trenches, where they came under heavy musketry fire. A Minsky battalion, under the command of a Major Evspavlev, 'broke into the defences of the batteries opposite No. 6 and No. 5 Bastions and spiked fifteen guns'. The French moved up reinforcements, ten battalions according to a Russian estimate; but Timofeev's aim was already achieved, and he began to withdraw in good order, bringing back his own wounded and those of the enemy. Timofeev was then further reinforced by a battalion of the Brestsky and one of the Vilensky Regiments and a further six guns. The French reinforcement under Lurmel followed up, but when they came close to the Shemiakin battery 'they were caught in the concentrated fire of other

Sevastopol batteries'. Suffering great losses, Lurmel's troops withdrew in disorder. Timofeev, having lost a third of his force, had done all that was expected of him.

Menshikov's main hopes were centred, however, on Prince P.D. Gorchakov's Chorgun force of 22,000 men and 88 guns that was to make an attack on the Sapun mountain escarpment in the south, drawing on itself Bosquet's reserves. The infantry component of the force belonged to 12 Infantry Division, commanded by Liprandi, said by Chodasiewicz to be a man of great energy; but General of Infantry Gorchakov had been put in overall command of troops that were not his own, according to Bogdanovich, 'only because of his seniority'. Gorchakov 'successfully denied himself any possibility of making a decisive contribution to the Sevastopol battle when he positioned half his force, seven battalions, 32 squadrons and 48 guns, *behind* the Chernaia, and scattered the rest of his force, nine battalions, 20 squadrons and 40 guns, between the Fediukhin heights and the No. 1 Redoubt'. The troops west of the Chernaia went forward to 'a distant cannon range from the Sapun and opened artillery fire'. This was answered by the enemy. 'This almost harmless activity', continued Bogdanovich, 'lasted until 9 a.m., until the French became convinced that this was so and ordered their guns to stop firing'. Gorchakov remained inactive, holding his distant ground until the late afternoon when he withdrew to his earlier positions.

Bosquet, knowing that Gorchakov's activity was only a demonstration, thinned out his troops continuously in order to send aid to the British, so that, by 11 a.m., only 3,000 men remained facing Gorchakov's Chorgun force. About ten French battalions and 20 guns had already arrived near the Cossack Mountain, 'and although the troops of Pavlov's 11 Infantry Division met the French fearlessly, the new reinforcements and the case-shot of their artillery drove our men back'.

Sixteen battalions of the Butyrsky, Uglitsky, Vladimirsky and Suzdal'sky on the Cossack Mountain had still not been brought into action, yet Dannenberg decided to call off the action and withdraw. Pavlov was ordered to fall back across the Inkerman bridge, but, as this was already blocked by wounded and transport, all the guns had to be withdrawn to Sevastopol. To enable his infantry to break contact Dannenberg ordered the brigade commander Baron Del'vig to take forward the Vladimirsky and Suzdal'sky to threaten the British right, beyond the Quarry. Del'vig was seriously wounded and many officers and men lost in this action.

The enemy made no attempt at a co-ordinated counter-offensive but limited his follow-up to the action of artillery and riflemen. The artillery, firing at distant range, did little damage, 'but the same could not be said of the skirmishers that hid in the scrub, for these, undeterred by the covering fire of the *Vladimir* and *Chersonese* steamers, closed in on the Russian guns', which by then were near the sapper road. The guns were only saved by the intervention of Totleben, who sent some Butyrsky and Vladimirsky infantry to extricate them. The losses of artillery horses had been so heavy that Istomin ordered two naval battalions out of the fortress to assist in dragging back the guns, but they were not all back in Sevastopol until late that evening.

Kir'iakov, the Commander of 17 Infantry Division, had been present near the Inkerman bridge earlier that morning, apparently as a spectator. According to Chodasiewicz, he complained to any who would listen to him that Menshikov had taken his formation away from him to share it out between Soimonov and Pavlov; he caused even greater surprise to a number of English prisoners who were waiting there, when he rode his horse at withdrawing Russian stragglers, slashing at them with his whip. Another Tarutinsky soldier present overheard the conversations of the groups of officers standing about. Some put the blame for the defeat on their lack of mountain experience; some thought battalion preferable to company column; all thought that the Russian training system was entirely unrelated to the conditions of modern war.

The soldier continued:

> A weak sun lit up the hill, where bodies were strewn about, some still stirring in their dying torment. There was little firing and everything became quiet as we crossed the bridge on the way to our previous day's billets, taking our wounded with us on carts and limbers; the men marched listlessly and unhappily, looking round and asking the fate of their missing fellows. We took possession of the same huts, but whereas last night there had been six or seven of us in each now there were but two or three. Where yesterday there had been chatter, noise, and mirth, today there was melancholy and emptiness.

Of the 35,000 Russian troops engaged in the north-east, 10,729 became casualties, this figure being increased to 11,959 if the Sevastopol garrison loss is added. Of this total, Gorchakov's Chorgun force suffered 15 men lost. The enemy casualties listed only 2,610 British and 1,726 French.

* * *

On 8 November Dannenberg wrote to Menshikov a formal and lengthy report, full of 'aforesaids' and 'above-mentioneds', placing the blame for the defeat on the dead Soimonov. Soimonov had been ordered, or so thought

Dannenberg, to advance, resting his left flank on the west side of the Kilen-balka (Careening Ravine). He continued:

Unfortunately, Soimonov, instead of taking the direction ordered, crossed on to the right [east] bank of the Kilen-balka and, without waiting for the appearance of the left column, quickly went forward at dawn until he was engaged by heavy rifle fire. The enemy, not being threatened on the left flank [the Victoria Ridge] was able to concentrate all his forces between the upper Kilen-balka and the Inkerman valley, on broken ground highly suitable for defence.*

Two days earlier Menshikov had sent a laconic, inaccurate and misleading despatch to the tsar:

On the night of 4 November a sally (*vylazka*) was made from the side of Bastion No. 1 [*sic*] in which the following troops took part:
   10 Infantry Division – Ekaterinburgsky, Tomsky, Kolyvansky
   11 Infantry Division – Seleginsky, Iakutsky, Okhotsky
   16 Infantry Division – Butyrsky, Borodinsky, Tarutinsky
Our first attack was entirely successful and the English fortifications were taken and 11 guns spiked. Then French reinforcements arrived and the English brought up their siege artillery which our field guns could not engage. The enemy won the battle on account of his numerical superiority and the effect of his rifle fire.†

The only comfort which Menshikov could offer to his sovereign was 'in commending the two princes [Nicholas's sons] for their conduct under fire', and suggesting that they be awarded decorations. In a private letter to Nicholas, however, Menshikov laid the responsibility for the defeat on Dannenberg.

According to Miliutin, who at the time was a staff officer in the centre of the administration in the capital, the Emperor Nicholas paid the closest of attention to all military operations, nightly sending packets of handwritten memoranda to the Ministry of War where they were hastily copied and despatched to the south; and the tsar knew most of his senior officers personally. But Nicholas was a very poor judge of character and ability, and it is difficult to understand how Menshikov's despatch escaped proper investigation. Miliutin said that even Prince Dolgoruki, the Minister for War, was aware that the Commander-in-Chief in the Crimea was failing because he had no one about him with command ability, for Menshikov

---

* Dannenberg, *Russkii Invalid*, 1854, No. 251.
† Menshikov, *Russkii Invalid*, 1854, Nos 245 and 247.

would not employ anyone who might eclipse him in the eyes of the sovereign. When Nicholas tried to improve the situation by appointing a Colonel A.E. Popov, said to be an outstandingly able officer, to be Menshikov's chief of staff, 'the tsar personally briefing Popov on his duties', Menshikov used Popov badly and merely detached him to a succession of subordinate posts before returning him to St Petersburg.

Menshikov openly admitted that he had no talent for tactics and said that he did not regard himself as a general; and yet he apparently did not consider that this should disqualify him from holding the post of Commander-in-Chief in the field, for, as Tarle said, he avoided embarrassment merely by keeping aloof from anything that he did not understand. Menshikov had had no wish to attack at Inkerman because he had little confidence in his own ability, but he went into battle notwithstanding, partly because logic told him that this course was inescapable, and partly to deliver himself from the bothersome pesterings of the tsar. It is doubtful whether his offensive had an underlying strategic or tactical theme; and, in spite of Dannenberg's protests that the arrangements were too vague, Menshikov made the strange decision to retain personal responsibility for the movement of the troops to the battle field, relinquishing the command to Dannenberg only when the battle had begun. When subsequently asked why he had entrusted the conduct of the main battle to Dannenberg, the Commander-in-Chief is said to have replied that since he had no faith in any of his generals it was immaterial who had the command. There was some suspicion that Menshikov indicated the scape-goats about him who could be dumped (*svalit'*) in the event of failure, for, with real or feigned indifference, he wrote that 'the command should be given to Dannenberg, though this might prove to be a real misfortune'.*

Earlier, when Menshikov had learned that Dannenberg was coming from Bessarabia with the two divisions, he had written a letter in French to Prince M.D. Gorchakov, the Commander-in-Chief there, asking him to be so good as to send the divisions without their corps commander; Gorchakov, however, thought that Menshikov should learn to take the rough with the smooth, for, in his reply from Kishinev on 19 October, he said that it was 'not possible to rid you of Dannenberg, for, in accepting the benefit of the troops, you must also accept the disadvantage'. And Gorchakov protested that he could not take such a serious step as to remove a corps commander from his post, but he thought it proper to advise Menshikov that Dannenberg's ability was not such that one could rely on

---

* *Russkaia Starina*, 1875, VXII, p. 314.

him to undertake independent operations.

On the day before the battle Dannenberg had accepted his allotted task, although under protest; he then redrafted the Commander-in-Chief's orders, so that Tarle surmised that Dannenberg could not and would not have been so bold as to have prepared new plans different from those issued by Menshikov, unless Menshikov had allowed him some discretion. Be this as it may, Menshikov, when he saw them, cancelled Dannenberg's orders to Soimonov later that same evening presumably without informing Dannenberg that he had done so. But if Menshikov was playing some crafty game (*khitril*) with Dannenberg, then Dannenberg was not above suspicion of doing the same to Soimonov, for, not only did he try to set aside Menshikov's dispositions, but he himself issued two contradictory sets of orders during the course of that night. As Totleben said, Soimonov needed clear and binding orders, without suggestions or hints. Both Soimonov and Pavlov considered themselves to be far more competent than Dannenberg, as well as being his military and intellectual superiors.

Dannenberg did not know the ground to the south of Sevastopol, although he said that he did. Nor were there *any* maps of the hinterland of Sevastopol, the Sapun or the Chernaia Valley in Menshikov's headquarters; in St Petersburg itself there was only one set of maps and these had not been copied, nor had Menshikov set his own cartographers to work. Command, as Bestuzhev said, 'was to be exercised by eye'. This had prompted Nakhimov the day before the battle to reply to Dannenberg, when he apologized to the admiral for not having paid him an earlier official courtesy visit, 'that your Excellency would do better to visit the Sapun rather than coming to see me!'.

The day after the battle, Nicholas's son, the Grand Prince Nikolai Nikolaevich, wrote a letter to 'Dear Sasha', his brother Alexander, shortly to become Tsar Alexander II; he supposed that Alexander knew, what was common knowledge, 'that Menshikov and Dannenberg simply could not abide each other'; and he went on to describe what he had seen the previous day:

We [Nikolai and Mikhail] had been waiting for Prince Menshikov near the Inkerman bridge but he did not come out of his house until 6.30 a.m. when our troops had already taken the first position. We stayed with the prince all the time [in the Georgievsky Ravine] on the right flank, and not once did any of the generals send him a report on the course of the battle. Finally the prince went to see what was happening on the left flank; on the way he met Dannenberg, who reported that he had ordered a general withdrawal on account of the increasing enemy fire which was causing fearful losses to the gun crews. After this the prince became completely unnerved.

Once again Menshikov blamed all about him, even condemning the men for cowardice, and he repeatedly told the royal princes that 'the troops would not fight (*voisko ne dralos*')'. Nikolai Nikolaevich, however, already had Menshikov's measure. Nikolai visited the formations and reported to his brother Alexander that the regiments were thinned by casualties and in disorder, 'disordered because they had been badly directed'. Nikolai also saw the Ekaterinburgsky, because he had heard that the regiment had been reluctant to close with the enemy; but there he found that 'many of the men carried blooded bayonets and the officers had English rifles'. Nikolai concluded:

The disorder originated from Menshikov. Staggering though it is to relate, Menshikov had no headquarters at all, just three people who work at those duties in such a fashion that if you want to know something you are at a loss to know whom to ask. Yesterday, for the first time, Menshikov went among the troops to thank them for what they had done, and when he returned he remarked to me on the fine morale of the Vladimirsky, who said that they were ready to give battle again. The Vladimirsky was one of the regiments that he had just been cursing.

For the first, and the last, time during this war, Russian troops had a decisive superiority in numbers of men and in artillery. Yet Menshikov failed to commit more than a third of his force, for the Tobol'sky and the Volynsky, the eight reserve battalions of 13 Infantry Brigade, all the cavalry and the seamen, Gorchakov's force and the covering troops on the Mackenzie heights did not come under fire. Of Soimonov's and Pavlov's artillery only part came into action, most being left down in the valley near the sapper road. Menshikov's manoeuvre had involved the movement, without maps, reconnaissance or proper preparation, of a large body of troops on concentric axes, over difficult and unknown ground during mist and darkness, on to a plateau too small to allow deployment. Colonel Men'kov, a close witness to Menshikov's actions, wrote:

It was the story of the Alma all over again, for no one knew the aim of the offensive, let alone how it was to be executed. Columns became confused, artillery got mixed up, and infantry, attacking without the support of artillery, lost thousands of men. We did not make any use of our advantage in artillery or cavalry, none of which saw action that day.

The artillery just crowded together, losing men and horses. We lost, so it is said, 12,000 men, nearly all our regimental and battalion commanders and senior officers. And all for nothing! Neither Dannenberg nor Menshikov did anything at all during the battle.

Yet the Russian columns advanced bravely in the face of superior artillery and rifle fire and, thought Bogdanovich, were it not for the mistakes of their leaders, would have won the day. For, he continued, 'if only Gorchakov had attacked with determination, and if only Moller had supported Timofeev', then the battle might have turned out very differently. This opinion was shared by the Frenchman Guérin.

Prince P.D. Gorchakov took issue with Guérin, writing to him in his own illogical and offensive style; and he offered this letter for publication. It began:

It is not without good cause that it is said that contemporary events are not history; your collection of works, my dear Sir, prove that point.*

Gorchakov blamed Liprandi for the lack of success, and Liprandi too was censured by Bogdanovich for 'advising Gorchakov, for reasons best known to himself, to confine his action to a cannonade'. Bogdanovich considered Gorchakov to have been brave but lacking in judgement. Krylov, the head of Menshikov's chancellery, however, had this to say of Gorchakov:

It is difficult to emphasize what a disastrous influence this character had on the course of the campaign. Of those not actually in overall command he did more harm than any others and it is hardly possible to explain how, with such a character, he could have achieved such high rank; for he was stupid, cowardly (*trus*), muddle-headed, vain and excitable. With each promotion he became more negligent.

According to Krylov, Menshikov knew that Gorchakov was unfitted for command and he neither liked nor trusted him, but he kept on good terms with Gorchakov since he was well thought of by the tsar and was the elder brother of the Commander-in-Chief in Bessarabia who was sending Menshikov reinforcements.

It was said of P.D. Gorchakov that he could not bear any of his subordinates to show any initiative. During the week before the Inkerman battle he plagued Liprandi's troops with frequent and constant alarms, having the horses kept saddled and the men at stand-to, so that he rapidly reduced them to exhaustion. For Liprandi himself has told how Gorchakov would beat the alarm 'for no apparent reason' when the troops were about

* P.D. Gorchakov, *Voennyi Sbornik*, 1859, No. 4.

to dine, so that they marched off hungry and the food was wasted. According, however, to an artillery officer on Liprandi's staff, Gorchakov was the leader only in name, for the real commander was Liprandi, who tended, as far as he could, to ignore Gorchakov's presence. It was widely said that Gorchakov spent his day in field reconnaissances of his own devising, sending gallopers back to Liprandi, demanding reinforcements and giving news that the flank was being enveloped by enemy cavalry, mounted troops which turned out to be Russian dragoons. The officer continued:

> I do not know whether this story is true. If it is, it needs no comment. If not, it gives the reader some idea of the extent to which the senior commanders were held in such low regard.*

The same officer gave evidence, and the details were published in the literary press, of the maladministration and corruption in the Crimea 'seen by all from the Commander-in-Chief downwards, but everyone kept silent'; of the starving horses and of the incredibly large sums of paper money being issued to units for the purchase of fodder when there was none to be had in the peninsula; and of rascally paymasters who demanded for themselves eight per cent of the cash before they would issue the fodder allowance. After Inkerman, he continued, 'there was a general depression everywhere, and all knew that in the whole of the Russian Army there were hardly three or four names in which anyone had confidence or which were in any way popular'.

Khrushchev doubted whether the Inkerman battle could have been won even if Gorchakov had driven home his attacks with determination, 'for the main attack was so muddled and our forces on the Inkerman heights [Cossack Mountain] were committed so irresponsibly through the lack of any ability on the part of the Commander-in-Chief'; conditions and personalities being what they were, 'the Commander-in-Chief would have been unable to exploit any success [that Gorchakov might have had] and so have smashed the English'. Or, as Bogdanovich said, the Commander-in-Chief, as on the Alma, did not display those qualities of generalship needed to direct and co-ordinate forces entrusted to his command. For there was an almost total lack of control over operations; and in this way victory fell from the grasp of a commander who lacked any powers of decision.

After Inkerman, Menshikov said that he could entertain no hope of annihilating the enemy unless the winter would do it for him. His prayers were almost answered, for the great storms of 14 November destroyed allied shipping, supplies, tents and roads. Sickness and cold did much of the rest.

* *Russkii Arkhiv*, 1870, No. 11.

CHAPTER 8

* * * * *

GORCHAKOV IN COMMAND

Tiutchev, who was close to the tsar, said that Nicholas 'could, when necessary, mask his true feelings and thoughts, but between the Alma and Inkerman, and especially between Inkerman and Evpatoria, he gradually lost faith even in those few people he had trusted up to that time'. Nicholas no longer troubled to disguise his emotions. The defeat at the Alma had dismayed him; his spirits had been temporarily restored by the false reports after Balaclava, only to be dashed when the truth became known. The tsarina was so seriously ill that the doctors feared for her life, and the atmosphere at Gatchina had become unbearable. The maid of honour Tiutcheva wrote in her dairy on 6 December:

> The Gatchina court is gloomy and silent: everywhere there is depression, people hardly daring to talk to each other. The sight of the sovereign is enough to break one's heart. Recently he has become more and more morose; his face is careworn and his look is lifeless.

Nicholas was a broken man, for suddenly, as Grunwald said, 'the brilliant insubstantial pageant of his reign had vanished'.

All hope of avoiding defeat had disappeared after Inkerman, and Nicholas turned for solace to those whom he had formerly disregarded as being pessimists; he sought crumbs of comfort in talking to Paskevich, because he knew that the old field-marshal had always been reluctant to risk war and still regarded the Russian position in Central Europe as fraught with the greatest danger. And the tsar came to rely on the opinions of his son Alexander and of Alexander's wife, for he recalled that they had made no secret of their opposition to the Russian occupation of the Principalities. He bitterly regretted his hasty action in going to war, for, although the allies were suffering from the Crimean winter and had as yet failed to win a decisive battle, they seemed as determined as ever to prosecute the war. Pogodin, the historian and publicist, reported to the tsar:

We thought that Louis Bonaparte could not find 20,000 men and yet he has already sent 100,000 and is said to be preparing a further 100,000. There is now talk of half a million! The war can be conducted more easily from London and Paris than from Moscow.

Only after the Alma did Nicholas and the ruling circles begin to reckon the cost of the war. After Inkerman they began to realize how irremediable had been their actions.

On 2 December 1854 Austria had concluded an alliance with France and England, and, in January 1855, Sardinia joined the anti-Russian coalition. In February, Palmerston, who understood Nicholas well but who had no liking for him, became the Prime Minister of Great Britain.

The Austrian alliance with Russia's enemies made the tsar fear that Russia would be attacked by a coalition, and he prepared to resist invasion from Central Europe as his brother Alexander had done in 1812, making plans to retire beyond Moscow, even behind the central Volga. He was ready, he told Prince M.D. Gorchakov, when the moment came 'to appeal to Russia in the knowledge that it will act as it did in 1812'. Yet, in reality, the enthusiasm for the war instigated by Nicholas had quickly waned and the tsar well understood that the circumstances of 1854 were entirely different from those of 1812. People already spoke in public advocating Nicholas's abdication.

Although Menshikov had no intention of resigning, he had been much depressed after Inkerman so that Nicholas, himself bent by worry and strain, was obliged to write to him frequently, urging him not to despair. In supporting Menshikov, Nicholas had to remove Dannenberg from the command of 4 Corps and replace him by *General-Adiutant* Baron von der Osten-Saken. Nicholas was not going to permit Menshikov to remain idle, however, and, since 8 Infantry Division had recently arrived in the Crimea, he used this as grounds for pressing his Commander-in-Chief to undertake yet another offensive operation.

The tsar had heard from his sons Nikolai Nikolaevich and Mikhail Nikolaevich about Menshikov's strange behaviour during the Inkerman battle, and he had been baffled by it. He turned to Paskevich for his opinion. When the aged field-marshal knew that the seeds of doubt had been sown in the sovereign's mind, he sided strongly and openly against Menshikov:

I certainly expected nothing of him. After all, a person that for the last thirty years has done nothing but make puns and jokes is hardly suitable for the task.

Dolgoruki, the Minister for War, took his cue from Paskevich and, although he continued to write to Menshikov in cordial, even lyrical, terms, he began to show Menshikov's replies to the tsar. The ladies of the court were already well informed, through their husbands' letters, of Menshikov's incompetence and indifference. It was widely known in court and government circles that the successful defence of Sevastopol had rested almost entirely on the Russian Navy and Nakhimov, who, according to Miliutin, 'personally took upon himself the allocation and control of all military forces in the base'. Menshikov's sneer that 'if he wanted a man to tar a few ropes he would, without a doubt, chose Nakhimov', when relayed to St Petersburg caused much indignation and prepared the way for the Commander-in-Chief's fall.

During the fighting in Sevastopol, the Commander-in-Chief was rarely to be found there, for his main headquarters remained 12 miles to the north at the Belbek camp; even his advanced headquarters was sited not in the base but at No. 4 Battery on the Severnaia. Menshikov wanted to give up Sevastopol. When he wrote to Dolgoruki on 15 November he complained about the lack of ammunition. 'Sevastopol will hold out', he concluded 'only as long as No. 4 Bastion holds *and we have powder* [Menshikov's italics]'. He had asked for a supply from Kiev and from Novocherkassk, the capital of the Don Cossacks. 'I cannot see where we can get any, anywhere else.' Menshikov was preparing the Minister of War for the evacuation of the base and looking for a pretext to give it up. But he lived in fear of Nakhimov and of the sailors, and of the day when he might have to order the withdrawal, presumably because he was afraid of a mutiny. He continued:

> I can do nothing about destroying anything in Sevastopol until the last minute, because of the effect that this might have on the sailors, who link the defence of the base with that of their country and their fleet.

Four days later the Grand Prince Mikhail Nikolaevich wrote directly to his father:

> The French have already begun to appear in sheepskin coats, but our young fellows have not got any. The weather is bad . . . Menshikov talks about sheepskin coats but nothing has been done.

Menshikov had his own conception of personal honour, even though it might have been difficult to define. Yet he tolerated the corruption and the thieving of the rascally officials and contractors who enriched themselves by withholding the soldiers' clothing and rations. He saw no virtue in sharing the danger and privations of the Sevastopol base. He regarded himself as high-born, close to the Romanovs, the Dolgorukis and those in the

Winter Palace, with nothing in common with 'sailor' Nakhimov, 'sapper' Totleben or the bourgeois Kornilov and Istomin: nor did he seek a closer understanding with them. As for the great grey mass of sailors and soldiers, they were completely foreign to him. They, however, thought that they knew Menshikov. The sailors called him 'Prince Anathema'; to the soldiers he was 'Prince Izmenshchikov' which, with its undertones of fickleness and treachery, might be translated as 'Prince Judas'.

During the Crimean War a striking difference had become apparent between the Sevastopol sailors and the soldiers, in their characteristics and in their efficiency. They were all, for the most part, Russian, and all fought either as infantry or artillery. Menshikov had originally taken a naval battery and a naval rifle battalion to fight on the Alma, but they had failed to distinguish themselves there. Under Kornilov's and Nakhimov's command, however, a naval battery or a naval infantry battalion was much more formidable than its army counterpart. For the Russian admirals were young, energetic, and closer to the ratings than the generals were to the army rank and file. The easy familiarity of the naval system was a source of wonder to army officers and other ranks, for 'under Nakhimov's informal approach, officers and ratings would talk freely – the ratings with their caps still on their heads – yet, when duty needed or volunteers were required none hung back'.

The Russian Army was not, however, without good officers, and these were often outspoken in their comments to the capital. Colonel Prince Vasil'chikov, one of the bravest and most reliable of Nakhimov's deputies, had the highest praise for the sailors. Vasil'chikov wrote to his wife:

Everything is fine here. We have two problems only: [firstly] that the Dear Lord above does not send us enough ammunition and [secondly] that Prince Menshikov is a traitor.

General Semiakin, writing to his wife on 26 December, said:

You ask whether there are any fortifications on the Belbek and the Kacha. None at all! The only ones on the north side are at No. 4 Battery where Prince Menshikov and his parish live in a state of near-insensibility.

Again, on 28 December:

There is something to eat here at times, just enough, so it could be worse. But be careful and keep all this to yourself! The troops are marvellous. As for some of those on high, I say nothing. May God be their judge!

Meanwhile Menshikov continued his life of ease and leisure on the

Belbek. On 31 January, however, he was rudely awakened by a not too happily worded letter, dated 19 January, from Krabbe, one of his spies in the capital:

> There is a ruthless party opposed to you here which is trying to get the ear of the sovereign; it includes Nessel'rode, Kiselev, Lieven and others. News is arriving in the capital from the Crimea through the ladies and N.N. [Nikolai Nikolaevich], and the arrival of Shenshina and his verbal description of Your Highness's abdication from command [sic] has produced a surprise sensation and given rise to a new unpleasantness; Field-Marshal Paskevich, whom unfortunately they [Nicholas] continue to believe, has even insisted that they convene a general commission of inquiry to judge you and your conduct. But what is more vexing is that Orlov and the General-Admiral who [formerly] took your side in some measure, have yielded to the general blindness and are even indignant at the conduct of Your Highness.

It would appear that the receipt of this unexpected and unwelcome news was one of the factors which forced Menshikov to undertake a new offensive.

*   *   *

In the view of some strategists, both allied and Russian, Evpatoria and its hinterland held the key to the Crimea. The port had originally been gar- risoned by only 300 French troops, but the allies had begun to land there good quality Turkish formations transported from Omar Pasha's victorious troops on the Danube, and Nicholas feared that two reinforcement French divisions might be brought to join them. An enemy force of such strength could move eastwards and cut Sevastopol's communications with Perekop and the mainland, so trapping the Crimean Army. Nicholas and Dolgoruki had frequently brought this danger to Menshikov's attention, and their warnings may have been responsible for the Commander-in-Chief's earlier obsession with safeguarding his communications and line of retreat to the north.

It had already been suggested from St Petersburg that an attack should be made on Evpatoria, and when Lieutenant-General Baron Wrangel, who had succeeded Korf in command of the cavalry corps in the Evpatoria area, rounded up and removed 10,000 beef cattle without interference from the allies, this had encouraged Menshikov to consider that an attack upon the port might have some prospect of success.

Evpatoria was believed to be defended by a force of over 20,000 Turks under the personal command of Omar Pasha, supported by the guns of part of the allied fleets; its defensive works, which included 34 pieces of heavy artillery, were formidable. Wrangel had been ordered by Menshikov to reconnoitre the area and prepare plans for the capture of the port, but, having completed his reconnaissance, Wrangel told the Commander-in-Chief that a successful offensive was out of the question. Menshikov ordered him to reconsider the matter but Wrangel insisted that he would not be responsible for such an undertaking.

Wrangel's deputy was a Lieutenant-General Khrulev, an artilleryman who had been recommended to Menshikov by M.D. Gorchakov as 'a disciple of Shil'der – not much in his head, but very active and brave, who will do exactly what you tell him'. Khrulev, when asked, told Menshikov that he thought an attack could be made on Evpatoria with prospect of success; he was then directed to take over the command, and Wrangel was transferred to Kerch.

Khrulev's force consisted of five infantry regiments of 22 battalions, 24 squadrons and 108 guns, in all about 19,000 men. The offensive began at daylight on 17 February and lasted barely three hours; the Russian troops were repulsed with a loss of 800 men and Khrulev did not renew his attacks. Menshikov wrote to Nicholas on 19 February describing the failure.

Meanwhile, in mid February, Nicholas had written to Prince M.D. Gorchakov in Bessarabia telling him that he was satisfied with the rate of build-up of troops in the Crimea and that he foresaw a battle at Evpatoria in the event of the landing there of the two French divisions shortly expected to arrive in the theatre. He added that he doubted whether it would be advisable to continue to hold Sevastopol in the event of such a French landing, particularly if the Sardinian corps should be involved. He thanked Gorchakov for sending twelve battalions to Menshikov, and ended:

> I agree with you that in the event of defeat in the Crimea it would be best to allocate the responsibility for the defence of Nikolaev to Menshikov, using the remnants of his army. Let us trust to God that it will not come to that.

On 21 February, not having yet received news of Menshikov's intention to attack or of his defeat in front of Evpatoria, Nicholas had changed his mind, for he wrote a letter to the Commander-in-Chief Crimean Army in which he set out newly found doubts about the wisdom of attacking Evpatoria:

> I fear that Khrulev might be impetuous, for the enemy appears to have strong forces there. I am not sure either what advantage Evpatoria would

be to us even if we did take it, for it is controlled by the guns of the enemy fleet. It might be better to let Omar Pasha move first and then attack him in the flank or rear; perhaps we might be able to do it with horse artillery and cavalry without much loss . . . The English seem to be the worst off; perhaps an attack on them would be easier then elsewhere . . . Cannot you find a weak point where we can break in?

Three days later, on 24 February, Nicholas received Menshikov's despatch notifying the repulse in front of Evpatoria. Although the St Petersburg court and the War Ministry knew that the initiative for the Evpatoria venture had come from Nicholas, all hastened to blame Menshikov.

The tsar had been sick with influenza from the evening of 16 February and his doctors had advised him to stay indoors. He did not do so, however, but continued his daily routine which included the inspection of march battalions about to leave the capital, often in temperatures of 23 degrees below zero. According to Mandt, the tsar's physician, 'the news of the reverses at Evpatoria stunned him and struck the final blow'. On 27 February Nicholas took to his bed, having instructed Alexander, the crown prince, to remove Menshikov from his appointment. The letter of dismissal, sent over Alexander's signature, read:

The Sovereign, whose health is not too good, has ordered me, my dear Prince, to answer, in his name, your despatch of 19 February. His Majesty was most grieved by the unsuccessful attack on Evpatoria undertaken by General Khrulev at your order, and by the considerable losses which our brave troops have suffered yet again – without any profit whatsoever. His Majesty could not be other than surprised that you let three months go by without attacking this point – at a time when its garrison was insignificant . . . but have waited till the present time when, according to all reports, there are considerable Turkish forces there under Omar Pasha. His Majesty cannot but remind you that he, unfortunately, foresaw this unhappy result.

By the morning of 2 March, Nicholas, the author of this dishonest letter, was dead.

* * *

By Nicholas's order, Menshikov was to leave the Crimea immediately. Osten-Saken, who, since 22 December, had been the Commander of Sevastopol, was to take over temporary command until the arrival of Prince M.D. Gorchakov, who would assume the command of the Army of the Crimea while still retaining the post of Commander of South Army in Bessarabia.

Menshikov was completely unfitted for any military command, diplomatic appointment or government post, and the fault was entirely Nicholas's
that he had employed this nobleman for more than 30 years without
discerning his lack of worth. Miliutin said of Menshikov:

> Of all the roles enacted by the most important actors in the bloody
> Sevastopol drama, the most contemptible was that played by Menshikov.
> Right from the beginning of the war he was distrusted both by his own
> troops and in St Petersburg. For his was a morbid character and a sick,
> disordered mind. In the end, the succession of testing failures shattered
> his energy and self-confidence. Although he was fully aware of his own
> incompetence, not once did he think of asking the tsar to replace him on
> the grounds of ill-health.

Yet the wording of Menshikov's dismissal was entirely unjustified for, as
Miliutin said, 'the tsar had pressed Menshikov to take advantage of the
enemy's disarray and to attack, and this was continually repeated in the
letters from the War Ministry which stressed the dangers in Menshikov's
rear'.

Menshikov's temporary successor, Osten-Saken, was 65 years of age and
was of a different stamp; he had said some very hard things about the worth
of many of the Russian generals 'for they did not, with a few exceptions,
match up to the officers and men'. In these opinions he was of course right,
although Tarle thought Osten-Saken to be in error in including himself
among the exceptions. Osten-Saken's presence went largely unnoticed by
the troops for he lived in a comfortable apartment in the Nikolaevsky
Battery away from the shelling and the bombing; he was rarely seen in the
bastions and then only in the quieter periods. A large part of his time was
occupied in study, in religious services, in discussions with the priests and
in writing eloquent and grandiose despatches and orders. Yet he was an
honest and a just man who never doubted the heroism of the defenders; he
valued Nakhimov, Istomin, Totleben and Vasil'chikov highly and he gave
them all the support of which he was capable.

Prince M.D. Gorchakov was a veteran of the Napoleonic, Persian,
Turkish and Polish Wars, and his fame rested on the energy he was said to
have shown at the time of the Hungarian capitulation at Vilagos. Whether
Gorchakov was an improvement on Menshikov as a Commander-in-Chief,
appears to have been a matter of opinion. One officer, writing at the end of
March, said 'Saken was rubbish (*drian*')' but not much was known about
Gorchakov except that Khlebnikov, who had served with him for two years,
said that we might yet regret the going of Menshikov'. Nikolai Vasil'evich

Berg said of Prince M.D. Gorchakov that he was an aristocrat who believed that all aristocrats of this world came from a better and more blessed mould than commoners. Tarle considered that Gorchakov was 'entirely unlike a Commander-in-Chief' for he was prematurely aged, absent-minded, muddle-headed and incoherent in thought and speech; his eyesight was so weak that he could not recognize many of the faces at his own table. But worst of all, like many of the court at the time, he talked, wrote and thought in French, so that his spoken Russian was poor and hardly under-standable by the men in the ranks; for this reason some regarded him as a joke. Others, however, thought that Gorchakov made a much better impres-sion than Menshikov. For as Pirogov said:

Menshikov sat hidden, silent, secretive as the grave, just watching the weather; and in the course of half a year he had tried to rescue the Russian Army by writing a few verses. Cold and merciless, he laughed only to mock, and if one complained to him about wants and privations he answered only that it must have been worse before! Gorchakov rarely appeared on the bastions, but when he did so he took the trouble to make himself agreeable, knowing of the dislike which everyone bore his predecessor.

After Inkerman the intensity of the allied bombardment of Sevastopol had slackened, except in the area of No. 4 Bastion, but as the winter changed to spring it resumed its former fury, the newly arrived enemy rocketry outranging the Russian guns. Nakhimov continued to be the breath of the defence. On 14 March he had been appointed deputy commander of the garrison and head of the port, and, on 8 April, he was promoted full admiral. But he still said quite openly that he had no faith in St Petersburg. His own quarters adjoined the naval hospital and he spent as much of his time there as he did in his bed. Much of his own personal salary was given to the sailors' families. Nakhimov had already chosen and dug his own grave, next to Kornilov's, on the St Vladimir mount.

On the morning of 19 March Istomin, the Commander of No. 4 Sector, was killed instantly by a shell when returning from the Kamchatka Lunette to the Malakhov. Nakhimov wrote that day to Konstantina Istomina, the dead man's spinster sister, sending her what was left of Istomin's orders and medals. Osten-Saken, in reporting the news to the capital, said that Nak-himov had given up his own burial plot to Istomin 'as he was the first to enter eternity'. From this time onwards Nakhimov became even more sombre and morose.

Prince M.D. Gorchakov had taken over his new command with confidence, but he, too, shortly began to lose heart, and he blamed Menshikov's costly foray at Inkerman for his own misfortunes; he hinted to Alexander that he might have to evacuate the south bank of Sevastopol. Gorchakov feared that he would be trapped south of the water and he ordered General Bukhmeier, his engineer-in-chief, to have a 1,000 yard long pontoon bridge constructed ready to link the town side with the Severnaia. Gorchakov, like Menshikov, feared to tell Nakhimov that he was thinking of giving up the south bank, but, because of the collection of pontoon material, the intention could no longer be concealed. Nakhimov was emphatic that he 'would not cross the bridge dead or alive'. Bogdanovich listened to the testimony of Captains (1st Rank) Kern and Voevodsky, and both were convinced that Nakhimov had no faith that the garrison would ever be relieved. But he was determined to stay in Sevastopol and he impressed on his naval subordinates that it was their duty to remain there whatever the outcome. Nobody in Sevastopol, except Nakhimov, wore gold epaulettes; in doing so he took a deadly risk.

*　*　*

The Russian troops in the Eastern Crimea were divided between Theodosia and Kerch. At Theodosia there was a static garrison consisting of 500 men, together with a 2,600 man strong mobile infantry column of sailors and Black Sea Cossacks, and an independent cavalry column of eight cavalry squadrons and 16 Cossack *sotni*, totalling a further 3,000 men and eight guns. The Kerch detachment consisted of another 2,600 sailors and Black Sea Cossacks. These 9,000 troops in the east of the Crimea were under Wrangel and formed part of the command of *General-Adiutant* Khomutov, whose headquarters was at Taman across the straits of Kerch. In fact Menshikov, and M.D. Gorchakov after him, frequently drew on the Theodosia-Kerch grouping for reinforcements.

The allies were suffering from cold and sickness, from divided counsels in the Crimea and in London and Paris, and from the heavy casualties of the Sevastopol siege. They sought, above all, an alternative operation which would bring them some relief and an earlier victory. It was therefore agreed that a force of 7,000 French, 5,000 Turks and 3,000 British should be landed in the bay of Kamish Borun near the Kerch peninsula, with the object of destroying the artillery installations covering the straits, thus allowing allied vessels to enter the Sea of Azov.

The disembarkation took place without opposition or incident at daybreak on 24 May, the allies intercepting a messenger from Gorchakov to Wrangel carrying orders to send all cavalry to Sevastopol immediately. Wrangel avoided giving battle but sent word to Gorchakov and to Khomutov, who happened at that time to be visiting Krasnov, the *ataman* of the Don Cossacks at his capital at Novocherkassk. M.D. Gorchakov believed that it was the allied intention to seize the Perekop either overland by way of the Arabat road, running over the causeway which marked the eastern confines of the Lazy Sea (the Sivash), or by naval landings from the Sea of Azov in the area of Genichesk. Such a stroke would have sealed off the Crimea from the remainder of the Russian Empire, and, if carried out with resolution and in strength, it might, thought Gorchakov, have ended the war. Gorchakov despatched Cossacks and infantry northwards to protect Genichesk and the Chongarsky bridge, while Khomutov returned post-haste to Taman, having first procured the assistance of the *ataman* of the Don Cossacks in sending detachments to the vulnerable points along the Sea of Azov. Wrangel began to withdraw his troops in front of the advancing allies and destroyed much of his coastal artillery.

On 25 May the allies had sounded and buoyed a channel through the straits into the Sea of Azov and the allied land forces reached the town of Kerch the next morning; a few hours later they had occupied the straits at Eni Karle. Having entered the hitherto closed Sea of Azov the allied vessels gave chase to the Russian naval squadron there, and this was beached and burned out. Thereafter, however, the allied operation degenerated into the raiding of towns and of fishing settlements on the Sea of Azov coast, the capture or burning of Russian merchant vessels and the sending of a small expedition to Anapa on the Black Sea coast. The allied troops remained virtually idle in the area until 19 October 1855 when they were withdrawn.

* * *

In June 1855 the Russian strength in Sevastopol stood at 78 battalions of infantry totalling 45,000 men, together with 9,000 naval gunners; in addition there were 39 battalions (21,000 men) and 100 field guns on the Mackenzie heights and on the Belbek. The army infantry strength within the Sevastopol garrison had been so increased that it had been thought necessary to attach a major-general to each of the defence sector headquarters. Lieutenant-General Khrulev had been sent to the Korabel'naia suburb to co-ordinate the operations of the 35 infantry battalions there.

The enemy forces in the area of the naval base were estimated by Russian sources to stand at 170,000 men; of these 100,000 were thought to be French, 45,000 British, 15,000 Sardinian and 10,000 Turkish.

The French Commander-in-Chief Pélissier had obtained permission to launch a major offensive on the Korabel'naia on 18 June, the fortieth anniversary of the day of Waterloo, using 44 French battalions (30,000 men) to attack the sector from No. 1 Bastion to the Malakhov; meanwhile the

British were to engage No. 3 Bastion and the Peresyp with a force of 14,000 men. The allied generals believed that the attack should be preceded by a two hour bombardment, but Pélissier insisted that, after a day long bombardment on 17 June, the Russian artillery would be in no state to interfere with allied operations. The French attack was set at 3 a.m., an hour before dawn, and the signal was to be given by the firing of three rockets from the site of the Lancaster Battery.

In the event, the offensive was poorly planned and executed, for many of the French battalions had not completed their preparations. And whereas the French parallels and trenches were only 70 yards from No. 4 Bastion and only 110 yards from the Shvarts Redoubt, the enemy infantry had to cross over 400 yards of open ground in front of the Malakhov and No. 3 Bastion and over 600 yards in front of No. 2 Bastion.

The French approach march to the Korabel'naia was detected just after 2 a.m. by the listening posts of the Briansky Regiment forward of No. 5 Sector, and these reported to the commander of No. 1 Bastion that there were large bodies of men in the Careening Ravine. Khrulev thereupon brought all troops in the Korabel'naia to combat readiness while Prince Urusov, with No. 5 Sector, sent fighting patrols out to engage the enemy. Knowing that they had been discovered, the French troops went into the attack against Nos 1 and 2 Bastions without waiting for the rocket signal. Since Pélissier had not even arrived at the Lancaster Battery by that time no action was taken to bring the other French or British troops into battle.

The attack on No. 1 Bastion was defeated by the fire of the musketry of the Kremenchugsky, artillery case-shot, and the guns of the steamers in the Careening Bay. No. 2 Bastion was successfully defended by the Vladimirsky. The Kornilov Bastion and the Zherve Battery came under heavy and repeated attacks, however, and the defending Poltavsky were driven off in disorder so that the guns of the Zherve Battery were captured by the French. Khrulev appeared on the scene shortly afterwards with a company of the Sevsky, and, rallying the Poltavsky, he led the troops back into the attack. By then the French had already occupied the huts on the side of the Khurgan and were turning the captured guns round. A further reinforcement of four battalions of the Eletsky, sent by Vasil'chikov, decided the issue and the French withdrew into the Dock Ravine. In this action the Sevsky company had lost 105 out of its total strength of 138 men.

The British attack was the last to develop – at some time after 3.30 a.m., but it continued after the French assaults had been repulsed. No. 3 Bastion was defended by the Briansky while the Peresyp was held by men of the Tomsky. The attackers in front of No. 3 Bastion were driven back at the first assault and they made off, 'leaving their scaling ladders and fascines behind them'; but they then returned and, closing in, began to break down the palisades until they were finally repulsed by the fire of the Briansky. According to Tarle, the British attacks were not pushed home with as much vigour as those of the French: Alabin, who was present in No. 3 Bastion, afterwards viewed the British dead and wounded and, according to him, 'none of the attackers would have got into the bastion anyway because they were not provided with ladders or fascines'. The British lack of success was severely criticized in the Paris press; many of the British blamed Raglan, their Commander-in-Chief, for the defeat.

By 6 a.m. the enemy had been repulsed everywhere and, except at the Peresyp, was already back in his trenches. The object of the offensive had been to storm the base and take it with the bayonet; but the allied attacks had made no headway, and the French had lost 3,553 and the British 1,728 men. The total Russian casualties were 3,950 over the two days of 17 and 18 June, the larger part during the bombardment of 17 June, for in close quarter fighting the Russian musket was in no way inferior to the British rifle. The calling off of the attacks left the allies subdued and the Sardinians demoralized. Raglan died shortly afterwards.

The spirits of the Russian defenders rose enormously. The success was notified to St Petersburg together with a note of caution that the position in the base remained grave because of the lack of numbers of defenders and of the shortage of powder. But the news delighted the new tsar. The Russian Army's success, for such it was, and its growing resolution and skill were noted elsewhere in Europe, and Prince Alexander Mikhailovich Gorchakov, the Russian Ambassador in Vienna, 'found that the attitude of the Austrian Foreign Affairs Minister had changed overnight'.

Vasil'chikov and Totleben, who had been seriously wounded in the engagement, received the George Order 3rd Class; Khrulev and Urusov were awarded the Order of St Vladimir 2nd Class; Vice-Admiral Panfilov received a sword set in diamonds; Buturlin and Semiakin were promoted; Osten-Saken and Nakhimov were granted an *arenda*, a supplementary increase of pay. When Nakhimov was told of the grant he is said to have replied that he wanted powder not an *arenda*. In the event, he had only three days left to spend it.

*   *   *

On the morning of 28 June Nakhimov rode out with two aides-de-camp to tour the defences. At No. 3 Bastion they found that the commander, a Lieutenant Victor, had been severely wounded, and Nakhimov sent one of his aides to fetch a replacement. Nakhimov then moved on together with

Lieutenant Koltovsky to No. 3 Sector, starting at the Nikonov Battery and then calling at Panfilov's dug-out to drink lemonade before inspecting No. 4 Sector and returning to No. 3 Bastion, where the fire was said to be heavy once more. His aide subsequently recounted:

> Bombs, shells and bullets were falling around, but Nakhimov strode on quite dauntless. He was that day positively cheerful, contrary to his usual glum demeanour, and he was kind enough to tell me 'how pleasant it was to have a good fellow with you'. 'Whether or not one is going to be hit', he continued, 'is God's will, but not to brave the fire would show a weakness of character. One should always be ready for death and meet it calmly when it comes, for only a coward fears death'. For him this was eloquence, and he then lapsed into his customary silence.

When they arrived back at No. 3 Bastion, Nakhimov met Panfilov once again, and together they sat on a bench talking to the many officers who stood around. Suddenly came the sentry's warning shout of 'Bomba!', and all flung themselves under cover except Nakhimov, who continued to sit hunched upon the bench. He then rose, called for his horse, and rode off to the Kornilov Bastion.

Dismounting at the Kornilov, Nakhimov thanked the sailors and soldiers for their valiant efforts in refortifying the bastion, and said that he wanted to inspect the fire-step at the top of the bastion. The sector commander and his staff tried to dissuade him but he ignored their protests. When Nakhimov arrived at the fire-step, Captain Kern told the admiral that a religious service was being held within the bastion in honour of the Saints Peter and Paul (Nakhimov's name) and asked whether they should attend. Nakhimov replied gruffly, 'I am not stopping you!'. Taking a telescope from a sentinel, he got up on the fire-step and began to view the French battery below.

> Immediately a bullet struck the sandbag at his elbow. Nakhimov took no notice, merely remarking: 'Their shooting is pretty good today'. A moment afterwards there was a second shot, and the admiral fell as if pole-axed. The bullet had hit him in the face, passing out of the back of his head.

Nakhimov was removed, still living, and carried to his quarters where he lay unconscious for two days.

A visitor on the morning of 30 June has left this account:

> Coming into the room where the admiral was lying, I found the doctors there together with the Prussian physician-in-ordinary . . . Nakhimov

was quite still, breathing steadily, and from time to time his eyes were open. But at about eleven o'clock the breathing became laboured; elsewhere in the room there was absolute silence. The doctors went over to the bed and Sokolov, who probably did not realise that Voevodsky, who was present, was Nakhimov's nephew, said loudly and distinctly, 'Death is near!'. Several minutes later Pavel Stepanovich began to sink. For the first time he actually moved and his breathing became quieter. But then, after several deep sighs, he moved once more and groaned; there was a convulsive movement and several more sighs and then, without anyone actually knowing when it had happened, he was breathing no longer. The silence was broken by Sokolov who said, 'He is dead!'. And so, at seven minutes after eleven that morning, died the Hero of Navarino, Sinope and Sevastopol, a warrior without fear or reproach, at the end of a glorious career.*

A Sevastopol nursing sister has described Nakhimov's lying in state, surrounded by his many orders and covered by the flag he had flown at Sinope; and the crowds of visiting sailors who were given leave of absence from the bastions and the trenches. The day of the funeral was dark and still, for the very enemy ceased all action and lined their epaulements to watch the great funeral cortège passing by below.

I cannot find words to describe to you the saddening impression made by his funeral. Below was the sea and the great enemy fleet; above, the hills and the bastions where Nakhimov had spent all his hours, and these said more than words can express; and the threatening batteries from which the enemy could view and fire on the funeral procession. But even their guns were respectfully silent and not one round was fired against us during the service. Over the whole scene, and particularly over the sea, hung dark lowering storm clouds . . . the doleful dead march of the bands, the tolling of the bells, and the sad solemnity of the choirs. In this way the sailors buried their hero of Sinope, and Sevastopol interred its own fearless and heroic defender.

So Nakhimov, the last of the trio, was buried on the St Vladimir Hill, next to Kornilov and Istomin.

---

* *Kronshstadskii Vestnik*, 1868, No. 17.

CHAPTER 9

* * * * *

FINAL DEFEAT BEFORE SEVASTOPOL

Although for the first few months of his reign the new tsar, Alexander II, made a pretence of following in his father's footsteps both in diplomacy and in the prosecution of hostilities, in reality he remained firmly opposed to the war. Nor did he believe in holding on to Sevastopol to the very end; the successful defence of 18 June did not change his mind in this, delighted though he was with the outcome, for the daily Russian casualties began to mount again in the fury of the renewed bombardments. Alexander wanted to get out of the war as quickly and as cheaply as possible, and was determined to stake all in a final battle which, he hoped, might inflict such a reverse on the allies that they would be pleased to come to terms with him. The strategic aim of such a battle would be to force the enemy off the Sapun plateau and so raise the siege of Sevastopol.

The Commander-in-Chief of the Crimea, however, regarded the whole position as hopeless. On 8 July he had written to the War Minister:

If I were to attack the enemy . . . I would be smashed by the third day with a loss of between 10,000–15,000 men. On the fourth day Sevastopol would be lost. But, if I do not attack, the enemy will take Sevastopol anyway in the course of the next few months, and your obedient servant will be back between Perekop and the Dnieper.

Prince M.D. Gorchakov was unwilling to risk his reputation in an attack on well fortified positions occupied by an enemy superior in numbers and armament. Alexander, however, continued to press for offensive action and the weak and vacillating Gorchakov was unfitted by nature to refuse his demands.

In the St Petersburg court the tsar had a trusted military confidant, *General-Adiutant* Baron Pavel Alexandrovich Vrevsky, one of those who had made his army career in the corridors of the Winter Palace. Since Vrevsky saw the virtue of the tsar's proposals, Alexander despatched him to Gorchakov's headquarters in order to bring influence to bear on the Commander-in-Chief and his staff. Officially Vrevsky was held on the strength of the War Ministry and detached to the Crimea only for liaison duty, but Vrevsky represented himself as being sent with the special mission of interpreting the sovereign's intentions and thoughts, as, in reality, he was. But, by extension, Vrevsky built himself up as being authorized to comment upon the highest plans, so that he was soon acknowledged to be Gorchakov's guide and mentor. Yet Tarle considered, probably rightly, that Vrevsky could not be dismissed as a careerist; he was more the court parrot, repeating what Alexander had said; and there is no reason to suppose that Vrevsky did not honestly and wholeheartedly agree with the views he expressed, and this, of course, gave him eloquence and sincerity.

Meanwhile Alexander kept up a relentless pressure on Gorchakov. On 30 July he wrote to the Crimea that he had heard from Brussels that the French were about to send another 24,000 men to the theatre, and he warned his Commander-in-Chief that the allies might move directly on Perekop. The tsar continued:

> *I am convinced of the necessity that we should attack; otherwise all the reinforcements recently sent to you, as has happened in the past, will be sucked into Sevastopol, that bottomless pit* [the tsar's italics]. According to information received by me, the allies will storm the base by land and by sea during mid August. Therefore it is much to be desired that, with the arrival of 4 and 5 Infantry Divisions, you will not delay undertaking decisive operations. You cannot avoid significant losses, but, with God's help, you may achieve a momentous result.*

Yet the tsar did not actually bind Gorchakov to any particular course, for all his missives were framed and worded in such a way that the final choice – and the personal responsibility – was Gorchakov's. Alexander continued:

> These are my thoughts which I reveal to you with my customary frankness in order that you should execute them if you should consider them to be possible either now or later, i.e. after the arrival of the *opolchenie*.

For such was the shortage of Russian military manpower that the Kursk *opolchenie*, the equivalent of the citizen home guard, had been embodied and was on its way to the front.

Four days earlier Gorchakov had bent so far to his sovereign's will that he wrote him a letter saying that he was 'preparing an offensive to be mounted after 4, 5 and 7 Reserve Infantry Divisions had arrived [these

* *Russkaia Starina*, T. XXXIX, 1883, p. 207.

were due about 1 August]', but that he would 'only attack if it were absolutely necessary to do so, for failure in battle would involve the fall of Sevastopol'. Gorchakov considered that it would be impossible to attack the enemy on the Sapun plateau and that the offensive must be limited to the destruction of that part of the allied force on the left bank of the Chernaia Rechka stream on the nearby Fediukhin and Gasfort (Hasfort) heights. But Gorchakov could see little advantage to be gained in doing this except that the occupation of these heights 'would threaten the enemy's watering places' and, so the Commander-in-Chief believed, 'constitute a threat on the enemy flank so that he could not attack Sevastopol – and maybe open the way for further advantageous operations'. Gorchakov ended his letter with the devastating admission: 'But one should not deceive oneself, for there is little hope of success in such an attack'.

Gorchakov wrote several times in this vein, expressing 'weighty reservations' and pointing out the many dangers, but he could not bring himself to refuse to attack. Alexander, however, was determined not to understand, and he wrote on 3 August:

> Your daily losses inside Sevastopol [about 250 men] emphasize what I have told you many times before in my letters – *the necessity to do something decisive in order to bring this frightful massacre to a close* [the tsar's italics].

Alexander well understood Gorchakov's character and limitations, and he knew that this military courtier, who all his life had stood in such awe of Nicholas and Paskevich, wanted to retain his appointment without its responsibilities. Alexander concluded:

> I want a battle, but if you as Commander-in-Chief fear the liability, then convene a military council to take it for you.

Gorchakov thought this to be his salvation, but, before convening a military council, he turned to Osten-Saken for an opinion. Osten-Saken's qualities as a military leader may not have been of a high order, but he was honest and his conduct was ruled by his conscience. He had been much affected by the death of Nakhimov and had become convinced that the continued defence of the besieged base was no way out of Russia's difficulties. Osten-Saken was appalled that Gorchakov should undertake an offensive merely because of 'a mistaken appreciation by the tsar'; he considered an offensive on the Fediukhin to be an absurd idea, and told Gorchakov so, 'for the enemy held the dominating ground and during the last ten months had lost no time in fortifying it'.

On 9 August the military council met in Osten-Saken's quarters under Gorchakov's chairmanship. The questions on which the vote was to be taken were tabled in the following form:

> The urgent matter to be decided is that of the future operations in the Crimea. Should the passive defence be continued, playing only for time without having any object in view? Or should the Crimean Army go rapidly over to the offensive when 2 Corps and the Kursk *opolchenie* have arrived? If we are not to remain on the defensive then what form is the attack to take, and when?

The individual members of the council were told to prepare their own views in writing and reconvene on the morrow with their papers to cast their votes.

The next day the papers were read and the votes taken. Vrevsky was present throughout. Osten-Saken maintained his earlier opinion against an offensive and, in view of the 65,000 casualties already suffered in Sevastopol, pressed for an evacuation of the south bank of the naval base. This irritated Gorchakov who interjected 'I will not give it up!'. But when Osten-Saken rounded on him with the words: 'Why should your Highness get angry with me? You did, after all, ask for an opinion, and an opinion must be honestly given', Gorchakov 'cooled down immediately'. Osten-Saken, Novosil'sky, Semiakin and Ushakov were against an offensive; Liprandi, Khrulev, Kotsebu, Buturlin, Bukhmeier and Serzhputovsky were in favour of some form of attack, but their papers were hedged in doubts and provisos with no common pattern of recommendation.* For, as Suponev said, all the generals knew that an attack into the enemy's rear must be a dangerous undertaking and that the Fediukhin was strongly held, that the banks of the Chernaia were boggy and that the Russian artillery was generally of too small a calibre to engage the enemy long-range guns.† After the closing of the meeting Vasil'chikov said to Osten-Saken:

> *J'admire votre abnegation, je voulais dire la même chose, mais le courage me manquait.*

Gorchakov, as Tarle said, 'with the tsar's letters in his pocket and Vrevsky by his side', had got the majority vote in favour of an offensive, a decision which he regarded with foreboding. He had produced not a single argument to refute Osten-Saken's objections. The Commander-in-Chief decided that the offensive should be made on 16 August across the Chernaia Rechka

* Bogdanovich, *Vostochnaia Voina*, Vol. 4, *Prilozheniia*, pp. 1–22.
† *Russkii Arkhiv*, 1893, T. III, p. 261.

on the Fediukhin and Gasfort heights, near the end of the North Valley along which the British light brigade had made its celebrated charge nearly nine months before. Both of these heights were far removed from each other and from the Sapun plateau.

On 14 August, only two days before the offensive, Gorchakov, together with Vrevsky and Kotsebu, the Chief of Staff to the Crimean Army, visited the wounded Totleben in a Belbek hospital to hear his views on the intended operation. Totleben spoke strongly against such an offensive for he doubted whether the Fediukhin would be taken and could not in any case discern an underlying strategic aim; he reasoned that the loss of the Fediukhin by the enemy was hardly likely to cause the raising of the siege from the Sapun. Gorchakov was much affected by what Totleben said and, thrown once more into doubt and confusion, was ready to cancel the operation. Vrevsky, however, in an extraordinary outburst of anger, told the military engineer that 'he alone bore the responsibility of trying to dissuade the Commander-in-Chief from an undertaking which had already been agreed by the military council'. Gorchakov, still wavering, told Totleben that he intended to postpone the attack. But on returning to his headquarters, Gorchakov again came under the influence of Vrevsky, Buturlin and others who had no field command or responsibility. The new offensive was therefore confirmed for first light on 16 August.

On the eve of the offensive Gorchakov wrote a last letter to Dolgoruki, beginning – for he wrote indifferent French as well as speaking poor Russian:

> *Je marche à l'ennemi parceque si je ne le fesait point, Sévastopol serait tout de même perdu dans un tems très court.*

He listed all his difficulties, emphasizing the strength of the enemy position and that he was outnumbered by 60,000 to 43,000; he had, he thought, little hope of success. If he failed, he would 'try to evacuate Sevastopol with as little loss as possible. But he reiterated that if matters turned out badly it was not his fault (*il n'en y a pas de ma faute*), for the whole Crimean situation had been too difficult for him. Rarely can a Commander-in-Chief have attacked with so little confidence in the outcome of his undertaking.

* * *

Although the Fediukhin heights appeared in the distance as a single mass, it was in fact three close lying features separated by steep ravines, with the Sapun plateau and escarpment about 1,000 yards or more to its rear. Its steep front, facing north-east, was covered by the Chernaia Rechka stream flowing close to the foothills, and by a broad aqueduct which ran parallel to the little river, about 100 yards behind it. The river was up to 25 feet in width and from two to six feet in depth, and in places was edged by marsh. The canal was a more formidable obstacle to infantry because of its depth and because it was bounded by vertical masonry sides. The main road from Sevastopol was led over the river by a stone bridge at the *traktir*, and continued over the aqueduct by a wooden bridge on its way to Balaclava, crossing the south-east part of the Fediukhin heights by a narrow pass in a deep gorge.

The Fediukhin heights were held by about 18,000 French troops with 48 guns, all under the overall command of Herbillon. Faucheux's division was deployed on the right, on both sides of the main road which cut through the Fediukhin by way of the gorge. Camou's division was in the centre and on the left; Herbillon's own division was in reserve at the rear. In addition the French held a small bridgehead forward of the river beyond the *traktir*, entrenched and protected by earthworks, and these were covered in their turn by the fire from two epaulements behind the river. The greater part of the French artillery had been positioned on the mountain, covered by riflemen sited in tiers high up on the hillside.

The Gasfort feature, also on the south side of the Chernaia Rechka, was about 2,000 yards upstream from the Fediukhin and formed an outcrop of a mountain range unconnected with the Fediukhin or the Sapun plateau. Its steep face fronted on the Chernaia Rechka and on the aqueduct source and junction where the waters were diverted from the river, and both of these were crossed by small wooden bridges. Immediately forward and to the north of the river was a solitary hill – the Telegraph Hill – one of many of that name in the Crimea. The Gasfort Hill was held by 9,000 Sardinians with 36 guns, with an infantry and artillery detachment forward of the river on the Telegraph Hill. The Gasfort feature was nearly three miles distant from the Sapun escarpment.

Although the allies had only 27,000 troops in the forward positions, there were substantial forces in reserve: Morris's 20 cavalry squadrons were picquetted between the Fediukhin and Gasfort; Scarlett's 30 squadrons stood at Kadikioi; d'Allonville's 20 squadrons, two battalions and 12 guns held the Baidar Valley; and Osman-Pasha's 10,000 Turkish infantry and 36 guns were stationed at Komary. By including these reserves, the Russians estimated the enemy strength in the area at 40,000 men and 120 guns, a figure which could be further increased, by the movement of troops from the Sapun, to 60,000 men– the number quoted by Gorchakov to the War Ministry.

While Gorchakov had been awaiting the arrival of 4, 5 and 7 Reserve

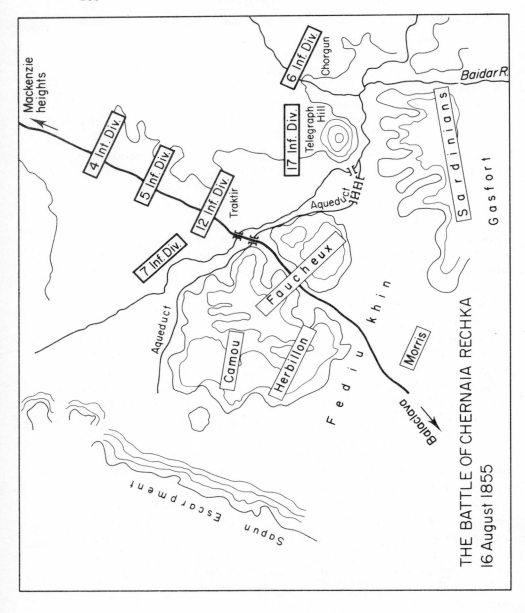

THE BATTLE OF CHERNAIA RECHKA
16 August 1855

Infantry Divisions from 2 Corps, he had begun to concentrate his field force on the Mackenzie heights and reconnoitre the approaches to the Fediukhin. This activity was well known to Herbillon, whose own scouts had told him that the Russians were busily engaged in constructing portable infantry and artillery bridges suitable for crossing canals and small rivers. But the Russian preparations had appeared so obvious that Herbillon was inclined the treat the implications with reserve. The Russians for their part knew that Herbillon was aware of this activity and what it might portend, for a line-crosser arriving in the Mackenzie camp on 14 August said that the French 'were expecting an attack to be made on them across the Chernaia Rechka'.

Gorchakov had not come to a decision as to whether he should make his main effort against the Fediukhin or against the Gasfort and what he was to do thereafter, and he went into battle on 16 August still in this unhappy state of mind. Gorchakov intended to take the field as the tactical commander, but, instead of a plan of battle, he produced only a long written movement order which was to convey his force into close contact with the enemy. On the right, *General-Adiutant* Read, the Commander of 3 Corps, was to advance with Ushakov's 7 and Martinau's 12 Infantry Divisions to the area of the *traktir* bridge, 'engage the Fediukhin by artillery fire and prepare to cross the river'. *Before* crossing, General Read was 'to await the orders of the Commander-in-Chief'. In the centre, Liprandi, commanding 6 Corps, was to move Veselitsky's 17 Infantry Division and clear the enemy from Telegraph Hill, *but he was to await the Commander-in-Chief's orders* before attacking the Gasfort on the other side of the river. Liprandi's left hand column, formed by Bel'gard's 6 Infantry Division, was to go to Chorgun, but its purpose was not clear except that it had to engage the Telegraph Hill, the Chorgun Valley and the Gasfort by artillery fire and *await the order of the Commander-in-Chief before attacking the Gasfort.* Following behind the two leading corps, came the main infantry reserve under Shepelev, with his own 4 Infantry Division and Vranken's 5 Infantry Division, the artillery and the cavalry reserves. Gorchakov's force totalled 47,000 infantry, 10,000 cavalry, 224 field and 48 horse artillery guns.

Gorchakov said afterwards that he was hoping that the preliminary artillery bombardment might serve to uncover the enemy's dispositions and intentions, enabling him to decide whether to direct his two infantry divisions in reserve against the Fediukhin or the Gasfort. So it came about that neither Gorchakov nor his subordinate corps commanders had any idea of the action which was to be taken as soon as they reached the river.

On the evening of 15 August Herbillon was warned of the approach of

Russian troops towards the main road and the *traktir* bridge across the Chernaia. The message, which was sent from d'Allonville, commanding the cavalry division on the extreme right in the valley of the Baidar, was transmitted by semaphore and the failing light prevented the whole of the message from being received. Herbillon, however, had received sufficient warning, except that such messages were the commonplace and, in fact, rarely signified an attack. However that may be, the French and Sardinian troops were already aware of the Russian movement at sundown on the eve of battle.

The Russian movement took place as planned, but when Gorchakov arrived in the field in the early hours of the morning of 16 August there was silence everywhere. Gorchakov ordered his aide, a Lieutenant Krasovsky, to hurry out to Generals Liprandi and Read and tell them it was 'past time to start (*pora nachinat*')'. Liprandi opened fire with his artillery shortly afterwards in accordance with the written orders issued by Gorchakov before the action; when Read heard Liprandi's cannon on his left, he ordered his own artillery to begin the preliminary bombardment against the Fediukhin. Soon afterwards, Gageman, the chief of artillery in 3 Corps, reported to Read that the fire was ineffective since the target was out of range and the shells were bursting at the foot of the mountain. The order was given to cease fire, and Veimarn, the 3 Corps chief of staff, went back to the artillery positions with Gageman. Krasovsky then arrived at the gallop with Gorchakov's verbal message that it was 'past time to start'. Read, having pondered on these words, asked the obvious question: 'Time to start what?' Krasovsky did not know, for such was the lack of training and experience of this aide-de-camp, that he could merely repeat Gorchakov's exact words. Read considered further and reasoned aloud: 'It cannot mean to open artillery fire because we have already done so. Does it mean to attack?'. Krasovsky did not know. 'Right!', concluded Read, 'Go back and tell the prince that I will attack now and that I would like him to send me further formations'. This is one witness's version of the conversation, and it is borne out by Read's subsequent action and dialogue. Read himself was killed. It was widely believed that Gorchakov or Krasovsky lied when afterwards they gave their accounts of this chain of misunderstanding and error.*

When Veimarn returned from the artillery lines he was concerned to find Read giving out orders for the crossing of the Chernaia Rechka and the

---

* Gorchakov, *Russkaia Starina*, T. XVI, p. 166; Bogdanovich, *Vostochnaia Voina*, Vol. 4, pp. 29–30; Tarle, *Krymskaia Voina*, Vol. 2, p. 348.

storming of the Fediukhin; he remonstrated with his chief, urging him to await the arrival of the flanking cavalry and reinforcement divisions with the infantry reserve. But Read replied, excitedly, *'Général, il faut attaquer! Je ne puis pas attendre, j'ai l'ordre du prince'*. What happened when Krasovsky returned to Gorchakov is uncertain but, according to one account, that unhappy young officer tried to report his fears and doubts regarding Read's intentions, only to be brusquely silenced by the Commander-in-Chief who retorted that 'General Read knows exactly what he has to do'.

Gorchakov then rode out to Liprandi, where, encouraged by the ease with which the Sardinian outposts had been driven off Telegraph Hill, he conferred with Kotsebu and decided that he would make his main attack on Liprandi's left flank. Gallopers were sent back to bring up Vranken's 5 Infantry Division to Telegraph Hill.

At some little time afterwards Gorchakov was surprised when musketry fire could be heard from Read's flank in front of the Fediukhin. Then Read's aide, Volkov, arrived saying that Read had already crossed the river and was asking urgently for reinforcements. Gorchakov decided that he must throw his main effort in on the right and not the left, and Men'kov was sent hastening off to halt Vranken's division and reroute it to the *traktir*. When Gorchakov realized that he was about to attack in two places, with 5 Infantry Division marching to and fro and not knowing where to go, he knew, or so he said afterwards, that the battle was already lost (*dès ce moment je vis que l'affaire était gatée*).

Meanwhile all was far from well on the right flank. Read had deployed Martinau's 12 Infantry Division astride the road against the enemy *traktir* bridgehead. Further to the right, downstream, Ushakov's 7 Infantry Division had reached the edge of the water while the Elisavetgradsky Uhlans and 37 Don Cossack Regiment had yet to come up to cover the far right wing. Read was occupied giving out his instructions to 12 Infantry Division; but his order to 7 Infantry Division, sent by a mounted aide, had again consisted of that one word made so infamous on that day: 'To begin! (*nachinat'*)'. Ushakov said that he was at a loss what to do. He feared that it must mean to attack, but his own bridging equipment had not yet arrived and he well knew that 4 and 5 Infantry Divisions were still on the Mackenzie heights. Ushakov sent back to Read for more precise instructions. He chanced to meet Major-General Grotenfel'd, the chief of operations of 3 Corps, but he, too, said that the significance of *nachinat'* was completely unknown to him.

Then came the sound of heavy musketry firing from the 12 Infantry Division sector in the area of the *traktir*, and Ushakov felt that he could delay no longer. The Mogilevsky, Vitebsky and Polotsky, 12 battalions in all, were hurried across the river and canal as best they might, while the Smolensky were left on the right bank to protect the guns. Because the artillery bridges were still on the road from the Mackenzie heights, Ushakov's columns advanced through the mist without artillery support to what was to be certain destruction. The mist may have been their undoing, for they came to close quarters before the artillery and riflemen of Camou's division opened up their murderous fire. Ushakov lost over 2,000 men in less than 20 minutes to case-shot, bullet and bayonet, and his broken division streamed back across the water, many of the men not stopping in their flight until they had arrived back at the Mackenzie heights.

Meanwhile Read had directed Martinau's 12 Infantry Division, consisting of the Odessky, Ukrainsky and Azovsky, over the water in the area of the *traktir*. The bridgehead close guard was driven off and bridging materials were brought up to the water's edge under the cover of the mist. The river and canal were soon crossed and the men reformed into close columns, which came on in good style in spite of the heavy enemy fire. The Odessky even claimed to have taken a French battery, but, whatever the gains, they could not be held. Skiuderi and 400 Odessky men lay dead and the regiment, fiercely counter-attacked with the bayonet, fell back over the river. The Azovsky had been similarly repulsed on the east side of the Fediukhin. Martinau's men might have been broken had not the clearance of the mists enabled Kishinsky to support them by artillery fire from the distant slopes of Telegraph Hill.

By 7.30 a.m. 7 and 12 Infantry Divisions had been defeated and the enemy was back in control of the left bank of the river. Liprandi had not moved from Telegraph Hill. The battle appeared to have ended. But since Gorchakov had not used any of his second line, for 5 Infantry Division had not yet even come up to the river, he determined to renew the attack at the *traktir* as soon as the reserve formations should arrive.

The Commander of 5 Infantry Division, Vranken, a Caucasian, intended to commit the whole of his division to the attack; in doing this he was of course reinforcing defeat, and why he should succeed when Martinau had failed is not clear. Read, however, vetoed even this proposal and made the most surprising decision to attack the mountain using a single regiment. Vranken selected the Kostromsky for this task, but covered its front by a battalion of the Galitsky in company columns and by all the divisional riflemen thrown out as a skirmisher line. When the Kostromsky close columns began their march with colours flying and drums beating, ready to face the hail of case-shot, Read suddenly changed his mind and had the regiment halted; he ordered the company columns of the Galitsky to go on alone. The companies crossed the water and reached the foot of the hill before they were driven back. The Kostromsky battalion columns meanwhile stood waiting, within range of the enemy artillery, losing men all the time. Seeing that the Galitsky had failed, Read ordered the Kostromsky to continue its interrupted march. Vranken was already wounded and his replacement, Veimarn, the corps chief of staff, marching with the Kostromsky, was shortly afterwards killed. Stolypin, his aide-de-camp, tried to get three soldiers of the Kostromsky to help him lift the body back, but they would not leave their ranks and strode on, saying that their duty lay to the regiment. The Kostromsky men advanced steadily, the majority to their deaths, for the French were by then entirely confident in their ability to counter the Russian close column, and they held their fire until the enemy were close at hand before opening the deadly salvo of guns and rifles. Within minutes half of the Kostromsky had fallen. Read appears to have lost all judgement, for he instructed Kuzmin, the operations officer of 5 Infantry Division, to order the Galitsky to renew the attack.

There could have been few sadder sights than the remnants of that once proud regiment advancing yet again in column towards the Fediukhin. It had already lost its regimental and battalion commanders and large numbers of officers and men. Its sole remaining field officer, a Major Chertov, who had been injured earlier that day in a fall when his horse had been shot down, limped along, a diminutive and elderly figure, at the head of the regiment. Its advance was repulsed, and, if it had not been cloaked from the enemy by mist and smoke, few would have made their way back again.

A peremptory order from Gorchakov put an end to Read's bungling. 5 Infantry Division was ordered back into the attack using all of its four regiments, the Galitsky, Kostromsky and the Arkhangelogorodsky, with the Vologodsky at their head. The French were again driven off the *traktir* bridge, the water was crossed and the division approached the heights moving in three great columns towards the gorge south of the bridge. By then, however, the mists had cleared once more and the French artillery began its deadly work. In 5 Infantry Division alone, the divisional commander, both brigade commanders, the four regimental commanders, nine battalion commanders and over 100 officers became casualties. The division fell back and the French, following up, recrossed the river.

Read had already been killed by a shell splinter and, at about 8 a.m., Gorchakov appeared near the bridge to take over the command of the corps. The enemy fire was so intense that the Commander-in-Chief told the remaining members of his staff to disperse; only Vrevsky and Kotsebu stayed with him. Gorchakov decided to continue the attacks and, as 4 Infantry Division was still far away, he called on Liprandi to move eight battalions of 17 Infantry Division over from Telegraph Hill to attack the eastern end of the Fediukhin. The battalions, commanded by Gribbe, moved down the Chernaia Valley, already under enemy fire, crossing the water by a ford, the Butyrsky in front of the Moskovsky, until its men began to fall in the cross-fire from the Fediukhin and the Gasfort. The Moskovsky then took the lead until driven back by the bayonets of the French and the fire of the Sardinians who had been moved over from the Gasfort to protect the open flank. Gribbe and the Butyrsky regimental commander, and nearly all the battalion commanders, were wounded. The troops fell back to Telegraph Hill, covered by the Borodinsky.

Vrevsky was already dead, killed by a shell. According to Tarle, it was 'as if Gorchakov was waiting for this', for at 10 a.m. he ordered the chief of the Kursk *opolchenie* to return to the Mackenzie heights. Then there followed a general withdrawal from the river, the left flank only remaining at Telegraph Hill. The dead and many of the wounded were left behind. The Russian field army remained in this intermediate position for four hours while it tried to reorganize, hoping, Gorchakov afterwards said to the tsar with a touch of bravado, 'that the enemy would follow up and attack'. Then, 'since there was no water', the troops withdrew to the Mackenzie heights.

The allies, mainly the French, lost 1,800 men on the Chernaia Rechka in dead and wounded. Gorchakov lost 2,273 dead, 1,742 missing, and a few short of 4,000 wounded, in all 8,000 men. In terms of casualties it was, with the exception of Inkerman, the most costly battle of the war.

Gorchakov, writing to Dolgoruki the next day, said that he had proposed 'to move Read's infantry divisions over to support [the main attack of] Liprandi, leaving only 3 Corps artillery deployed against the Fediukhin, . . . but then suddenly, for no known reason, Read moved his divisions against the Fediukhin'. He thus put the entire blame for the defeat on the dead Read. To the tsar Gorchakov wrote, that same day, on 17 August:

You will know from yesterday's despatch that our attack had no success. I did not count on success but I did not reckon on such heavy losses . . . it is grievous to think that if Read had carried out my orders to the letter we might have ended with something like success and that at least a third of those brave warriors who are now dead might have been alive today. . . . The enemy has not attacked me on the Mackenzie heights though I would be very pleased if he would do so. But the renewal of the terrible bombardment will soon force us to evacuate Sevastopol.

Alexander, however, thought otherwise. He who had once told Gorchakov that he must be prepared for 'significant losses' replied: 'Our glorious troops have had enormous losses, *without any gain* (the tsar's italics)'. Alexander was still waiting for the success which could take him to the peace table. Although he wanted to end the war he did not intend to do so on terms damaging to Russia. Suddenly, he showed himself to be entirely unwilling to evacuate Sevastopol. He continued:

I hope that the bombardment will lessen and that if there is another enemy storming it may be beaten off. The evacuation of the south bank would in any event be a grave undertaking.

Both Alexander and Gorchakov bore a terrible responsibility for this needless slaughter. Alexander for insisting on an offensive when no offensive action was possible; Gorchakov for failing to withstand the tsar's pressure and for going into battle without concerting a plan or giving out any orders. For when Stolypin, the aide to General Veimarn, asked his chief for an explanation of Gorchakov's intentions, Veimarn was unable to give it. Veimarn believed that 'even if we take the Fediukhin, we will be unable to hold it and will have to withdraw by nightfall'; the chief of staff could only conclude that the general aim was to take the enemy's attention away from Sevastopol.

Gorchakov had committed first 12, then 7, then 5 and finally 17 Infantry Divisions throwing the formations in piecemeal; much of Liprandi's force, the many reserves and the cavalry saw no action at all that day. Once Gorchakov had committed troops to battle he seemed to forget about them for hours at a time, leaving them without support and without orders. Read was no better, for his judgement and command ability were seriously at fault in that he interfered with his subordinate commanders in the exercise of their duties; by his express orders, single battalions were sent into battle.

Paskevich, who had himself showed a lack of moral courage in his relationship with Nicholas, dictated from his deathbed a bitter letter to Prince M.D. Gorchakov. Paskevich accused Gorchakov of cowardice in failing to counter the tsar's wish to give battle, so becoming responsible for the destruction of thousands of men (Paskevich put the true loss at nearer 10,000). Paskevich called Gorchakov's plan 'castles in the air (*delom nesbytochnom*)', and said that Gorchakov had gone bull-headed, almost 'on the off-chance', to attack positions which he himself had admitted to be stronger than those of Sevastopol. In summarizing the battle, Paskevich 'arrived at the sad conclusion that it was without aim, without calculation, without necessity, and worst of all, finally eliminated the possibility of attacking anything thereafter'.

Gorchakov replied, excusing himself as best he might, 'that the offensive was in accordance with the sovereign's opinion and therefore was necessary as an expression of the common Russian view'. This angered Paskevich to retort that it was unpardonable for the Commander-in-Chief to blame the tsar or Read 'since the brave Read and Veimarn could not answer from the grave'. The sovereign, having sent Gorchakov the whole of the Russian Army with the exception of 1 Corps and the guard, had a right to demand that some action be taken; and Gorchakov 'could have told the sovereign that he should replace him as Commander-in-Chief, and then he would not have had the blood of 10,000 men on his conscience'. Paskevich concluded:

> Finally I must add that you have written your despatches with an eye to future historians, confident that no one would challenge what you have said and that, in the course of time, everything written by you would be accepted as historical fact. It is a misfortune that cunning of this nature often succeeds in Russia.

The papers taken by the French from General Read's body indicated that the Russians were desperate for any success, however small. The allies took heart accordingly, for they reckoned that the end could not be far away.

*　*　*

On 26 August Prince M.D. Gorchakov wrote to the tsar, once again echoing the sovereign's wishes rather than stating his own opinions:

> I have decided not to evacuate the [Sevastopol] south bank but will continue to put up a determined defence until I am sure that we can no longer withstand the attacks.

The Commander-in-Chief concluded on an inconsequential note, hoping that he could beat the enemy off and force the allies to give up their attacks. But neither Gorchakov nor Alexander really believed this, for, according to Tiutcheva's diary, the tsar and the tsarina and the Winter Palace court were filled with the deepest anxiety. Yet Alexander had begun to show himself as obstinate as his father, for he was determined that he would not talk of peace until he had a victory to Russia's credit. The loss of Sevastopol would not, he thought, end the war. He was already calling up the *opolchenie* in Central Russia and he told Gorchakov to prepare for a winter war.

Information had been received in the capital from diplomatic circles in Berlin and Brussels that the enemy offensive would be renewed at the end of August.

Totleben had said that the Malakhov Kurgan was the key to the defence of the Korabel'naia, and therefore of Sevastopol; and, although Totleben was not entirely happy about the layout of the Kurgan defences because of earlier differences of opinion between himself and Istomin, the military engineer believed that the Kornilov Bastion and the Malakhov were still very formidable, in spite of the loss to the enemy on 7 June of some of the covering works, the Selenginsky and the Volynsky Redoubts and the Kamchatka Lunette.

On 17 August, the day after the Chernaia Rechka battle, the artillery bombardment against Sevastopol was renewed in all its fury, and it continued almost without cease over the next three weeks. The allies were reckoned to have 800 guns and 300 mortars, a total of 1,100 against the defenders' 1,200 pieces; but in calibre and range the Russian artillery was inferior. Sevastopol still suffered from a grave shortage of shells and powder, and all artillery had been put on economy rates of fire in order to conserve ammunition against the awaited enemy offensive. The defenders' losses began to mount to over 2,000 casualties a day, so the Russians subsequently said, of which total the larger part were troops struck down at night in the open while repairing the defences. On 27 August the enemy fire began to weaken and from 1 September the daily losses dropped to half of what they had been formerly. From 5 September, however, the cannonade was fiercer than ever, an estimated 17,000 shot and shell and 16,000 bombs falling in 24 hours, mainly on the Korabel'naia and the Malakhov. More than 2,000 of the defenders died that day. Shipping, jetties and buildings were hit and set on fire. Gorchakov wrote to the tsar:

From dawn on 5 September the enemy increased the intensity of his bombardment to an absolutely unbelievable degree, smashing up our defence line throughout its whole length, sometimes by artillery salvoes sometimes by barrage. This infernal fire, much of which is counter-bombardment, clearly indicates that the enemy intends to destroy or neutralize our guns and make a ground assault. It is impossible to repair the fortifications and the best that one can do is to try to keep the powder magazines and the shelters intact; the broken parapets are filling the ditches and we are for ever keeping the embrasures clear. The losses among the gun crews have been heavy and can hardly be replaced.

On 5 September the strength of the Sevastopol garrison stood at 96 battalions of infantry, three of *opolchenie* and one rifle battalion, in all 42,000 bayonets; in addition there were two battalions of sappers, 2,200 army and 4,000 naval artillerymen bringing the total to 49,000. Semiakin was in command in the old town and Khrulev commanded in the Korabel'naia.

Gorchakov and his commanders knew that the ground attack was imminent but they could not know exactly when it was to be launched; for this reason infantry were kept in the forward area and suffered heavy casualties. The south bank of the base was ringed by the enemy and the sapper road could no longer be used, but Gorchakov made some pretence of posting a strong force on the heights of Inkerman ready to threaten the enemy rear as soon as the garrison should be attacked. The French troops being concentrated against the Korabel'naia had to move up to their forming up places through communication trenches which, though camouflaged with foliage, were in full view of the Russian force on the Inkerman heights.

On Wednesday 6 September Captain-Lieutenant Karpov, the Chief of No. 4 Sector, of which the Malakhov formed part, reported that the Kurgan defences were in a very bad state, and that unless he received immediate aid then the Malakhov would fall on the Friday. But that night the enemy fire increased to an unheard of violence. By the break of day on 7 September the fortifications were in a much worse state than they had been at dusk, as it had been impossible to carry out repair work during darkness; this was the first time that this had happened during the 349 nights of the siege. Of the 63 guns on the Kurgan 22 were still in action, of which only eight covered the area to the immediate front. The flanking Zherve Battery was still fit for battle, however.

Just before dawn on 8 September the listening posts forward of the Malakhov and No. 2 Bastion reported the movement of troops in the enemy trenches. The Russian infantry reserves were immediately brought forward on to the banquettes, the gun crews were stood to, and the guns were loaded with case-shot. But no enemy attack followed. Then the allied bombardment, increasing in its intensity, began to take a heavy toll among the defenders exposed on the ramparts. Three mines were detonated by the enemy under the Malakhov glacis, and these, although they did not penetrate the underground galleries, blew further holes in the defences. The order was then given to withdraw all reserves in order to spare them further losses.

Although Tarle would have his readers believe that the Malakhov was held by only 1,400 men, including those of the Zherve battery, Bogdanovich's detailed list gives a considerably larger total. For the garrison consisted of four battalions of three separate regiments of 15 Reserve Infantry Division, the Modlinsky, the Pragsky and the Zamostsky, in all 1,400 men;

the men of the fourth regiment, the Liublinsky, except for a working detachment in the mines, had been withdrawn for rest. In addition to 500 artillerymen, there were also 1,000 sappers and labourers, the Orlovsky Warsaw Regiment and men of the (49) Kursk *opolchenie*. In reserve beyond the gorge of the Kornilov Bastion were three regiments of 9 Infantry Division, the Eletsky, the Sevsky, and the Briansky, six battalions in all, totalling another 2,400 men. Major-General Bussau's command on the Malakhov, according to Bogdanovich, would appear to have been more than 4,000 bayonets.

The enemy fire always slackened a little each morning, but after 9 a.m. on 8 September, the day of the allied assault, there was a noticeable lull in the bombardment. Two hours later Russian look-outs on the Inkerman heights could discern unusual movement in the enemy trenches in front of the Korabel'naia. A message was semaphored into the besieged base at 11 a.m., but the signal 'strong columns approaching the Korabel'naia' was received and presumably transmitted as 'enemy fleet approaching the Korabel'naia'. This nonsensical message was referred back to the sender for verification. Meanwhile, however, the presence of large numbers of French troops in the forward trenches had already been seen from the Malakhov, and, what was more unusual, it was noted that the enemy were dressed in full field service order. Yet, according to the Russian account, no one expected that the French offensive would be launched at midday 'for their attacks were usually made at dawn or at dusk'. Most of the defenders of the Malakhov were thereupon sent to their dinners, the Russian soldiers' main meal of the day.

So it came about that at noon only skeleton gun crews and a few riflemen remained on the banquette ramparts. Bussau, the Malakhov commander, was below cover preparing to confer George Crosses on a number of junior ranks at a parade to be held after the troops had finished their meal. Karpov stood chatting to *Fligel' Adiutant* Voeikov, who was on a visit with a message from the Commander-in-Chief. Suddenly at 12 o'clock exactly, there were three distinct salvoes from the enemy guns, though these went largely unheeded down below. Then followed a short quiet, broken almost immediately by cries of alarm from outside 'The French!', together with the sounds of hundreds of cheering voices, and the shout of *Vive l'Empereur!* The men of Macmahon's division had doubled across the forty yards separating the French trenches from the counter-escarpment of the Malakhov, and were already pouring over the parapets. Only six of the Russian guns in the Malakhov had time to fire, and then only once.

The French were met by the men of the Modlinsky rushing back to the banquette, and fierce hand-to-hand fighting began everywhere in the Kornilov and on the Kurgan. Bussau, caught on the rampart without a weapon, was said to be seizing rocks to hurl down on the enemy when he was shot down by a bullet in the chest. The Modlinsky lost its regimental and battalion commanders; Karpov was wounded and captured.

The French then drove the *opolchenie* from the first courtyard and opened fire on two companies of the Pragsky covering the battery to the north of the bastion. Colònel Freind, the Pragsky regimental commander, surprised at the appearance of the French troops, rallied his men and tried to retake the battery and was killed. Remnants of the Pragsky, Modlinsky and Zamostsky fell back on to the last court in front of the gorge, where so many of them were to lose their lives that thereafter it was named 'the Accursed Courtyard'. By 12.30 p.m. the Kornilov Bastion and the whole of the Malakhov was in French hands, although small isolated parties of Russian soldiers are said to have remained hidden in the galleries from which they continued to harass and snipe at the enemy. Totleben had built a mine shaft into the Kurgan in order to blow up the bastion should the enemy occupy it. In the event, the shaft was two days off completion; the 200 men working there were taken prisoner.

Once the French had taken the Malakhov they could not be ejected from it, although their numbers were in fact relatively small. For the Kornilov was a redoubt with all round defence and a deep encircling moat which the counter-attacking Russians had to cross, unless they chose to enter by a narrow bridge. Having taken the Kornilov, French troops moved down to their left and attacked the Zherve Battery, defended by the Kazansky; Kitaev, the Kazansky commander, was among those shot down. But the enemy advance was held when the Kostromsky and Galitsky arrived on that flank from the old town.

The curtain wall connecting the left flanking Nikiforov Battery of the Malakhov with No. 2 Bastion, 800 yards to the north-east, was occupied by the Muromsky and two battalions of the Olonetsky. But the curtain was not yet under attack. No. 2 Bastion, however, had been overrun by the French at the same time as the Malakhov.

No. 2 Bastion was part of 5 Sector, under the control of Captain (1st Rank) Mikriukov; the acting bastion commander – in the absence of Prince Urusov – was Major-General Sabashinsky. The bastion garrison consisted of the two remaining battalions of the Olonetsky, while the sector reserve was made up of detached battalions of the Aleksopol'sky, Poltavsky and Kremenchugsky. As had happened in the Malakhov, nearly all the defenders in No. 2 Bastion had been sent to their dinner, and only a few riflemen and

Sabashinsky himself remained on the parapet. Sabashinsky, looking idly towards the French trenches, was remonstrating with Cherniaev, a captain of the general staff sent by Khrulev to arrange an exchange of troops, when to his astonishment he saw, only fifty yards away, enemy troops come swarming out of their trenches and cross the ditches which had fallen in during the bombardment. The alarm was quickly sounded and the Olonetsky came running up to the fortifications. It was too late, however, to save the banquettes or the guns, and the Olonetsky were soon in flight running down the Ushakov Ravine closely pursued by the French. There Lebedev's sapper battalion happened to be at work in the gully, and, learning of the situation from the Olonetsky fugitives, the sappers took up their arms and surprised and drove back the enemy. The French troops were too few for the task allotted. For meanwhile Sabashinsky had called up a Kremenchugsky battalion, and the enemy were soon driven out of the bastion, the retreating men being raked by grape from those cannon which they had earlier captured but had failed to spike.

Shortly afterwards the French mounted an attack against the curtain wall between the Malakhov and No. 2 Bastion. This was a more difficult operation since their men had to cross a greater expanse of open ground which was broken and full of obstacles; the Russian infantry meanwhile stood on the banquettes with their reserves drawn up in the rear in company columns, waiting patiently, with their drummers endlessly beating the alarm. Yet the French succeeded in taking the curtain and they broke through the first and second defensive lines, capturing a number of guns. Alekseev, commanding the Olonetsky, was captured, and Nichik, the regimental colonel of the Muromsky, was wounded.

Khrulev, the commander of all army troops in the Korabel'naia, was in his quarters in one of the casemates of the Pavlovsky Battery, together with Generals Lysenko and Rennenkampf. They were about to lunch, when Khrulev, noting, presumably through a telescope, the unusual movement near the front, suddenly shouted 'Shturm!'. All mounted their horses and galloped off to the Korabel'naia reserve area. Khrulev, imagining that the Malakhov would hold but that No. 2 Bastion – the weakest point – might fall, set out in that direction with the Shlissel'burgsky and the Ladozhsky Regiments. On the way he heard that the enemy were actually in the Kornilov, and he sent back to Lysenko ordering him to take 9 Infantry Division, the No. 4 Sector reserve, to the Malakhov.

When Khrulev arrived at No. 2 Bastion he and the two regiments found that they had made their journey in vain, for Sabashinsky was in control of the situation. Khrulev's force then moved south-westwards along the curtain wall in the direction of the Malakhov, when they came upon Tishkevich's light battery engaging the captured Gennerikh Battery with case-shot in an effort to dislodge the French hold. A battalion of the Shlissel'burgsky then retook the guns. Leaving the Shlissel'burgsky Regiment with Sabashinsky, who used it, together with the Sevsky, to recapture the second line behind the curtain wall, Khrulev moved on south-westwards together with the Ladozhsky.

Sabashinsky regrouped his forces and began to clear the enemy from the curtain, and his attacks were successful except in that part of the wall which was commanded from the high ground at the Malakhov. At 3 p.m., however, Sabashinsky ceased all further counter-attacks on the curtain as the French had once more obtained a foothold inside No. 2 Bastion; he was obliged to return there to drive them out once more.

Khrulev and the Ladozhsky had by then arrived in front of the Kornilov. It was there that the final battle was to be decided.

* * *

The British attack against No. 3 Bastion (the Great Redan), in the centre of the line, did not develop until after the French had taken the Malakhov.

The Russian defenders of No. 3 Bastion and the curtain, together with the adjoining batteries, numbered about 7,500 men. Inside the bastion itself were two battalions of the Vladimirsky; to the left stood two battalions of the Suzdal'sky, together with the Iakutsky, and the (47) Kursk *opolchenie*; on the right, there was a composite reserve battalion and the Kamchatsky. The Okhotsky held the Peresyp, while the Selenginsky was in reserve.

The British riflemen ran forward across the 300 yards of open ground which separated the trenches from the counter-escarpment, followed by sappers and fatigue parties carrying storm equipment. Then came the line infantry. The British force, which was reckoned to total about 11,000 men, suffered heavily from the fire from a projecting corner of the bastion until the red-coated infantry changed direction by making further to the right. Then, seeking out the damaged areas of the bastion defences, they broke in, crossing the ditches by portable bridges and scaling the walls by ladders. In vain did Perelishen, the Commander of No. 3 Sector, try to rally the Vladimirsky, who ran back to the second line. But the English, said Bog-danovich 'made no attempt to follow up, but merely engaged the retreating Vladimirsky companies with rifle fire'. Ventsel, the Vladimirsky commander, arrived on the scene to reorganize his men, who, reinforced by the Selen-ginsky and Iakutsky, counter-attacked with the bayonet. After a bloody engagement the British were thrown out again down into the ditch, leaving 150 prisoners behind, among whom was a Colonel Hammond, wounded by eight bayonet stabs. The enemy fell back, some to the trenches and some to the intervening hollows.

The British soon returned to the attack once more. By then, however, it was already too late, for General Pavlov had had sufficient time to move two battalions of the Selenginsky into the bastion. During this second attack the British advanced against the connecting batteries as well as against the bastion, and although this new movement on the Russian guns was easily beaten off, the second assault against the bastion, according to Tarle, was made 'with great determination and bravery'. The ditch appeared to be full of enemy dead, row upon row. The attack was beaten back, however, by the men of the Selenginsky who fought with musket and bayonet and manned the unspiked cannon, for most of the Russian gun crews were dead. Only a handful of the British succeeded in getting into the bastion and these were taken prisoner or driven back into the ditch. Pavlov came to the conclusion that the bastion was no longer in danger, and at about 2 p.m. when the second attack had been repulsed, he ordered the fire of the left flanking battery of No. 3 Sector, together with that of the steamers *Bessarabia* and *Gromonosets*, to be moved on to the Malakhov. The third British attack was no more successful than the second. Thereafter Pavlov's attention was taken up by the repeated attacks made on the gun lines between the Zherve and No. 3 Bastion. 'In repulsing these attacks', said Tarle, 'the Russian troops excelled themselves'.

On the far left, on the old town side, the French attack on No. 5 Bastion, the adjoining Belkin Lunette and Shvarts Redoubt had no greater fortune than the British assault in the centre. The French force, believed to have been 15,000 strong, opened the offensive at 2 p.m., the first attack being made across the 50 paces of open ground on to the right face of the Shvarts Redoubt. There the French infantrymen broke in through the embrasures and drove the defending Zhitomirsky battalion firstly to the left face and then down into the town ravine. But any further advance was stopped by the fire from No. 5 Bastion, from which the Podolsky had already beaten off a separate attack. The enemy were said to have left 150 prisoners in the Shvarts, and renewed attacks against both the Shvarts and No. 5 Bastion were again driven off. Near the Belkin, a four cluster (*gnezda*) mine, exploded electrically from within the redoubt, was said to have caused great enemy loss.

These attacks, and those against No. 3 Bastion, were, in the Russian view, entirely unnecessary and against the allied interest. 'For Pélissier continued to attack everywhere when, in reality, he already held the Malakhov, the citadel and key to the fortress.'

When Khrulev arrived on the Malakhov below the Kornilov Bastion, Lysenko was already there with the reserve regiments of 9 Infantry Division. Adding his own troops to Lysenko's, Khrulev went to the head of the great six rank column and dismounted. Having sent his horse away, he called for the regiments to advance. With drums beating the Russian column began its steady march towards the Kornilov gorge entrance, to be met almost immediately by the intense fire of French riflemen sheltering in the traverses.

At 30 paces from the traverses, so says the Russian account, Khrulev was wounded. It is not clear how grave the wound was, for Bogdanovich said that Khrulev 'lost a finger and suffered a contusion in the head'. However that may be, Khrulev gave up the command of the column to Galkin, commanding the Ladozhsky, and went to the rear. Galkin fell immediately afterwards. The column faltered and halted and then dropped back in disorder. Lysenko rallied it, and, with the Ladozhsky and (48) Kursk *opolchenie* in the van, led the column back against the French. Lysenko was mortally wounded. Iuferov took his place and managed to close with the enemy before being cut down dead, together with Voeikov, in the slashing of swords and jabbing of bayonets near the entrance to the Kornilov.

The Commander-in-Chief, Prince M.D. Gorchakov, was on the north side at the Nikolaevsky Battery, from where he had ordered the Azovsky, the Ukrainsky, the Odessky and the Smolensky across the pontoon bridge to the south bank. When the messenger arrived from Khrulev saying that he had been wounded, Gorchakov ordered Martinau, the Commander of 12 Infantry Division, to replace him. When Martinau arrived at the Malakhov, the defeated Russian troops had already fallen back. The position was already hopeless. But Martinau formed up the Azovsky and Odessky and, putting himself at their head, bravely marched forward into the attack. He was among the first casualties, struck by a bullet. In a matter of minutes nearly all of the officers had been shot down, and the leaderless column began to break up. 'There was', said one witness, 'no commander, no officer and no ammunition save for that taken from the bodies of the dead or wounded; and the dead were piled high as if they were a breastwork.'

Such was the system of control that the replacement commanders had to be appointed personally by Gorchakov back at the Nikolaevsky Battery. For none seems to have had a deputy. Shepelev was then sent forward to replace Martinau. Only then did Gorchakov himself go forward to the Malakhov to judge the situation. 'There at 5.30 p.m.', said Bodganovich, 'standing among the many dead and dying, he decided that a renewal of the attack would have no useful purpose'. Gorchakov subsequently reported in his despatch to the sovereign:

The Commander-in-Chief was in the second line behind the Malakhov, and seeing the height occupied by a great mass of French, with strong reserves still coming up, he was convinced that the retaking of the Kornilov Bastion would result in enormous sacrifices. As he had already decided to evacuate the city by a bridge of boats constructed across the roads to the Severnaia, he resolved to profit by the situation in that the assault had been repulsed at all other points; the enemy, being utterly exhausted, was in no condition to interfere with the evacuation.

Gorchakov returned to the Nikolaevsky Battery on the Severnaia shortly after 6 p.m., and gave the order for the south bank defenders to be withdrawn by boat and across the floating bridge. The evacuation was carried out in a remarkably orderly fashion, since the fires and explosions, starting at 5 p.m. with the chance igniting of a powder store in the curtain between the Kornilov and No. 2 Bastion, made the allies extremely cautious; recalling the burning of Moscow in 1812, they appear to have believed that the whole fortress area was heavily mined, a belief that was further reinforced later that evening by the sound of the many detonations. For 35 powder magazines were destroyed, 7, 8 and 10 Batteries and the Alexandrovsky were blown up, and six men-of-war and seven other naval vessels were sunk by Russian demolition teams. The movement northwards across the bridge had already been noted by the allies at dusk, however, and throughout the night their long-range artillery attempted to destroy both the pontoon causeway and the steamers and barges which were plying to and from the north shore.

The night was dark and starry, the weather clear and the water calm; Sevastopol itself was covered with a pall of smoke that glowed by the glare of the many fires. From time to time bombs and shells fell on both sides of the bridge sending up great columns of water, unheeded by the many tired columns of men crossing over the Severnaia. Each phase of the withdrawal was signalled by a series of rockets sent up from the old town. When the bulk of the marching troops were over, the bridge was broken up and Gorchakov himself was rowed back in a naval cutter. At 8 a.m. the rearguard, the Tobol'sky, was withdrawn, and the last to leave, together with the rifle outposts, was Osten-Saken attended by the Sevastopol veterans – Panfilov, Khrushchev and Vasil'chikov. About 500 seriously wounded were left behind with a doctor, the bearer of a letter from Gorchakov to Pélissier asking that the allies should give them medical attention and care.

The Russian losses on the day of 8 September had totalled nearly 13,000 men, compared with the enemy casualties which were estimated at over 10,000. Since the enemy took more than 24 hours to occupy the south bank, the Russians returned there to blow up the Pavlovsky Battery at 2 a.m. on 10 September. But when the allies did close up to the shore, the intensity of their gunfire against the shipping moored off the Severnaia was such that Gorchakov had to order its dismantling and sinking.

When Gorchakov crossed the roads early on the morning of 9 September, he had, according to Il'insky's memoirs, 'appeared, or succeeded in appearing, cheerful'. But looking at the dark sky and speaking, as usual, in French, he had said: '*Je vois mon étoile de malheur*'. This it was not to be, for Prince M.D. Gorchakov lost not a whit of his sovereign's favour and was soon to replace Paskevich as the Commander of the Western Army.

CHAPTER 10

*   *   *   *   *

EPILOGUE

During the autumn of 1854 Nicholas I had instructed the diplomat Prince A.M. Gorchakov to begin preliminary talks in Vienna about the four peace conditions demanded by the allied powers; but the tsar insisted that he would 'agree to nothing that was incompatible with Russia's honour and rights'. Nicholas's instructions to Gorchakov made it clear that the tsar was the aggrieved party and that the talks were intended to bring Russia's enemies round to his point of view. Nicholas told his two representatives, Gorchakov and Titov, that Russia could not be in the wrong over its protectorship of the Principalities 'because this subject had not been defined in any of the earlier treaties with the Porte', and that the free movement of shipping on the Danube 'should be decided in accordance with the demands of trading precedents'. On the third point, the limiting of Russian maritime sovereignty over the Black Sea, Gorchakov was to explain that, 'on the basis of former agreements, the Black Sea could never be shut to any merchant ships; it should of course remain open to both Russian and Turkish warships, but in order to placate the fears of the West Europeans, Russia agreed that navigation on the Black Sea should be free to the naval vessels of all powers, on the understanding that Russian warships had the right to go in and *out* of the Bosphorus and Dardanelles at will'. Nicholas did not for the moment commit himself to precise terms on the fourth point, but merely 'insisted on the equality of all the sultan's Christian subjects, irrespective of their particular faith'. Although Nicholas proclaimed afterwards that he had accepted the four points, he had not in fact done so: he was willing to bargain, provided that his own conditions were accepted. In December 1854 the talks had been broken off.

When Nicholas died, the Austrian Emperor Francis-Joseph visited Prince A.M. Gorchakov, then the Russian Ambassador in Vienna, to express his condolences to Alexander on the death of his father; for, said Francis-Joseph, he had lost 'a tried friend at a time when he hoped to give him [the former tsar] proof of his gratitude and of a sincere wish to return to the old paths [of friendship]'. Alexander II, in his turn, made a public announcement that he would be faithful to the principles of the Holy Alliance (that frothy declaratory undertaking, framed by Alexander I in 1815, that 'the sovereigns of Russia, Austria and Prussia would be guided in their internal administration and foreign policy by the lofty principles that make up the ethics of Christianity'). Since the Russian and Austrian attitudes seemed favourable, the preparatory peace talks were resumed in Vienna; these lasted until June but failed to make any progress.

In spite of his emotional announcement at the time of his father's death, Alexander differed very much from his predecessor in character; he was cautious and there was nothing quixotic about him; he was more interested in internal politics than in diplomatic affairs; on matters of foreign policy he listened carefully to the opinions of his many advisers, yet came to his own decisions. Although many believed that Russia could, notwithstanding its defeats, continue the war indefinitely, Alexander measured the war in practical terms, in casualties and in rubles. The new tsar wanted peace; he considered that the war was finally lost and that one of the main reasons for the defeat had been the long and costly defence of Sevastopol. And he subsequently told Canrobert that all the advantages lay with the allies because Russia could not overcome the problems of supply and transport, time and space. Russia had won only a single victory, for during the autumn of 1855 the Army of the Caucasus had defeated the Turks and taken Kars; this, so Alexander believed, must strengthen the Russian position in any diplomatic talks that might follow.

The first peace move came, however, from the French, when Prince A.M. Gorchakov heard from Count de Morny by devious unofficial channels – through a Viennese financier and his French agent – that Paris was interested in reopening talks. Gorchakov, knowing that de Morny was close to Napoleon, for he was reputed to be his half-brother, and believing that de Morny was in favour of a Franco-Russian alliance, replied that Russia was ready for talks 'provided that certain conditions were met'. Meanwhile, however, Napoleon, aware that the wife of the Saxon Ambassador to France, von Seebach, was Nessel'rode's daughter, had instructed his own Foreign Minister Walewski (a natural son of Bonaparte and therefore Napoleon's own cousin), to use von Seebach for exploratory moves towards peace negotiations. Although it was believed in St Petersburg that de Morny had greater influence than Walewski over Napoleon, Nessel'rode chose to deal direct with Paris through his own son-in-law; St Petersburg instructed Prince A.M. Gorchakov to make no further use of his Vienna channels.

It is unlikely that Nessel'rode would have made these decisions on his own responsibility, for the Chancellor and Foreign Minister, who had served the two previous tsars for a total of more than 40 years, was in his last few weeks of office. He was moreover incapable of original thought or of adroit manoeuvre. The preference for the direct contact with Paris probably originated from Alexander, for Tarle tells of the existence in the imperial archives of a rough draft, in the tsar's handwriting, of a personal letter from himself to Napoleon, a clever and cunningly worded missive which played on the French Emperor's vanity, suggesting that all future conferences should be held in Paris and not in Vienna.

Although Prince A.M. Gorchakov had already been designated as Nessel'rode's successor as Foreign Minister, he had no idea that secret talks were being held between St Petersburg and Paris. Yet the Austrian Emperor received intelligence during December, from some unknown source, that Napoleon was conducting his own clandestine negotiations in breach of earlier Franco-Austrian understanding. Francis-Joseph was determined that Austro-Hungarian interests should not be ignored, and he directed Esterhazy, the Austrian Ambassador in St Petersburg, to deliver an ultimatum to Nessel'rode, demanding the immediate acceptance of the four points. To the original four points, Austria added a fifth, said to have been included at Britain's insistence, that the allies should retain the right to raise further questions or demands at the time of the peace conference 'in the interest of lasting peace'. If Russia did not accept the five points by 18 January, then Austria would, by the terms of the ultimatum, declare war on Russia.

On 1 January 1856 the tsar held a council to discuss the Austrian ultimatum, Nessel'rode, Kiselev, Vorontsov, Orlov and Bludov being present. Nessel'rode was in favour of peace but was against the blind acceptance of the imprecise fifth point, which he viewed 'as having threatening implications'. All those present, except for Bludov, were in favour of ending the war immediately, Kiselev giving his view that if Russia suffered any more serious defeats, then the Caucasus, Poland and Finland might be lost from the Empire. The council then recommended, and Alexander accepted, that a reply should be made to Vienna agreeing the four points but rejecting the fifth, and adding the condition 'that there should be no loss of Russian territory'.

On 11 January, when A.M. Gorchakov handed the answer to Francis-Joseph's Minister in Vienna, he was told that the note was unacceptable, and that Austria would not consider communicating it to London or to Paris. Von Buol-Schauenstein repeated the Austrian Emperor's demands.

If Russia did not agree the five points there would be war; and there remained only six days in which to accept them.

At 8 p.m. on 15 January, Alexander held another council meeting in the Winter Palace. As before, Alexander presided, and Nessel'rode, Dolgoruki, the Grand Prince Constantine, Vorontsov, Orlov, Kiselev, Bludov and Meyendorff, the former Ambassador to Austria, were present. The proceedings were in French and, as no protocol was taken, the only full account of what was said was that recorded afterwards by Meyendorff.

The tsar reminded the council that only three days remained before Esterhazy was due to ask for his passport; he asked Nessel'rode to open the discussion by giving his view. By then Nessel'rode favoured peace almost at any price and he advocated accepting the five points without further argument; to wait, he said, would merely add to the list of Russia's enemies. Orlov spoke out plainly against the Slavophils and, by implication, against Bludov and Bludov's daughter. The people, Orlov said, were tired of the war, and he reminded his listeners that Finland and Poland had been part of the Russian Empire for less than half a century and might be regarded as the booty of others at a peace conference. Kiselev and Meyendorff sided against Bludov, 'for the Slavophils might want to emulate Dmitri Donsky, preferring death in battle rather than dishonour', but even that would not stave off financial bankruptcy. The meeting ended by voting unanimously in favour of accepting the five points, Bludov resignedly quoting the words used by Louis XIV at the end of the Seven Years' War 'if we no longer have the means to make war, then let us make peace'.

On 1 February a protocol was signed in Vienna by Austria and by all the belligerents accepting the five points as the basis for the subsequent peace talks which were to open in Paris on 25 February.

* * *

Alexander appointed Count Orlov as the main Russian negotiator in Paris, and before quitting St Petersburg Orlov was given advice and instructions by both Nessel'rode and the tsar. Nessel'rode, the timid Austrophil with outmoded ideas, advised Orlov to try to isolate England by creating a Russian, Austrian and French bloc. Alexander was more realistic. He had already tried to wean Napoleon away from Britain and Austria by suggesting earlier that the peacemaking be transferred to Paris and by offering to send Orlov to Napoleon as the tsar's personal representative. Alexander told Orlov that Russia might hope for a future understanding with France; but that was not for the present. Orlov was not to show himself to be reliant on French goodwill during the negotiations because Alexander mistrusted Paris; 'Napoleon III was the most needy and the most dangerous of the

223

allies because his designs were unknown'. Europe should be made to remember the Corsican Bonaparte – to Russia's advantage – for any coalition against the latter-day Napoleonic dynasty would be ineffective without Russian help. And Alexander well understood that Russia's position in Europe in 1856 was wholly different from that which had existed in 1853. For Russia's voice had lost its authority. The relationship with Sweden and Turkey must henceforth be very delicate; with England it had certainly not improved; and Russia had irretrievably lost its two allies Austria and Prussia. The neutralizing of the Black Sea was a most hurtful condition, and Orlov was told to introduce any argument, from smugglers and pirates to length of coastline, if this would permit Russia to maintain her fleet on those waters; he must use his skill and experience and do his best to salvage what he could. In any event he was not to come home without a signed peace. The experienced Orlov hardly needed this advice, and he was firmly of the opinion that his principal adversaries would be Austria and Britain.

By the peace treaty that was signed on 30 March 1856, Russia came out of the war on better terms that it had expected. For the allies were in disarray. Napoleon was tired of the war and his ambitions had been satisfied when the Sevastopol south bank had been occupied. He believed that France was bearing the main burden of the war and he was determined on peace, whatever the allies might think. The French Emperor was resentful against Francis-Joseph for rejecting the French nominee as the ruler of the Principalities, and, behind their backs, he poured scorn on his British allies in London. Walewski, his Foreign Minister, went so far as to give Brunnov, the second Russian representative at the Congress, the following 'very confidential' information, which Brunnov forwarded to his sovereign posthaste on 20 March:

> At the end of 1855 the English proposed to Paris that another campaign be undertaken for 1856. The French Emperor replied that he was fully in agreement. 'But', he continued, 'war involves an enormous expense and a great sacrifice of lives' and he 'would like to know exactly what the English contribution is to be'. The English had hedged. Napoleon concluded that the English were of little account (*les gens de peu*). 'For they want me to do all the work and pay for it too'.

The Russian historians noted that Walewski seemed 'determined' to blacken the English in Brunnov's eyes'. In this Walewski did a disservice to the French as well as to the allied cause. But Napoleon, as Orlov soon realized, 'was playing a game on two fronts, courting Russia but not wanting to be separated from England'.

Orlov conducted his negotiations with skill. Although his tsar had ordered him to secure a peace, at one time, when the allies were too pressing, Orlov threatened to break off the talks and return to St Petersburg. When Napoleon and the half-Polish Walewski proposed to table certain questions concerning Poland, he refused even to have the word 'Poland' mentioned at the conference. He was forced to agree that Kars should be restored to Turkey but he persuaded the Turkish representatives that the redrawing of the Russo-Turkish border should be deferred for a more propitious occasion, synonomous in Russian with the Greek Calends. The question of the navigation of the Danube was relegated to various commissions which were to be convened at a future date, but Orlov could not escape the condition that Russia should cede to Moldavia that small corner of Bessarabian territory on the mouth of the Danube. Russia lost its self-assumed role as the protector of the Christians living in European Turkey and of the Danubian Principalities of Moldavia and Wallachia, for these latter were henceforth to be united as an independent European state. But he opposed British demands that Russian forts and bases in the Caucasus be demolished. Nor did the neutralizing of the Black Sea prove the bogey which St Petersburg feared. The allies had wanted to ban all warships from plying on those waters; Orlov replied simply that the Russian Black Sea Fleet had already been destroyed and the allied troops in Sevastopol were fast demolishing the remainder of the naval base; therefore, said Orlov, the condition had already been met. But he resisted strongly all allied efforts to control Russian shipbuilding on the Black Sea. This Franco-British demand for neutralizing could not be translated into action unless the allies were prepared to enforce it for all time by a strong naval presence in the Black Sea; and even this would not have prevented the Russians from building new warships in the riverside wharfs at Nikolaev and elsewhere.

Britain had had an interest in preserving the ailing state of Turkey, yet it also favoured the self-determination of the new Balkan national states. In Russian eyes this contradiction was inexplicable and it was commonly believed in St Petersburg that Britain's actions were motivated by jealousy and distrust, 'for even the younger Pitt saw a Russian presence near Constantinople as a threat to British interests in the Levant and in India'. The British politicians of the nineteenth century were charged with hypocrisy in clothing self-interest with altruism. Russia's deeply inbred hostility to Britain continued as a corner stone of Russian foreign policy, the self-same enmity which was to be carried forward into the twentieth century. Palmerston and Disraeli on the other hand were not blind to Russian pretensions in the Balkan and Caucasian states, expansionism which did not cease with the end of the Crimean War. Russia professed to speak for the Slav peoples and those of the Orthodox religion, whether they liked it or not; for many Greeks, Serbs and Bulgarians hated the Russian as much as they did the Turk. The population of Russia already numbered millions of non-Russian subjects, even Moslem Turkic peoples that were closer to the sultan by ties of blood, religion and tongue, than a Moldavian was to the tsar. It is therefore understandable that Britain's statesmen of that age were unable to subscribe to the protestations of sincerity that came from St Petersburg; and London took the view that, when the time came, the tsar would pay scant heed to the wishes of the smaller nations as he took them into his embrace, whatever their nationality or religion, particularly if they should show themselves unwilling to support his imperialist and expansionist policies.

Russian expansion was not the forced result of the pressure of population, for the vast territories which Russia controlled in 1850 were only thinly populated. The main motive for Russian aggrandizement was political, the desire for international power; the secondary motive was to acquire outlets for trade.

The loss of the Crimean War hardly retired Russia's frontiers – it merely held them temporarily in check. Within three years Alexander II secured by conquest all the lands between the Black Sea and the Caspian, and then, by breaking a treaty with the British covering the neutrality of Turkestan, he overran that territory, finally taking the capital of Samarkand in 1868.

In 1863 the Foreign Minister Prince A.M. Gorchakov became Chancellor, in which post he was to rival Bismarck as one of the most influential and powerful statesmen of the age; together with his sovereign he sought to achieve what Nicholas I had failed to do. In 1871, taking advantage of the defeat of Austria and France by Prussia and of the emergence of Imperial Germany as the dominant land power in Western Europe, Alexander unilaterally declared as null and void that part of the Treaty of Paris which had closed the Black Sea to all warships. In 1872 Russia entered into a Triple Alliance with Germany and Austria, so succeeding in isolating Britain, its main enemy. St Petersburg, determined on the destruction of the Ottoman Empire, had a hand in nearly every Panslavic and anti-Moslem intrigue in the Balkans and the Middle East. By 1875, when Turkey was nationally bankrupt, Russian influence was paramount in Constantinople and the sultan and the grand vizier were already Alexander's creatures. But in 1876 sultan quickly succeeded sultan and Abdul Hamid II was not so compliant. The 1876 Slav and Christian insurrection and the massacre of Moslems in Bulgaria were believed in London to have been instigated by

St Petersburg as a pretext for interfering in Balkan affairs. It was only
Alexander's personal intervention that saved Serbia from annihilation by
Turkey.

In an abortive attempt to check Russia's political and territorial ambitions,
Britain proposed a Constantinople conference to give the Balkan provinces
administrative and local autonomy within the framework of the Turkish
Empire. But by 1877 Russia had a conscript army newly reorganized on the
Prussian pattern, and, as the United States military attaché affirmed,
Alexander had revived the popularity of the Little Father so that the
Russian peasants were no less ready than their forebears to take up the war-
ring crusade. This time there was to be no shortage of reinforcements, and
Alexander and Gorchakov considered it unlikely that any allied expeditionary force would come to Turkey's aid. By April Alexander's preparations
were complete and he declared war, using the same worn pretexts that his
father had advanced. The Balkan provinces were already beginning to fall
apart; the lost Bessarabian territories and the whole province of Kars
were soon regained, and together Alexander and Gorchakov contrived to
annex vast lands beyond Nicholas's most ambitious dreams.

SELECT BIBLIOGRAPHY

This list is not a comprehensive bibliography but indicates the principal works to which reference has been made in the writing of this book.

I Books

Alabin, P.V. *Chetyre Voiny*, Moscow 1892.

Alexander III. *Souvenirs de Sébastopol*, Ollendorf, Paris 1894. (2nd edition).

Andriianov, A. *Inkermanskii Boi i Oborona Sevastopolia*, St Petersburg 1903.

Anichkov, V.M. *Voenno-istoricheskie Ocherki Krymskoi Ekspeditsii*, St Petersburg 1856. (In German as *Der Feldzug in der Krim*, Mittler u. Sohn, Berlin 1857, and supplement 1860).

Bariatinsky, V.I. *Vospominaniia*, Moscow 1904.

De Bazancourt, C. *L'Expédition de Crimée*, Amyot, Paris 1856 (Two volumes).

Bestuzhev, I.V. *Krymskaia Voina 1853–1856*, Moscow 1956.

Bogdanovich. M.I. *Vostochnaia Voina 1853–1856*, St Petersburg 1876. (Four volumes).

Chodasiewicz, R. *Within the Walls of Sevastopol*, John Murray 1865.

Curtiss, J.S. *The Russian Army under Nicholas I 1825–1855*, Duke University Press, Durham, N.C. 1965.

Dubrovin, N. *Materialy dlia Istorii Krymskoi Voiny i Oborony Sevastopolia*, St Petersburg 1871–74. (Five volumes).

De Grunwald, C. *Tsar Nicholas I*, Douglas Saunders and MacGibbon and Kee 1954.

Kinglake, A.W. *The Invasion of the Crimea*, Blackwood 1899.

Krushchov, A.P. *Istoriia Oborony Sevastopolia*, St Petersburg 1889.

Men'kov, P.K. *Zapiski*, St Petersburg 1898.

Tarle, E.V. *Krymskaia Voina*, Moscow 1941–5. (Two volumes).

Todleben, E. *Défense de Sébastopol*, St Petersburg 1863. (Two volumes).

Tolstoi, L. *Sebastopol*, Ann Arbor, University of Michigan Press. (1961 edition).

Zaionchovsky, A.M. *Vostochnaia Voina 1853–56*, St Petersburg 1908. (Volume 1 and *Prilozheniia*).
Zhandr, A. *Materialy dlia Istorii Oborony Sevastopolia i dlia Biografii Kornilova*, St Petersburg 1859.

II Anthologies and Journals
Opisanie Odezhdui Vooruzheniia Rossiiskikh Voisk, St Petersburg 1899–1902. Edited by Viskovatov. (Nineteen volumes).
Russkaia Starina.
Russkii Arkhiv.
Russkii Invalid.
Sevastopol'tsy, Sbornik Portretov Uchasnikov Oborony Sevastopolia v 1845–55 godakh, St Petersburg 1904. (Three volumes).
Voennyi Sbornik.

INDEX